THE GARDEN CLUB
of AMERICA
CENTENNIAL
1913-2013

The Garden Club of America

100 YEARS OF A GROWING LEGACY

William Seale

Smithsonian Books
Washington, DC

To Gina Miller Bissell

This book may be purchased for educational, business, or sales promotional use. For information, please write:
Special Markets Department
Smithsonian Books
P. O. Box 37012, MRC 513
Washington, DC 20013

Published by Smithsonian Books
Director: Carolyn Gleason
Production Editor: Christina Wiginton
Editorial Assistant: Danielle Villalovos

Edited by Robin Whitaker
Designed by Kate McConnell

Library of Congress Cataloging-in-Publication Data

Seale, William.
    The Garden Club of America, 1913-2013 / by William Seale.
      p.   cm.
    Includes bibliographical references and index.
    ISBN 978-1-58834-328-4
    1. Garden Club of America. 2. Gardening—United States—Societies, etc. I. Title.
    SB403.Z5S43 2013
    635.0973—dc23   2012006212

Manufactured in the United States of America
16 15 14 13 12   5 4 3 2 1

Contents

Foreword

In 2013 the Garden Club of America marks one hundred years since its founding in 1913. This history, commemorating that century, begins in Philadelphia in the founding year. Most of the rest of the story takes place in New York.

Working through documentary records, both official and personal, both scattered and swept up together, I have been challenged to build a narrative history of an organization that rarely looks back, but keeps moving ahead along its chosen paths of education and civic improvement. The GCA seems always young. Its fortunes have passed through the hands of many generations of its members. It has never fallen under a dictatorship. This book has more characters than I would even try to count. My tendency to stop and get to know every one of them conflicted with the objective of writing one volume, not ten. Many compelling biographies of women lie between the lines here.

This is a work commissioned by the Garden Club of America. Not in a single instance have I been pressured to direct the narrative or details in any particular way; rather, I have been free to write the history as I have seen fit. Any mistakes the reader may find are entirely mine, as is the interpretation of the historical materials.

My objective, which I established after a preliminary review of the existing sources, has been to chart the development of the Garden Club of America as a national organization and to detail its representative work. The GCA is mainly a women's organization by membership but not by charter; a number of clubs have males on their rosters. Yet the GCA can be seen as part of the feminist movement in America, which began to flourish early in the twentieth century, after some rougher years in the nineteenth. The GCA's story belongs to feminism in the sense that the women involved in it were entering public activities; however, while it has been part of the larger feminist current for over a century, historically the GCA stands closer to the shore than to midstream. Its business is gardening, not politics, yet you will see that at times gardening has required some politics.

Besides presenting the history of an organization's first century, this book offers the reader a different slant on the women's movement and women's pursuits outside their homes.

Chapter One
THE FOUNDING GENERATION

$\mathscr{T}$he vision for the Garden Club of America took shape in the garden of Elizabeth Martin, in the Philadelphia suburb of Chestnut Hill. Her neighbors' daughter Ernestine Goodman often crossed the Bethlehem Pike to visit, and the two agreed that since a "rage for gardening" had "swept across this country" there was good reason to link American gardeners through an association of garden clubs. They might be somewhat like the guilds of old that, through mutual support, maintained standards of the crafts. The two women had led in the founding of the Garden Club of Philadelphia, which had flourished for nine years already, friends sharing information on horticulture. Why not something more ambitious?[1]

It was the spring of 1913, in the midst of a new era of gardeners. As gardeners themselves, Elizabeth Martin and Ernestine Goodman were part of a long period of transition. In the city during this period, their parents and grandparents, who were of the post–Civil War generation, were largely replacing the earlier home vegetable gardens with flower gardens. Their approach was in a sense the farming of flowers. Miss Goodman remembered there were few gardens in the area that could be called

1

artistic at that time. Mrs. Martin's flower-filled acre or so in Chestnut Hill had begun with her family as a terraced strawberry garden nearly a century before. The domestic garden, with its mix of as many edible plants as decorative ones, had always been the purview of women on the farm. Edited in its translation to city life, the flower garden was probably shaped by sentiment; however, with the concentration on flowers, the gardeners' love of beauty was magnified. While Victorian gardening had been for everyone, women were more apt to remember, as one of them put it, "the Delphiniums, Columbine, Fox-glove and hundreds of other charming plants" in the flower gardens their grandmothers had cherished.[2] They wished to know all the details of what made the past gardens so appealing, so that they could re-create in their artistic gardens the charms of the past.

Evidence that many shared this wish was everywhere. Other garden clubs had been founded on the Philadelphia model, not only as amateur study groups, but also as associations of friends. The shared interest was widespread enough to attract more gardeners. At the White House where the Rose Garden grows today, Edith Roosevelt, wife of Theodore, had created her own "colonial garden," with paisley-shaped, box-bordered beds, brimming with hollyhocks, sweet William, and black-eyed Susans, to mention a few. The early years of the 1900s were a period also of women celebrating women, although these women were hard to categorize: Some wanted the vote, some did not; others wanted public libraries, better hospitals, and the banning of prostitution and alcohol. Some saw the garden as a place of expression, where genteel-looking hands, protected by gloves, turned the soil with farmhand energy, introducing seeds and roots that would eventually fulfill as shade or flowers or even food—although in this case not so much food as in the past, for green grocery stores had begun to proliferate.

Old-fashioned flower gardening was a movement that, in a modest way, re-created the simple truths of planting the land. It can be seen as a reaction to the standardization imposed upon an individual's personal prerogative by urbanism and the attendant conformities of suburban life. Taste should originate in the soul. In garden terms the unhappy transformation could be seen in the sculptured junipers and monolithic spreads of bedding plants espoused by architects and professional landscape gardeners as flattering settings for new buildings.

The Garden Club of Philadelphia was one of the first of a scattering of American garden clubs founded in different locales at the time. Although the earliest, usually called horticultural societies, dated from the 1880s, the Philadelphia club was different, in that its membership consisted of mutual friends. Thus, in addition to the subject matter it espoused, it also had a social basis. Books on gardens of the past became familiar on the market, and none more so than Alice Morse Earle's *Old Time Gardens*, a nostalgic return to garden ideas and concepts of gardening for modern women. Edith Roosevelt's worn copy remains on her nightstand at Sagamore Hill, where she left it.

Elizabeth Martin, who was known to her friends as Lizzie, was forty-one; and Ernestine Goodman, thirty-three. Mrs. Martin was married to a distinguished Philadelphia jurist whose physical condition was precarious. Their permanent residence was in the city on Rittenhouse Square, which she herself had landscaped. She and Judge Martin, despite apparent limitations of his health, were active and stayed on the move with travel, work, and civic causes. Miss Goodman lived with her parents, both in Philadelphia and at the summer residence in Chestnut Hill.[3] It had been in one of their gardens in 1904 that the idea for the Garden Club of Philadelphia evolved. Looking back on that success, in 1913 they conceived of a second organization that would carry farther afield the successful ideas of the first, to bring about "mutual help and inspiration." Their concept cannot have been imagined without some idea of where member clubs might come from. Friendships made through family associations or contact during summer residence in the cooler climes of New England and California made more promising the possibility of a national organization.

Working through the Garden Club of Philadelphia, the organizers invited various clubs of similar purpose to meet in Philadelphia on May 1, 1913. Twelve attended. The occasion was designed in a way that was to be reflected in Garden Club of America meetings for a century to come. The setting for the meeting was carefully selected to illustrate the history and heritage the new organization would represent. Stenton, a colonial-period house in Germantown, was selected. Preserved by the National Society of the Colonial Dames of America, eighteenth-century Stenton was being landscaped as a "colonial" garden celebrating the botanical achievements of its builder, James Logan, William Penn's agent in America, and a colonial statesman. The handsome old Georgian house, which had welcomed Benjamin Franklin, George Washington, and the Marquis de Lafayette, was now garlanded with flowers to greet a group of founding ladies.

On the last day of April, a preliminary organizational meeting took place to create a framework to facilitate the seminal meeting scheduled for the next day. This meeting took place at Wyck, another of Germantown's landmarks and the home of Mrs. Bayard Henry. Elizabeth Henry was more a civic activist involved in good works around Philadelphia than a gardener, but she loved flowers and liked to arrange them artistically. At the "most delicious luncheon" the ladies were supplied with pink tablets and pencils, so that their notes would complement Elizabeth Henry's decorations of spring flowers. One participant remembered the fragrance fifty years later.

This luncheon was the first meeting of what would, on the next day, be the founding of the Garden Club of America. But the name did not present itself immediately. "The Garden League" was tried. No one much liked it. "The Garden Guild" was discussed at length. Mrs. Martin asked how the gathering felt the organization should go—as purely a social group or on a broader plane, "undertaken in the certainty of great future expansion."[4] The latter was by far the preference. Then there was the question of how to organize on a national basis. Grouping members by state was rejected, fearing "jealousies," in favor of leaving each member club to function independently, with its own approach to membership. The binding central organization would be as simple in structure as possible, serving the clubs with needs they could not satisfy locally.

On the next day, May 1, 1913, which would be remembered as the founding date, the group of twenty-four gathered in the sublime interior of Stenton. Such light as there was in the paneled room had to have fallen from the tall windows, sunshine from a lovely day outside. Artificial light at Stenton was still provided by candles and coal-oil lamps. The officers, duly elected at the conclusion of the lunch at Wyck, took their places and presided. Elizabeth Martin became the president; Ernestine Goodman was appointed secretary and treasurer. Helena Rutherford Ely, the well-known garden writer from New York, was a vice president; among the other five vice presidents were Albertina Russell, of New Jersey, and Kate Brewster, of Lake Forest, Illinois. Dues were set at fifty cents per year per member. Beginning a tradition that prevails today, all further organization lay with the Executive Committee, composed of the officers.

Many items of business, already discussed privately, were established as directions for the new club. "The Garden Guild" was first to be the name but was challenged in final discussion, and the matter was tabled for a while. Fields of endeavor were proposed in quick succession, suggesting a few GCA interests in the years to come: forestry and grass; structural uses of green planting in a landscape design. The horticulturists and flower arrangers pressed the need for using the color chart in determining combinations of flowers in vases and plants in gardens. Five new clubs were admitted. Much of the discussion seems at first glance rather random for a founding meeting, yet time would place each item, as pieces in a puzzle, in the organization to come.

The meeting was followed by a luncheon featuring "good things of olden times" taken from an ancient cookbook found in the house, and afterward a paper was read on James Logan, of Stenton, based upon his garden notes. As the assembly broke up and the motors lined up to carry the delegates to the railroad station, the "May day of divine beauty" fixed itself in the memories of the participants, and as Elizabeth Martin later wrote, "So was joyously ushered into being the Garden Club of America" in the first Bulletin.[5]

During the founding meeting the absence of a statement of purpose or mission became painfully clear. Elizabeth Martin asked Ernestine Goodman to leave the room and not return without a mission statement. Obediently Miss Goodman retired elsewhere in Stenton and set to writing, producing the following, which has stood, with only slight changes, for a century: "The object of this association shall be to stimulate the knowledge and love of gardening among amateurs; to share the advantages of association through conference and correspondence in this country and abroad; to aid in the protection of native plants and birds; and to encourage civic planting."[6]

More flexible perhaps than most of the founders understood it to be at the time or even intended it to be, the mission statement reflected the interests of women gardeners as known to Ernestine Goodman through her association with fellow garden club members. It is possible, of course, that the statement was drafted at some point earlier, with other hands at work. Whatever the details, Miss Goodman was always credited with writing it, and whatever editing and alteration it may have gone through was completed by the time she carried it through the door into the meeting room.

After the meeting the officers got down to business. They lived in relatively close proximity. Elizabeth Martin, when residing in Philadelphia, did her gardening in the warm months at the old family home in Chestnut Hill. Ernestine Goodman lived in about the same manner, between city and country. Albertine Russell, though a New Yorker, was in Philadelphia frequently, because she had a country house near Princeton, which had belonged to her husband's family. Kate Brewster lived in

Chicago, but in fact spent much of her time in New York and California, so was likely to be available for meetings.

First, a constitution. For this purpose Mrs. Martin assembled a committee of four, including herself, a week after the May meeting had adjourned. They met at the home of one of the committee members, Letitia Biddle. Andalusia, her husband's family home, with its academic, temple-style, Greek Revival portico, brought yet another great American house into the history of the Garden Club of America. In the process of being remodeled, Andalusia had as yet no electrical wiring, so for the ladies Mrs. Biddle had appropriated the billiard room, an elevated out-building with a colonnaded upper porch, upon which they met, "to the song of a cardinal," as Mrs. Martin remembered later.[7]

Few other details of the constitutional meeting survive, except that it produced a brief document that established the purpose and structure of the new organization. Since the club was not incorporated, nothing more was required. What had been the Executive Committee became styled as the Council of Presidents, governing the national club and meeting at different places on a twice-a-year basis. Headquarters was to be where the president lived, there being no permanent office. In its essentials the constitution was to prevail.

Elizabeth Martin continued building the organization's foundation in the midst of a very busy life, using her small Rittenhouse Square study for headquarters. Communication, she realized, was essential to the individual clubs of the new national organization, so she founded the *Bulletin of the Garden Club of America*. The first issue, compiled apparently by her, was four pages in length. She wrote, "This little sheet goes forth in the hope that it will be the means of bringing into closer touch the Clubs composing the GARDEN CLUB OF AMERICA."[8]

This, at last, was to be the official name.

The first Council of Presidents met on March 25, 1914. Foremost in current events was the ominous tension among the European powers prefatory to the deterioration of that part of the world come June, when the heir to the Austrian throne was assassinated. Most American citizens could hardly imagine American involvement in a European war, but government officials were less dismissive and got to work preparing for the possibility. The Department of Agriculture urged the Council of Presidents to recommend that the various clubs intersperse vegetables with their flowers.[9]

An annual meeting—to be known as the second annual meeting in honor of the founding meeting—convened in Princeton, New Jersey, at Vice President Albertine Russell's estate, Edgerstoune. Elizabeth Martin remembered the luxury of the place, the "bowls of fine alamanders and white lilac" mixed with narcissus, all from Mrs. Russell's greenhouses.[10] The principal speaker at the annual meeting was Aldred Scott Worthin, a professor of pathology at the University of Michigan. A pioneer in the search for a cure and ideal treatment of tuberculosis, Professor Worthin took the opportunity to admonish the new organization to adopt a "democratic character" and to seek "the widest possible field of action" so that the GCA would "insure its vitality and real usefulness."[11] In its subsequent history, the GCA would follow at least part of the speaker's midwestern idealism.

An afternoon of touring old houses and gardens around Princeton, plenty of lunch, and later tea parties climaxed in an elegant dinner at Edgerstoune. Poems were read; plantings and flower arrangements, admired. On the following morning at the business meeting, committees were appointed. One was to promote the use of a color chart in horticulture and flower arranging, and another was to build up a program of lectures and a library of garden books to help bind the clubs together through knowledge. Last, a committee was appointed for the "beautification" of highways and towns. The work of the GCA was beginning to take on its future form.

During the year that elapsed between the Princeton annual meeting and the third annual meeting, in Baltimore, cannon fire from Europe seemed to resound in everyone's ears when Americans received war news. Anger rose against Germany and was fueled by an avalanche of British propaganda. President Wilson spoke before the Senate: "Every man who really loves America will act and speak in the true spirit of neutrality. . . . The United States must be neutral in fact as well as in name during these days that are to try men's souls."[12] They were words both terrifying and less and less credible.

Mrs. Martin, all too aware of what seemed inevitable, appointed a committee headed by Cora Sellers, wife of the noted Philadelphia architect Horace Wells Sellers, to propose instructions for vegetable gardening according to the latest techniques. This was the beginning of war work yet to come. Meanwhile, the council's responsibilities included admission, and new clubs applied for membership in a steady stream. By 1917 the member clubs numbered thirty-five.

Annual meetings in Baltimore and in Lenox, Massachusetts, were the last to be held before World War I. The fifth annual meeting, scheduled for Lake Forest and Chicago, was canceled because war seemed near. There were to be only business meetings until the war was over.

Mrs. Martin wrote, "The clubs were called into the service of their country." She sat with her council in June 1917, two months after the United States had declared war on Germany, and recalled simply, "The Garden Club of America laid aside its pleasures and met its duties."[13] This the GCA did with remarkable speed. Their cloth they cut carefully, not taking on too much. The focus would be farming and the production of food. Vegetable gardens and food preservation programs designed by the Sellers Committee were suddenly in demand. Enthusiastic participation in the Woman's Committee of the Council of National Defense was the GCA's ready response to the urgencies of the times. Mrs. Martin appointed herself delegate to the opening meeting held in Washington. This marked the first interaction of the GCA with national affairs in the capital.[14]

The Woman's Committee, on which Mrs. Martin served, was sometimes a bold and argumentative group, with every sort of agenda represented among its members. Far from its designed purpose, for example, was one of the first major resolutions it passed, which recommended that the secretary of war close all houses of prostitution in the vicinity of ports and army and navy posts. This was incorporated into the Selective Service Act early in 1917. A New Orleans madam soon had reason to quip, "The country club girls has put us outa business."[15] Time would give the famous remark, quoted in error, a broader social interpretation.

Among the "country club girls," only two organizations on the Woman's Committee represented food production, which was of vital interest to the government. One was the GCA; the other, the Woman's Farm and Garden Association. Among the founders of the FGA, which was only a year younger than the GCA, was Mrs. Francis King, who served as president and representative at the meeting in Washington. Mrs. King was the well-known garden author Louisa Yeomans King. Old and dear friends, Louisa and Lizzie returned to Philadelphia, determined to see that their combined members did big things for the war effort.

They appointed war work councils at their two clubs. For the GCA, that council was a committee of three: Mrs. John E. Newell, Mrs. Robert C. Hill, and Delia West Marble. When the Council of Presidents met in October 1917, the report of the GCA War Work Council was read, recommending the United States' formation of the Woman's Land Army on the model of the Women's Land Army in England. The Woman's Farm and Garden Association voted to make the same proposal to the secretary of labor.[16]

Britain's land army had been established when it seemed obvious the war would come, with the idea that women could take the place of men in the fields, planting, harvesting, and generally operating farms. The rapid launching and remarkable scope of the Women's Land Army had proved its worth to the British Empire.

Resolutions in hand, Elizabeth Martin, Delia Marble, Anna Hill, and Ernestine Goodman took the train down to Washington. In the office of the secretary of labor, William Bauchop Wilson, they were joined by Louisa King, who lived in both Michigan and New York, and other delegates from the Woman's Farm and Garden Association. Even though the successful result of the meeting is well-known, the event itself still gives flight to the imagination.

Wilson was already a monumental character in the birth and history of the American labor movement. The massive Scotsman had come to America as a child with his coal mining parents and nine siblings. He had grown up in the Pennsylvania coal mines, developing into a labor organizer early in his life and working against what he considered the wrongs committed by the class of people that his guests so well represented. A founder of the United Mine Workers, Wilson was no cynic, yet shrewd man that he was, he cannot have missed the irony of well-heeled ladies asking him to sponsor a program of hard physical labor for others of their class. But neither were the ladies strangers to self-made men. Harmony and ultimately friendship carried the day.

Wilson served on the Council of National Defense, which supervised the Woman's Committee, and knew that body's challenges. Also, privately, as owner of a working farm in Tioga County, Pennsylvania, he was sensitive to what likely would be involved in the project his visitors proposed with female volunteer workers. He rolled out the red carpet for the ladies. Already, under his guidance, the Labor Department had established an agricultural division. On the spot he made the Woman's Land Army an agency of that new division.

The Woman's Land Army, which boasted membership from many organizations besides the GCA, became a familiar part of the wartime scene. For work the volunteers dressed in jodhpurs and puttees, like the British models, with a similar long, loose coat of cotton or linen, belted, not unlike the "dusters" worn when driving on the open road. "Farmerettes" rose in number far beyond those of either the GCA or the FGA. Housewives' legions left their drawing rooms and kitchens, big houses and bungalows alike, to mount the farm bandwagon.[17] Miss Goodman wrote, "Ladies of every description, many of whom, with large places and excellent gardeners, who may have scarcely recognized their own vegetables except on the table, planted and hoed little strips side by side, with more fatigue than results. . . . Our Farm Units may have been hectic, our canning may here and there have exploded in a truly warlike way . . . but on the whole we did our bit."[18]

The farmerette uniform, crowned by a broad-brim straw hat, introduced a new chic, while the labor itself, hard work indeed, was an honor to the volunteers. Most of this patriotic effort centered upon vegetable gardening. But also some women drove tractors and grain combines; some raised pigs, chickens, and turkeys; and some filled silos with corn and grain and pored over agricultural guides that came off the presses of the Departments of Agriculture and Labor, giving step-by-step instructions on planting and canning. In their own kitchens they cooked their own produce, thus helping the food market provide for the war by reducing their own purchases as well as donating to public collection.[19]

The work of the Woman's Land Army was the most nationally visible contribution of the GCA to the defense effort in World War I. Women, it seemed, had come from the shadows to take important roles in the war, as nurses, ambulance drivers, office workers, and even in domestic aviation. Yet none were so numerous as those in the land army, and the GCA was there, nationwide. Delia Marble, at fifty, became one of the most famous members of the land army. She was one of those people who commanded respect; her own presence was stronger for the encouragement of her father, Manton Marble, who owned the *New York World* newspaper and was a powerful player in the Democratic Party, which then prevailed in Washington. She took to the rails, traveling to organize and promote the Woman's Land Army from town to town.

Kate Brewster, the Lake Forest, Illinois, garden club activist who paid for and edited the *Bulletin* for its first six years, assumed a strong voice when addressing her readers. Of the clubs and the war she wrote:

> Every woman's club has a department for garden work; the great newspapers are organizing allotment schemes; universities, schools, golf clubs and individuals have plans for increasing the food supply of the country. Possibly it will be best for our member clubs to join with some national or local organization, rather than duplicate their efforts. Large cities have had city gardens for many years and this year the number and output should be increased. Neighborhood garden clubs might help them. Instructors will be needed everywhere and every garden club could produce a few practical teachers from among its members.

She saw the greater challenge in deciding what to undertake: "Before starting new activities every club should make a careful survey of those already started in the neighborhood. Cooperation is what will win out this time rather than multitudinous and conflicting organizations."[20]

War work did take place largely in the clubs. Records suggest that every club participated. In moments of altruism a few clubs disconnected from the GCA, feeling that their money and energy were better spent on the war effort than on membership in a distant national garden club. The Council of Presidents gently discouraged secession with the warning that readmission would not be automatic. Clubs frustrated by ill treatment sometimes turned to the national organization, for example, when suppliers sent inferior seeds to the ladies working in the fields. Elizabeth Martin received these complaints in her study and took to heart every one. As for the bad seeds, she took those issues individually to her friends in the Labor Department, which responded by contacting the seed companies, warning them that federal wartime policy demanded they produce their own seeds whenever possible and that they could be held responsible for "faulty products."[21]

For Americans the war was of shorter duration than for Europeans but very stressful nevertheless. GCA officers, meeting for business only, missed the charms and good times of the past three annual meetings. "Dreary wartime recipes and resulting culinary atrocities abounded," agreed Mrs. Martin and Miss Goodman, summing up the situation.[22] Some key members focused their attentions elsewhere, such as Elizabeth Henry, who braved crossing to Europe to work with the Children's Aid Society of the Belgian Relief. Always claiming to be too busy to garden, she left a full house of local good works in order to give war service in Belgium every ounce of energy she had. Kate Brewster left her civic activities in Chicago, California, and New York to go to France and join her friend Mabel Boardman, powerhouse of the American Red Cross, in hospital work.

Elizabeth Martin assembled an annual business meeting at the Cosmopolitan Club in New York on June 13, 1917, with an attendance of some eighty women, thirty-four being delegates from the GCA member clubs, the rest "nondelegates" or representatives from the clubs to be admitted at the meeting. This was an amazing turnout for wartime, drawing women from far away, who journeyed all night on crowded trains and left family and other responsibilities at home behind them. In this attendance, Mrs. Martin, ever the optimist, had reason to feel good about the future of the GCA. Expressing hope, she asked those present not to neglect their gardens but to keep them "as a haven of rest and beauty for ourselves and others in the suffering, strain and turmoil of the world."[23]

In March 1918, when the Council of Presidents met at Emma Auchincloss's residence in Manhattan, spirits were low. The annual Meeting set for Boston in 1919 was canceled. New clubs had joined in

California and Virginia, increasing the spread of membership to a total total of thirty-nine clubs, but there was little else to celebrate. That summer the *Bulletin* closed down. Editor Brewster summed up the reasons with a wry smile, saying that in the first months of the war in Europe the *Bulletin* had "struggled on, trying to be interesting, hoping to justify itself, but always growing feebler, less self-confident. . . . Finally it dug itself in, canned itself, conserved paper, time, energy, by ceasing to be."[24]

The Armistice, declared on November 11, 1918, ended what was for some years simply called the Great War. Indeed in scale it had been the greatest war in history until that time, and it led to years more of human devastation. When it was over, no one really knew why so awful a sacrifice had been exacted from civilization. Over the world twenty million people died, some on the battlefields; many more were murdered for their politics or ideals or race or religion; still larger uncounted numbers starved or were the victims of disease. Influenza made its grim appearance in the United States, entering on the East Coast from Europe in the autumn of the Armistice. The epidemic then moved west, taking an estimated half million lives in this country.

For all the jubilation victory brought, the tragedies of war hovered nearby like smoke. The Americans fallen in battle lay buried on foreign soil. American families expressed their outrage, and thousands of mothers, organized, would journey to Europe to visit the graves of their sons. Garden clubs helped begin planning memorials in granite, which would rise on the lawns of American courthouses, to be surrounded by plantings of flowers and shrubbery. Peace did return, with change. The Garden Club of America had survived but had changed.

Chapter Two
The GCA Defines Itself

$\mathcal{B}$efore the national organization had tabled everything but wartime objectives, the last strong interaction of the elected officers and committees of the Garden Club of America took place at the annual business meeting in New York on June 13, 1917, at the Cosmopolitan Club. The general fixation on the European powder keg did not yet so dominate the members' minds as to preclude their concentration on GCA business. A motion was made to support Liberty Loans, but the GCA was ineligible because it was not incorporated. With that set aside, discussion in the meeting turned entirely from the war to gardening and related interests. Thirteen committees reported, and what they had to say foreshadowed a century's coming interests of the GCA. These committees and their objectives were what the members wanted to create and pursue:[1]

1. Color Chart Committee, to apply official standards of color to garden plantings and the arrangement of flowers
2. Beautifying of Roadsides Committee, to act in response to the highways being built across the United States by keeping their surroundings beautiful
3. Honorary Awards Committee, to consider awards to stimulate education

4. *Bulletin* Committee, to publish the literary voice of the GCA
5. Wild Flower Preservation Committee, to conserve and extend American wildflowers, particularly along the roadsides
6. Plant Testing Committee, to test new plants
7. Library Committee, to develop a library of gardening books
8. Historic Gardens Committee, to promote the use of old-fashioned garden design and plant material, notably flowers.
9. Lecture Committee, to work with the Library Committee to bring lecturers to GCA meetings
10. Photography Committee, to perfect the art of floral and garden photography and to keep a pictorial record of gardens and flower arrangements
11. Special Plants Committee, to study, record, and propagate rare and unusual plant material
12. Medicinal Herbs Committee, to study historical medicinal plants
13. Seedsmen or Nursery Committee, to identify and qualify appropriate nurseries and suppliers

In June 1919 in Lake Forest, the GCA held the first full annual meeting since the war. This, as we know, had been planned prior to the war but had to be postponed. The Lake Forest and Winnetka garden clubs were primed and ready to make it the best annual meeting yet. From all accounts, no one was disappointed. Delegates visited houses both beautiful and opulent, admiring the ambitious gardens, superb in execution and flawless in maintenance. They enjoyed the private train cars that shuttled between Grand Central and Union stations in downtown Chicago and the suburban towns that were their hosts. One of the grandest sights in Lake Forest was Kate Brewster's Italian classical garden, which was planted to her own design. The editor of the *Bulletin* and her businessman husband, Walter Brewster, were prime movers in the development of the Chicago Art Institute. There, the delegates at the annual meeting admired both statuary and paintings that were part of the collections donated by the Brewsters.

For all the horticultural splendors of this annual meeting and its "gardens of Eden," all was not well among the visitors to paradise. Hardly had America's war storm ended when some garden club members began to criticize the GCA, questioning the focus of its efforts. It happened that Martha Brookes Hutcheson, the well-known garden lecturer and one of America's first women landscape architects, had compiled a report, really an unsolicited essay, on her opinion of garden clubs in general and how they should be planning their futures. With her report, titled "A Wider Program for Garden Clubs," she encouraged universal interaction and cooperation among different clubs. Elizabeth Martin said when the report was first presented that she could not have improved upon it had she written it herself.

Mrs. Brewster tried unsuccessfully several times to obtain the report for publication in the *Bulletin*. However, Martha Hutcheson held it close and agreed to present it only orally at the annual meeting in Lake Forest. Its appearance was fortuitous. Her report made it clear that she was addressing all garden clubs, not only the GCA. But it was primarily targeted at the GCA, and she began by pointing out the "discontent with the old regime." She then set out to make suggestions intended to "help to add new life to garden clubs." Her program was based upon the following four points:

1. What had garden clubs stood for before 1914, and what had they accomplished?
2. What they did do during the war?
3. How could the present "discontent" among garden club members be understood and remedied?
4. What program for the future would include the "broadest range of usefulness" for achieving "true national beauty"?

Presumably, no one had asked for Mrs. Hutcheson's opinion, yet the questions were worthy of consideration. Although she was a member of the GCA and although the GCA was very much involved with landscape architects during this early period, she distanced herself from the organization in her critique of it. She called for a "wider program," saying that the GCA suffered a "lack of direction." Whether this was her idea or that of a dissatisfied group of other GCA members who encouraged her is not revealed in the surviving records. She concluded by calling for a council of "the most helpful minds in the country" to "map out our work."

Her proposals varied, but collectively they called for more extensive civic participation. She encouraged the building of public gardens and a new focus upon children's education in gardening. She also called for a serious approach to educating the membership in horticulture. This was to be done through lectures, competitions in flower arranging, exhibitions, collecting gardening books, and a more liquid exchange of information among individual clubs. What she wanted was a powerful civic women's movement through garden clubs: "The tendency of a common program with a common purpose would be to throw a magnetic cooperative and competitive interest into all the garden clubs in the newfound scope of their work." Furthermore: "The work of garden clubs would be turned out into this great land with its thousands of rapidly growing towns. . . . The influence would gradually go through the wives as members of garden clubs to the husbands who devastate roadsides."[2]

Although Elizabeth Martin seems to have thought the report mapped out the ideal future for the GCA, the majority of the delegates expressed their hesitation toward the whole concept, from the powerful advisory to the standardization of activities among member clubs. Mrs. Hutcheson was offended and perhaps a little angry over the rejection, and still felt the sting years later when she pointed out the various GCA activities that were similar to those she had originally recommended.

Mrs. Martin left the presidency at the Lake Forest meeting, passing on to new hands the job she had held since the founding, six years earlier. At the same time, Mrs. Brewster turned the *Bulletin* over to the board to select a new editor. The Lake Forest meeting thus launched a new generation of leadership, as well as an assertion of independence of the member clubs. Elizabeth Martin handed the gavel to Mrs. S. V. R. Crosby, of Boston, with the knowledge that she relinquished to her successor "an organization already influential, with unlimited possibilities."[3] She accepted the title "honorary president," which she kept for the rest of her life. Mrs. Martin faithfully attended the board meetings in New York, notwithstanding heavy commitments to other projects at home in Philadelphia. She often traveled to New York by train with Ernestine Goodman. They never ceased to be amazed at the rapid advance of the organization they had imagined in the tranquility of that other world before the Great War.

Henrietta Marian Crosby served as president for less than a year, and even in that short time, much of her responsibility was handled by her first vice president. Very suddenly she resigned and moved to Europe for an extended stay with family members. An active member of the Massachusetts Horticultural Society and active in the New England Wildflower Preservation Society, she seems to have filled the GCA presidency only as a transition and may have been part of the opposition of the so-called wider program for the organization. Yet, though she left the presidency early, Henrietta Crosby would reappear before a decade had passed, and she went on to become one of the most important figures establishing the GCA's conservation program.

Her place as president was taken by Katharine Colt Sloan, an energetic New Yorker and world traveler. She had the spirit and projected the image of a GCA leader. Although she felt at home in Manhattan in a town house on the Upper East Side, her permanent residence, where she gardened extensively, was a Hudson River estate, Lisburne Grange, built by her father-in-law, the railroad magnate Samuel Sloan. Under her direction the garden at Lisburne Grange became one of the East Coast's finest, a green jewel on a ridge overlooking the river. She enlisted the services of Fletcher Steele, a young landscape architect of great creative skill, immersed in modern European ideas. One of very few men members of the GCA and called the "most valuable" of that gender in 1920, he was becoming a major influence in his field, no small thanks to wealthy GCA clients like Mrs. Sloan, who were willing to indulge his expensive taste.[4] As president of the Garden Club of America, Kitty Sloan began a succession of presidents who remained in office full or nearly full term, giving the GCA stability in its role as the binding power and inspiration to member clubs all over the United States.

Before World War I, public activities by GCA clubs had been relatively few. During the war they had been limited to vegetable gardening and other related war work. All along there had been flower shows, more like horticultural shows, in which the featured exhibitors competed for prizes with their specimen flowers and vegetables as well as competing for ribbon prizes with some flower arrangements. Some of the shows were held in conjunction with county fairs, and some were already a tradition. The organization, however, also tended toward less traditional directions, and in the 1920s these came into their own, as projects and programs.

One of the two strongest efforts of the GCA clubs was related to the new highway system, but it would be difficult to say whether that effort ranked first or second. Many organizations were concerned about the highways. Traditionalists favored configuring them where historical roads and trails had been. A stronger voice addressed not the highways themselves but the business interests that advertised on billboards along the margins. The billboard companies paid handsome fees to rent prime locations, naturally preferring beautiful sites that attracted attention. Billboards were a great irritation to people who responded to natural beauty, and the GCA was one national organization that took up the pitchfork to eliminate them. First among the GCA clubs to create a public noise over this was the Warrenton Garden Club, of Virginia, which started a program in 1915 for "beautifying" the roadsides and "preserving their natural beauty."[5]

The billboard, or "outdoor advertising," lobby groups have proved a daunting rival that the GCA has dogged for all of its hundred-year history. Surely few campaigns have enjoyed greater public enthusiasm and support and less success than that to rid America of billboards. The first formal mention of the "sign board menace" in GCA records is in June 1920, but the sign issue had been tossed around from the outset. "Why may not offence to the eye," wrote one member, "be regulated by the courts?"[6] It was observed in response that even the courts were no help, seeing beautiful landscape as luxury, not a necessity. The fifty-two clubs of the GCA got down to work.[7]

Elizabeth Martin had appointed a preliminary billboard committee in 1920, but it was not formally established as a GCA committee until 1923. This committee decided to join forces with the Woman's Municipal League of New York City, the American Civic Association, the Society of Landscape Architects, the Municipal Arts Society of New York, the American Scenic and Historic Preservation Society, and the Movement in Behalf of Massachusetts State Roads. Had these organizations strongly united into one powerful political fist, more might have been accomplished. But each one went its own way. The National Association of Gardeners was conducting a war of its own, apart from the rest, which involved printing brochures and broadsides. Billboards continued to appear, ever larger, some with electric lights. By general consensus they were ugly, yet the American culture would not rise up and banish them. Even if a collective effort had happened, the battle would have been difficult, simply because the billboard lobby had superior power in state legislatures and Congress.

The uphill war was fought by billboard opponents in two ways, through the arousal of public opinion and through political pressure. With stirring drawings, editorial cartoonists denounced the billboards and their bold intrusion on citizens' heritage of natural beauty. Billboard advertisers seemed the butt of every editorial page, yet they won every time in the legislative hall and the courtroom, and they have nearly always won since the 1920s. The early battle was bitter and long. Its warriors consumed ever more time at club meetings, telling their plans and woes. For some it became a passion likened to that of a holy war. Cherished in GCA legend is the Pennsylvania woman who stood by while her chauffeur chopped down billboards with an axe. In Westchester County, New York protest led to the burning of more than a thousand billboards that guards had been stationed to protect.[8]

The preservation of wildflowers was another, more scholarly effort made on behalf of America the beautiful. Since the earliest days of settlement, people had shown an interest in wildflowers, from John White's drawings along the Atlantic coast, through Bartram's explorations, to amateurs like Lady Skipwith, of Southside Virginia, who kept notes and specimens of native plants and flowers, now housed in the archives of the College of William & Mary.

Destruction of wildflowers ignited opposition from many individuals who had loved them long before the lilies of the field became a preservation issue. Premier in the effort to save this feature of natural beauty was the Wild Flower Preservation Committee, and the leading lights of the committee were Delia Marble, of New York City; Eloise Payne Luquer, of Bedford, New York; and Mrs. F. C. Farwell, a member of the Lake Forest Garden Club. In 1916 Delia Marble was appointed chair of the Wild Flower Preservation Committee and forcefully carried the cause forward. Eloise Luquer had loved wildflowers since early childhood, when she explored the fields by horse and buggy with her minister father. Mrs. Farwell, who preferred to be known as Fanny Day Farwell, had been interested in the Wild Flower Preservation Society of America since its inception in 1902. This organization, incorporated in 1915 and run by its founder and Fanny Farwell's friend Elizabeth G. K. Britton, was housed at the New York Botanical Garden. Perhaps it was the preservation society's interest only in New York State wildflowers that turned these enthusiasts toward a national point of view.

Whatever the reason, in 1917 the GCA organized a committee "for the Study and Preservation of Natural Landscape Beauty." Under Miss Delia Marble, the direction of the committee quickly shifted its weight from study to actual preservation, more toward being a governing body than a mere committee. It was the first GCA committee of national scope. The activist chairman successfully pressed member clubs for one and even two representatives, demanding, until squelched, that they assemble at the annual meeting each year. With a 100 percent favorable response from the clubs, the Wildflower Committee—as it was still usually called—soon united with the billboard and highway beautification advocates. A study group for all the other horizons that the preservation efforts seemed to open conducted an admirable educational program, sending leaflets, lantern slide programs, and speakers to the clubs.[9]

The Wildflower Committee's span grew ever broader. Already in 1920 its chairman was concerned about the harvesting of Christmas greenery from the forests and along the edges of the highways. Beatrix Farrand, the well-known New England landscape architect and member of the GCA, protested, "Few people realize how much widespread destruction our cheerful demand for Christmas greens entails."[10] A campaign was launched to rescue not only the hollies in particular but also western pines, Montana mountain laurel, and the Toyan Christmasberry (notably in its native California), which were wantonly butchered in November by nurserymen and in December by nearly everyone to make holiday wreaths and garlands. Posters designed to discourage the clipping practice were mounted in town halls and along roadsides; clever bumper stickers preached the text, protesting the ruin of nature's gifts. Autumn's challenge was soon joined by spring alarms over blooming dogwood branches and even whole trees cut from the woods for decorative use in weddings and other events. The committee decided to pressure churches to prohibit the desecration. Several ministers protested against the GCA's efforts to no avail.

Elizabeth Martin took particular interest in the manner in which protest in GCA could be taken as "public." At her request, drafts of letters and articles that expressed or implied GCA support were sent first for her review. She was surprisingly generous in her approval, even when considered in the context of today, yet she had an acute sense about how the GCA should appear to the public, and she meant to protect its image. Her pencil quickly caught the questionable turn of a word or phrase. The following is a form letter she approved around 1923:[11]

> To the President of the _____:
> Dear Mrs. _____ etc.
>> There is a movement on foot in many states that if successfully carried out, will do much to prevent the unnecessary destruction of our natural American Beauty that is so fast disappearing.
>> The success of this effort will depend upon the vision and cooperation of all groups that are interested in their own locality in its characteristic scenic beauty, its natural contours and its native trees and plants. _____ has long been famous, but it is being depleted rapidly. It was only at the last moment that the Palisades of the Hudson, the Big Trees of California, and the Falls of the Genessee River were saved from annihilation. Much that is beautiful and characteristic in our neighborhood is also threatened, but by such gradual destruction that it is generally unnoticed until too late.
>> Will you and a delegate (a substitute if you are unable to come will be welcome) represent your [club, society] at a meeting at _____ on _____ to discuss what, if anything can be done?
>> Some valuable material has been collected by my club and will be shown.
>> I enclose a copy of the Resolutions that have awakened interest in this subject in widely scattered sections of America.

Surely _____ should not be without effective
participation.
Sincerely, etc.

These efforts with hollies, wildflowers, and billboards brought the Garden Club of America into the public eye in the political sense for the first time, and the debut did not please everyone in the GCA. Had they not rejected in Lake Forest the idea of being an activist organization? Had they not agreed at the time to the original mission statement written down by Ernestine Goodman that day at Stenton?

The Wildflower Committee and the Billboard Committee heard this but kept to their course and enjoyed enviable support in the clubs. Indeed, at first glance these two efforts might have seemed the strongest cord binding the national GCA together, but that was only because horticulture, landscape gardening, and flower arranging were so much less provocative. The leaders of the respective roadside movements wondered through 1923 if their ardor for a new, broader approach to "garden" did not merit a more comprehensive, all-inclusive name. *Preservation* was not quite right for it, perhaps a little open-ended and awkward. In New England preservation meant saving old houses. In 1924 the word *conservation* was introduced and the Conservation Committee was born.[12]

In the early years of the Garden Club of America, its business was conducted in Philadelphia in Elizabeth Martin's study in her town house at 1709 Walnut Street. Summer months she spent in Chestnut Hill, so such GCA business as there was followed her there. She was an extremely busy woman, one of the most visible civic leaders in Philadelphia, famous for instigating big projects and getting them done. By the fall of 1920, with the president in Boston and five of the eight members of the Executive Committee in or near New York and only three from elsewhere, New York seemed a more centrally located venue than Philadelphia, although the founders had determined originally that the headquarters would always be in Philadelphia. Early in 1920 the rule was broken, and the GCA leaders packed the organization's boxes and moved to New York. They were offered a place to meet in the East Sixty-seventh Street house of the widowed Emma Auchincloss.

Mrs. Auchincloss spent most of her time in Newport, and her servants accompanied her. Perhaps for that reason, her closed-up Manhattan house did not work out, so for GCA meetings Mrs. Harold Irving Pratt cleared a convenient, if small, space in the servants' quarters of her apartment at 820 Fifth Avenue. Harriet Pratt's husband was president of the Standard Oil Company, and they were part-time apartment dwellers in transition. At home permanently on an estate, Welwyn, on Long Island, they were in the process of building a house in Manhattan, on the corner of East Sixty-eighth Street and Park Avenue. Harriet Pratt was forty, energetic, and able. She had three teenaged children and a very busy husband; equipped with a staff to run her household, she was able to devote plenty of time to volunteer work. She joined her friends in planning the American Wing of the Metropolitan Museum of Art, among other things. Whatever she did, she did well. Very interested in gardening and the possessor and planner of notable gardens at Welwyn, she took an early interest in the GCA and its ideals.[13]

The other women who took leading roles in the management of the GCA lived more or less the same sort of life as the Pratts. They all benefited from circumstances that freed their time and gave them the leisure and means to pursue options in addition to the management of their homes. Their private lives were mixed with their other activities; much of the GCA work was, and still is, conducted at home. Those who met in the Pratt apartment remembered how Mrs. Pratt enlisted the services of the children's French-speaking governess to take minutes and cleared a closet to serve as office storage. The Pratts had a single telephone line, which became the New York phone number of GCA. In this setting, under these conditions, amidst the household activities of the Pratts, a little-known group of GCA members began building a firm nationally oriented foundation for the Garden Club of America.[14]

The records do not offer much in explanation of how the sudden move from Philadelphia to New York all happened. It was unlikely as simple a matter as it seems. Interest in building a viable national organization was not so strong among the Philadelphia clubs; except for Mrs. Martin's ambitions for the GCA, which were expansive, one wonders if left in Philadelphia the GCA would have grown as it did. As it happened a headquarters developed in New York, where there was no local GCA club. The participants lived in the city part-time or came in from elsewhere for GCA activities.

Besides Harriet Pratt and Emma Auchincloss, the builders of the New York headquarters included Effie Chandler Rhodes, Helen Thorne, and Katharine Sloan, all of New York; Louisa Yeomans King, of Michigan and New York; and Mabel B. Taft, of Cincinnati. Whatever other home base they might claim, their lives were all attached to New York City in one way or another, and none was a stranger to public sorts of work through charities and organizations. The press at the time dwelled upon the activities and extravagances of the rich, much as it does movie actors today, so these women's names were likely to appear in newspapers. Their weddings, funerals, dinner parties, receptions, new houses, trips to Europe—all were considered newsworthy. Most of the founders of the GCA doubtless questioned the propriety of this. But approve or not, no one could deny that the New Yorkers were spirited and effective volunteer workers and not women who would have tolerated exile behind closed shutters.

Whereas Philadelphians moved to the nearby suburbs in the summer, New Yorkers of means were likely to leave town for farther destinations from May or June to September. Yet the Executive Committee met in New York monthly without fail. Louisa King and Mabel Taft attended as faithfully as those close at hand. Well before Harriet Pratt's house was completed in 1923, the committee began to consider possibilities for other, more official headquarters. The American Horticultural Society occupied a suite of rooms in the new Bankers Trust Building, at 598 Madison Avenue. The GCA moved to one room in the society's suite in 1921 and installed a telephone, Plaza 3164. Soon they were too cramped again, and on May 1, 1924, Mrs. Sloan signed a three-year lease on an additional room within that suite. The Garden Club of America now had its own offices in New York.

Olive Barnewal, a Manhattan interior decorator whom they knew, was called in to give the "new room" some style. She built trellis work around the windows and had five screens made with matching radiator covers. A bookcase, a table, and five Windsor chairs were acquired, all in dark, shiny mahogany. The walls were painted a low-luster gray-green that complemented the Chinese rug. This "cheery new office" had an executive secretary, Antoinette L. Rogers, who had already reported part-time to the Pratt apartment. She was soon assisted by a second part-time typist. The GCA had now set its roots permanently in New York. This was the first of five Manhattan addresses the organization would occupy over ninety years.[15]

Among the prevailing interests of the Garden Club of America in 1923 were horticulture and flower arranging, but it was horticulture that embraced the interests of the most members. For both, the forum was the flower show. At the outset the flower shows were local, usually small, and not structured by more than the most basic rules, with the objective of recognizing excellence. Their evolution into more complex and instructive shows can be largely attributed to the hard work of the Garden Club of America over many long years. Already before World War I the International Flower Show had become for the GCA the most prestigious vehicle to developing useful concepts for its own flower shows.

The International Flower Show, established originally in 1914, was held for the third time in New York on April 5–12, 1916, and was sponsored by the Horticultural Society of New York in cooperation with the New York Florists Club. Making a notable appearance was the International Garden Club, founded two years before as an American version of the Royal Horticultural Society, in England. The main purposes of both the American and British societies were the dissemination of information to the general public and an open membership. The GCA had the same purposes, but the objects of its educational outreach were member clubs, which were in turn associations of friends. The International Garden Club was never a rival of the GCA, but the women at GCA Headquarters, in New York, suspected it might be.

The International Garden Club came on strong and actively sought an American base for its headquarters. Already raising money with apparent ease in the year of their club's founding, the directors obtained custody of the dilapidated Bartow-Pell Mansion, an elegant stone house of the 1830s, sitting in the midst of the twenty-seven-hundred-acre Pelham Bay Park, in the Bronx. William Adams Delano, a principal in the architectural firm Delano & Aldrich and later the architect for the Pratts, was engaged to restore Bartow-Pell Mansion, and on May 1, 1915, with great celebration, the International Garden Club dedicated it as their "club house." To begin its residency there, that May the club planted a young tree to replace the landmark Treaty Oak, blown down in a storm. In the now-vanished shade of the original, Chief Wampage had closed the land deal with Thomas Pell, transferring title to all the Bronx and more. After several more replacement oaks died, an elm was substituted, and it prevails.

So splendid was the International Garden Club's debut at the International Flower Show in 1916 that it gave a sheen to the whole event. The *New York Times* reported, "The most successful flower show in attendance and worth of exhibits, ever held in New York was staged in the Grand Central Palace. . . . To thousands of people it was a revelation of what a great indoor flower show can be."[16] The IGC had learned valuable techniques in two previous shows. What the IGC created and opened in April 1916 was a mighty trade show, mixed with amateur venues.

A cosponsor, the New York Florists Club monitored the commercial entries in the competitive classes. Landscape companies, architectural firms, landscape architects, and nurseries created wondrous gardens, walkways massed with flowers, urns, statues, and fountains. For New Yorkers, housebound in winter snow and March wind and rain, the International Flower Show was a stroll through paradise. A gate count at the show held in 1928 totaled over 108,000 visitors. It was an attraction not for the few but for the many. Or, one might rephrase, it was a show put on by the few to attract the many.[17]

The Garden Club of America enjoyed the International Flower Show and participated in it sometimes quite extensively, both as individual members and as individual clubs. During the Depression, the flower show was an inspiration to the great numbers who visited it. To be an exhibitor at the show was an uplifting honor to a flower arranger, and the conservationists were even able to use exhibits to graphically convey their messages. Yet the GCA watched the show's commercialization with suspicion over many years.

Through successive officers and executive committees, the GCA became more and more sensitive to its role as an educational organization and alert to any involvement with money making. Not that the members rejected interaction with nurseries and landscape architects— far from it. However, when the subject of advertising, fees, or profit in the use of the GCA's name appeared even briefly, the proposal was always struck down. In this there would be gray areas, but as a rule the opinion of "business" or "trade" remained negative. This was in no sense snobbery, any more than academics may avoid the cast of profit making in their endeavors, which could shade their efforts to seem somehow less pure in the pursuit of knowledge. Some might have argued, and probably did, that charities openly worked for profit to fund their good works. The GCA was not a charity.

In spite of the GCA's reservations, the International Flower Show became an anticipated part of the organization's year. For nearly half a century, 1914–53, it was held at the Grand Central Palace, the second exhibition hall of that name on Lexington Avenue at Forty-sixth Street, the initial structure in an ambitious complex built by the New York Central Railroad. Nearby would soon rise Grand Central Station and the new Waldorf-Astoria Hotel.[18] A more currently fashionable location in Manhattan could not have been found, although the luster of the Palace dulled after World War II, and in the 1950s the bulldozers ended its career.

Displays by the GCA at the International Flower Show began in 1921 under the Flower Show Committee, then a subcommittee of the Art Committee. Never a very active body and lacking focus, the Art Committee became the Exhibition Committee, and in 1922 the Flower Show Committee proceeded as an entirely separate body. For all practical purposes the Flower Show Committee could have been called the International Flower Show Committee, for in the activities at the Grand Central Palace lay its strongest interest. The involvement of the GCA began small, but already by the late 1920s, member clubs from California, Ohio, and Michigan were bringing entries to New York. At first the exhibits were notably models, miniature houses, and gardens, some with real plant material, some simulated.

The miniature models were always stars of the show, especially the dream gardens, for the Maxfield Parrish visions in architecture and landscape design that had flourished before World War I had not entirely died. Like many other interests of that seemingly distant time, the dream gardens had adapted to change, and in this case the GCA models related to ordinary folk, showing what average people with modest means might create at home at little cost. Most models were of suburban bungalows, complete with garage, driveway, and small yard with vegetables and flowers, carefully planned and executed. GCA exhibitors were strongly influenced in this pursuit by Horace A. Peaslee, who was both an architect and a landscape architect, a self-styled "suburbanist" and at that time director of the Office of Public Buildings and Grounds in Washington. Eager to involve the architectural profession in the many jobs that were beginning to go to landscape architects, he was a leader in the prevailing discussions of land use as it related to the suburban movement reaching out from American cities. The models proved a gratifying expression of the educational ideals of the GCA and were given to the Smithsonian Institution.[19] Most of the construction costs were absorbed by those who made the models.

With time the models evolved into "model houses," not full-scale but large enough for a person to enter. Around them were beds of real flowers always, vegetables sometimes, live boxwood hedges and iron seats and perhaps a table beneath a potted tree. The idea, introduced at the Philadelphia Sesquicentennial Exhibition, met with such success it was carried over to the New York show, where it was an immediate favorite with the public. Across from the house was always a "GCA Area," from which the proud parents watched the droves of New Yorkers admire their baby.[20]

Horticultural exhibitions brought garden club members together to compete in classes of tulips, irises, and seemingly endless numbers of other flowers, nearly all grown in greenhouses because of the March date of the show. Any gardener, commercial or amateur, could compete for acceptance into the show, but the show's prestige apparently limited entries to the top landscapists and gifted amateurs. Classes, or categories, included orchids, carnations, and sweet peas, along with other flowering plants and cut roses, as well as ferns, palms, and other foliage plants. The Brooklyn Botanic Garden entered with an exhibit, and the New York Parks Department had a large display.

There were classes of competition in floral decorations for parlor tables and dinner tables, for which fine glassware and china were used along with the flowers. The arrangements of flowers as independent creative essays did not appear in the first shows, except thematically as features of table settings, wedding bouquets, and miniature nosegays; flower arranging took its place in 1921, attracting more general GCA participation than any other class. "Commercial growers" were displayed in areas away from the clubs and amateurs because of the scope of their work. For each class, or exhibit category, prizes were awarded. Special gold medals and certificates of merit joined traveling silver cups at the presentation ceremony. Over the course of the 1920s the GCA became extremely active. At a board meeting on October 10, 1928, a member rose and ventured, "Some feel that the International Flower Show is the ultimate purpose of the Garden Club of America."[21]

Publication was an early and enduring part of the GCA's work in education. From the first a circulating library was set up on a shelf in Elizabeth Martin's study. Once a headquarters was established, the books were sent to New York, and the body of books grew yearly. Gardening-oriented books flooded from the presses in the 1920s and 1930s: books on botany, gardening in general, garden history, horticulture; books and pamphlets on irises, tulips, roses, landscape design. Botanical engravings and paintings joined the collections early on. Most came to the library as gifts from members, some from the authors, and others were purchased outright by what came to be known as the Library Committee. When the organization moved to 598 Madison Avenue in 1921, the books filled one shoulder-high bookcase that was about six feet across. Additional shelving was called for right away. Movable bookcases soon shared their task with built-in shelving, which was extended repeatedly.

The Library Committee developed exhibits at headquarters, especially when the new room leased in 1924 provided additional space. Records do not show a heavy borrowing of books; however, GCA members were free to borrow, and even rare books were mailed out to club members. Readers and researchers were encouraged to come to the library at headquarters and sit at a table in one of the Windsor chairs or sink into a leather armchair and read and take notes. Exhibits were placed on emptied shelves or tables at first. Books were propped open to some preferred page, or visitors were allowed to thumb through. This proved destructive, so vitrines were acquired, to place glass between the visitor and the book that lay open. One favorite was Robert John Thornton's richly illustrated *The Temple of Flora,* a classic published in 1799 and donated in memory of Edith Stanton. Gifts of botanic prints and original watercolors and oil paintings were accessioned by the library. A selection of framed works was hung on the walls, but most were left loose and kept in boxes for their protection, to be brought out for exhibit or study.

The most important publication, the *Bulletin of the Garden Club of America,* appeared first in 1913; the four-page journal was the work of Elizabeth Martin. It continued, if not always on schedule, all through World War I. On the resignation of Kate Brewster, effective in 1920, Mrs. T. H. McKnight, of Sewickley, Pennsylvania, took on the voluntary job of acting editor early in 1921. After four months she became editor, expressing the purpose of making the publication "a magazine of accurate garden information."[22] Mrs. Brewster had put the *Bulletin* together with assistance only insofar as she was able to call in her friends.

Martha McKnight organized a board of editors. Each of the editorial board's nine members had a subject specialty, and representation was scattered over the country. McKnight began a "new series" of the *Bulletin* on a strict schedule. Her publications literally lived with her in Sewickley and at her Nantucket summer home. In soliciting articles she suggested the following categories in 1922: garden literature, special plant societies, history of gardening, vegetables, plant material of exotic kinds, garden design, garden pests and remedies, wildflower preservation, and special correspondence.

Articles did not flood to her from GCA members. She cajoled members to write them and even wrote some herself. Like most nonprofit editors, she had to request some of the articles from other authors to give issues the balance she desired. Following the design tradition established by Kate Brewster, she kept the *Bulletin* going full-force. Its appearance was that of a literary journal, its content varied, including essays, articles, poems, photographs, and drawings. When editor McKnight spoke of the

GCA, to which she was warmly attached, she never described a women's club but wrote always of men and women, a reminder that no rule limited participation to one sex. In 1926 the board of directors created the paid position of editor at twenty-five hundred dollars per year. Martha McKnight was offered the job and accepted.

As the principal vehicle of communication among the three thousand members of the GCA, the *Bulletin* was many things, but in simplest terms it might basically be described as an elegant book. To hold the early volumes eighty years later is to enjoy the feel of the luxury of fine paper; the typeface molds itself slightly into the pages. It is a level of design that would have been admired by the celebrated printers of the era in Kyoto or Paris. The use of pictures varies, often illustrating gardens and garden plans, but rarely people. Martha McKnight, as the *Bulletin's* creator, traveled the paths of her readers' interests, with a devotion to deepening their knowledge. Some of the articles are as alive and useful today as they were when McKnight relaxed her blue pencil and cleared them for publication.[23]

It has been mentioned that the founders and early members had interest in historical gardens. In his address to the annual meeting in 1914, "A Quest for a Garden," the horticulturist H. H. Stockton praised garden preservationists. In the 1920s and '30s, the *Bulletin* abounds in articles about history, with forays to Napoleon's garden on the island of St. Helena and, closer to home, to the gardens of old Germantown houses like Stenton and the surviving Philadelphia garden and home of John Bartram, which remained an abiding interest of Elizabeth Henry following completion of her Belgian war work. Certain members of the GCA, active in New York and environs, wanted the organization to produce a book on historical gardens in America. The market was rich in books on British gardens and those in continental Europe, and Kate Brewster and Louisa King are remembered as published authors on the subject of gardens. In 1923 the Garden Club of Virginia, a member of the GCA, published *Historic Gardens of Virginia*, a seminal study of fifty early Virginia gardens, edited by Edith Dabney Tunis Sale, of the James River Garden Club. To the Publications Committee's surprise, by 1930 their book had gone into four printings and was on the market in a revision. It remains a classic.

Just who got the production of the GCA history book moving is not clear, but the answer is very likely the new board member in 1924, Alice Burnell Lockwood. Active on various committees before, she had been outstanding among the historical garden enthusiasts, so she brought to the board her devotion to the subject. Certainly a major influence upon her was her husband, Luke Vincent Lockwood, an estate lawyer and well-known antiquarian who collected early furniture and porcelains. His 1901 book, *Colonial Furniture in America,* was sold in three editions. At their Greenwich residence, Riverside, the rooms were filled with American antiques, amid which, from all accounts, they lived with traditional formality, rearing their two children. Lockwood was chairman and chief fund-raiser for the American Wing, dedicated at the Metropolitan Museum of Art on November 10, 1924. The American Wing was the climax of years of study and collecting, mainly on the part of men, who saw it to completion; the wing's rich exhibits and elegant period rooms conveyed an underlying theme of postwar romantic patriotism with a flavoring of Anglo-Saxon pride. Alice Lockwood's absorption in the colonial-style garden matched her husband's in collecting American antique furniture. She created at Riverside a reproduction of such a garden that reflected her knowledge of both garden history and historical plants.

In September 1925 the Committee of Special Publications was formed to attend to the publication of a book on early American gardens. With the American Wing's opening ten months behind her, Mrs. Lockwood had already been evaluating the garden material in hand, for at the next month's meeting she observed that the files were too slim for a "high class book." The board allotted two thousand dollars for the project, which was to be in print in two years. A year later Mrs. Lockwood

appealed for an extension of time. She had contacted each state represented in the GCA, asking for historical information and illustrations to
represent gardens in that region. The response was slow. Alice Lockwood
went overseas to engage an engraver, insisting that Americans could not
match the quality of European work. Her committee, apparently on its
own, called on Scribner's Sons for advice. Charles Scribner also had
friends on the committee, so with a personal interest as well as that of
a publisher, he recommended that they publish two volumes instead of
one and insisted that illustrations were most important, since even the
average garden reader might feel buried in so much specialized text. The
job of the book, after all, like the American Wing and the GCA itself, was
to educate and encourage appreciation of the sponsors' binding subject
through understanding.

Alice Lockwood began assembling volume 1 in September 1926.
On January 11, 1928, she reported to the board that the manuscript was
at Scribner's for "preliminary consideration and styling." While production was well underway, the contract was not signed with Scribner's until
the following month. Scribner's estimated the cost, which was far above
the board's allotment, and Helen Clay Frick, a devoted GCA member
from Pittsburgh and New York, underwrote the balance. The cover price
for volume 1 was twenty-five dollars. The original title, "Gay Old Gardens of Our Forefathers," fell quickly in favor of *The Gardens of Colony
and State*. Volume 1 was on the market by March 16, 1932.

Charles Scribner requested that the GCA delay publication of volume 2 "owing to the general financial condition."[24] The board decided not
to interrupt the work on volume 2 but to table publication until later. Nevertheless, the second volume soon followed the first. A classic was born.
In addition to being the first book publication of the GCA, the underlying theme of *The Gardens of Colony and State* represented an effort
to be national in scope with historical gardens, to break the "colonial"
mold established by the East Coast. Old gardens across the country were
depicted for the first time—Spanish mission gardens, Mississippi Valley
French gardens—drawing local attention through national notice.[25]

For all of its success otherwise, the Publications Committee suffered the malady of all publications committees, money problems. Even
the *Bulletin*, held in reverence by the membership, was sometimes in
fear for its life. Martha McKnight spoke of going to twelve issues. The
readership was there for it, but funds were not. A main topic of discussion in the fall of 1926 was how to pay for an expanded *Bulletin*. Twelve
issues had real promise, for some could be special numbers on gardening
subjects; others could contain reports of various other interests to the
readers. Eventually the question of advertising came up, creating a flutter
of objection to "commercializing" the GCA's finest product. An alternative was approved: a second publication, called the *Almanac*, along the
lines of the *Bulletin*, which would include news about gardens but also
appropriate advertisements, such as nurseries and suppliers. This was approved in 1924, and the new publication went into production in January 1927. The *Almanac* made some money but not enough to sway those
who thought it too commercial for the GCA. The board discontinued the
publication in February 1931.[26]

From the beginning in the GCA, horticulture shared importance with
flower arranging and conservation. Since the founding generation and
their immediate successors were dirt gardeners to one extent or another,
horticulture was the umbrella for every GCA pursuit. Plants and landscape gardening were familiar subjects in the pages of the *Bulletin*. Some
members had elegant private gardens, like Katharine Sloan's, which was a
dreamlike setting overlooking the Hudson River. As we've seen, this garden aided greatly in Fletcher Steele's rise to prominence as a landscape
architect, and in 1929 he was elected to the honorary membership status
of member-at-large in the GCA.

Louisa Yeomans King had inherited from her mother-in-law a
very fine formal garden in Michigan. Her friend, the British landscape
gardener Gertrude Jekyll, helped her design her later garden at South
Hartford, New York.[27] Mrs. King always made a point of being a "farmer"

of both vegetables and flowers. Harriet McCormick's Lake Forest estate, Walden, was landscaped in the grand naturalistic manner developed by the landscape architect Warren Henry Manning. Beatrix Jones Farrand, a GCA member and prominent landscape architect, maintained with her husband, the noted historian Max Farrand, acreage in Maine, called Reef Point, at Mount Desert. The Reef Point garden was a natural forest she ever enhanced with new varieties of plants, bidding them to survive on their own in the severe northern climate.

The gardens of most GCA members naturally were less ambitious. Design ideas appeared in the *Bulletin* and in the exhibits at the International Flower Show. Readers of the *Bulletin* looked upon the estates with admiration and obviously liked to read about them and when possible visit them. GCA members had the opportunity to tour gardens in England and France as well as to enjoy those in the United States, thanks to the Visiting Gardens program, which began in 1923 and continued to flourish in the following decades. Indeed the flower shows in the 1920s and '30s were venues more for horticulture than for flower arranging. Although both were featured, flower arranging probably accounted for less than 20 percent of the entries in a show. Public acclaim rose the most for the model gardens. It was of early and continuing interest to the GCA that those model gardens relate to what might be possible for the average citizen cast into suburban life by the urban prosperity of the day.

Apart from the tours and publications of the GCA, horticulture, like flower arranging, was actually more the pursuit of the member clubs than the parent organization. That is, the individuals who did the actual gardening were members of the clubs and, through those clubs, members of the GCA. In their monthly meetings the clubs offered programs on pruning, planting, propagation, and garden design. These programs could be checked out, like library books, from the New York office and from other member clubs, and they involved a set of scripts and "lantern slides" sent to the subscriber with instructions for presentation. The traveling programs were very popular. Most of them were assembled by club members or members of the Slide Committee. Yet, some were the work of professionals like Fletcher Steele, whose basic lecture on landscape design was the perennial favorite.

The library in the New York headquarters usually had several copies of each slide show. There were often waiting lists. Member clubs paid the postage. An individual show was sent out repeatedly until after several repairs it became no longer usable and was destroyed. Now and then a show, like Fletcher Steele's, was completely reproduced and updated for yet another episode of appearances "on the road." Surely hundreds of club meetings over the years had these GCA shows as their centerpieces, ranging from subjects such as flower arranging to the most modern methods of slug control, in addition to those already mentioned. This was one of the most effective educational outreach programs of the Garden Club of America. Activity in the member clubs grew through the 1920s. Clubs looked to the national office increasingly for advice and information, which helped bring their various programs and projects to high standards.

Public activities were more numerous in the later 1920s than previously, and GCA member clubs worked hard to make them succeed. The National Flower Show, in Hartford, Connecticut, in 1921, in which a dozen GCA clubs participated, attracted thirty-five thousand visitors; a few years later in Cleveland the crowds were even larger. In Philadelphia, the Pennsylvania Horticultural Society flower show brought similar crowds year after year and continues to do so. Member clubs held shows that were smaller but still well attended. The GCA published a booklet and kit with directions on how to stage a flower show, selling out several editions at eighteen dollars per copy. In the kit were five hundred entry blanks, five hundred entry cards, five hundred envelopes, an exhibition book, a judge's book, and one defining classes. "Since co-operating with the [Pennsylvania] Horticultural Society," Margaret McPherson wrote in the brochure, "we are learning a great deal more than we ever knew about running shows properly, and we are glad, even eager, to pass on to these Member Clubs who wish it, knowledge we have gained along those lines."[28]

The design of gardens and the cultivation of plants ruled the day in GCA participation in flower shows. If the issues of the flower arrangers were artistic, then the pursuits of the horticulturists were never far from what members sometimes called "dirt digging" or "digging in the dirt." Rules and concepts honored at the shows found easy adaptation to the home gardens. A real gardener was a "dirt gardener" who turned the earth herself, and even if the moniker seemed ludicrous when applied to some individuals, it was nevertheless probably true even when the woman looked too grand for such exercise and had a garden too elaborate to imagine her puttering in it with hoe and trowel.

Thus the GCA gardener's image in most of the members' minds was of a peace-loving, reflective individual, happy among her plants, her vistas, and her plans. Let the wildflower enthusiasts go out in public; gardeners wanted no part—until 1922, when their bell jar was shattered and gardeners through all fifty-two clubs found an issue on which they had to take a public stand. A decade before, the government, through the Department of Agriculture, had established a quarantine against imported bulbs, corms, and some rhizomes, which American gardeners traditionally purchased each year and planted in their flower beds. This quarantine had been suffered in silence during the war, in the belief that it would be lifted after the war was over. It was an old law of 1912, used on and off by the Department of Agriculture as needed, and also included many farm crops such as alfalfa and clover, in addition to flowers, especially bulbs. Most of the categories had been dropped by 1921, yet daffodils and narcissus remained under restriction, the villain being by name Quarantine Number 37.[29]

At the beginning of 1922 the GCA Horticulture Committee addressed the subject of the quarantine; its members were in no mood to be sympathetic. The chair was Louise du Pont Crowninshield. At first the battle did not seem so daunting, for the House had appointed

Congressman J. Horace McFarland to chair a committee to investigate the issue. His friendly association with several GCA clubs and his being as close to an environmentalist as one could find in those days made him seem the perfect ally. When he became ill and had to resign, waters became troubled, and Mrs. Crowninshield went into fighting mode. At forty-five, she lived on the move, sharing between campaigns four perfectly managed residences with her husband, Francis Boardman Crowninshield, a well-known sportsman and also an avid gardener. An activist to her bones, Louise was not a woman who took on projects in small measure or opposed public encounters.[30]

Her first volley against the stringencies of the quarantine was an article she wrote for the *Bulletin* and reprinted also as a pamphlet, which was distributed to all the clubs, *Plant Quarantine Policies and World Progress*.[31] Nearly three years passed with committee members taking continual trips to Washington, knocking on doors in the halls of the Capitol and office buildings, even calling upon President Harding at the White House. Still the quarantines remained. Louise Crowninshield was a big woman with a big presence. Impatient over the apparent dismissal of her committee's efforts by the Department of Agriculture, she stormed into Washington in 1925 and started making calls and pulling strings, grand scale.

First she met Walter G. Campbell, the solemn Kentuckian in the Agriculture Department charged with obliterating "plant pests." He stood pat on prohibiting daffodils and narcissus—products of the Netherlands and Turkey—from entering the United States. Not pleased, of course, she called next on Dr. Charles Marlatt, head of the department's Bureau of Entomology, the real power behind the control of plant imports. It is history's loss that the meeting of the two was not recorded in any detail. Marlatt was popularly known, indeed a little notorious, for ordering the famous Tidal Basin cherry trees, gift of Japan, to be pulled up, stacked, and burned for the diseases he said they carried. He allegedly set off a "string of horrors for U.S. hopes in Asia" by this act, but Japan soon sent fresh young, healthy trees, and Marlatt, with aplomb, saw that they were planted properly. After considerable discussion, Marlatt told Mrs. Crowninshield emphatically no.[32]

In desperation she contacted Elizabeth Henry, whose war work in Belgium had placed her in close contact with Herbert Hoover, now secretary of commerce. Together they called upon a very friendly Hoover, who had many memories in common with Mrs. Henry. His was a sympathetic ear. Hoover was not unaware of the political pressures that played upon the quarantine, nor did he deny there were good points to it, but he said that it was a battle that could be won and gave this advice: Go to as many experts as they could find to support their side; gather up a storm of essays and letters in their behalf; and literally flood Congress and the White House with them.

The commerce secretary observed that what they were really fighting was a political lobby, the American Nurserymen, who profited from the embargo. Secretary Hoover bid the ladies to make their approach to the Congress just as strong as that of the nurserymen. They were to remember that they had the advantage, because they had no monetary involvement. He told them never to present themselves as anything other than honest citizens with a strong belief that an improvement could be made in the system. Such appeals the lawmakers took to heart. In his advice, Herbert Hoover feathered the GCA's political war bonnet and sent them off to battle. His advice, well taken, was to cast a long shadow over the future of the Garden Club of America.[33]

The American Nurserymen announced that their membership would convene in Washington on November 15, 1925, the day before the Quarantine Commission met. Louise Crowninshield rallied her committee to go to Washington for a confrontation of the lions in their den. When she announced her aim before the board, Harriet Pratt rose in protest. Representatives of the GCA must by no means enter quarrels with nurserymen. The board of directors agreed with Mrs. Pratt that it would be "undignified for the Garden Club of America to attend this meeting," the reason being the "desire to keep free from all suspicion of commercial connection."[34]

The assault was canceled, but the issue was not dropped. In 1933 the first horticulture committee was established. Quarantine was their inherited battle. The members, invigorated once more by Louise Crown-inshield, gained the support of William M. Jardine, President Coolidge's secretary of agriculture. The former Kansas college president was in sympathy with the appeals of the GCA committee in the instance of importing bulbs and spoke at length with the ladies. Nothing advanced much from that point.

The quarantine was not to be lifted until 1947, after World War II. Pressure from the GCA was at least part of the reason it was rescinded. Even so, the problem simmered on many years longer. In 1987 the perspective reversed when Marjorie Sale Arundel sponsored a study of the mass digging of bulbs for commercial sale and their exportation. Two years later the study revealed that the United States was the sole exporter of trillium bulbs worldwide. At this writing the trillium is at the top of the Endangered Plant List.[35]

The quarantine was the Horticulture Committee's first battle and one of the few really bitter and continuing ones it had to face in its long history.

Chapter Three

POLICIES

$\mathcal{I}$n 1930 the Garden Club of America reached the age of seventeen. It had set up national headquarters in New York, could boast of an impressive membership of eighty-nine clubs nationwide, and could tally a list of activities that was extraordinarily full for so young an organization. Made a Delaware corporation in 1923, the GCA was soundly constructed on paper, yet by 1930 was still defining itself.

Such an organization naturally had growing pains, united as it was under the broad subject of amateur gardening, but beneath that umbrella it rather more precipitated than divided into three distinct approaches—horticulture, flower arranging, and conservation. Through the 1920s and '30s a group of its most active members kept watchful eyes on directions the club might take. They became editors of a sort, trimming, shaping, substituting so successfully that the organization in the course of its regular work took the form it has carried ever since.

The organization of the GCA was simple, as set up in its constitution, written in 1913 and amended in 1929. Officers and directors were nominated by a nominating committee appointed by the current president. At the top of the structure was the president, elected for three years and allowed only two terms. An auxiliary or advisory committee to the president was the Executive Committee, consisting of the officers, treasurer, secretary, and the four vice presidents. The board of directors came from the various clubs. They were appointed at the annual meeting, and while the constitution provided for nominations from the floor, one is left with a distinct impression that pop-ups were discouraged. The board of directors answered to the Executive Committee. Directors' terms were staggered into three-year "classes" of six members each. Six board members made a quorum. The president and Executive Committee appointed the heads of all committees, of which there were always many, attached to the varied work of the GCA. Some were standing committees; some were temporary. Through the years since, there naturally have been revisions, but the structure has remained close to what it was at the outset.

In 1931, after some discussion, Harriet Pratt's concept of dividing the member clubs into regional "zones" seemed a good idea for managing a large organization. Each zone was to have a chairman appointed by the president, and zones were to meet twice a year, assembling all their member clubs. The creation of zones was based upon "the hope that this plan would bring the clubs into closer touch with the officials and directors of the Garden Club of America." General policy and issues relating to it were to be reviewed and discussed at zone meetings. Moreover, the zones had no power to implement their conclusions but could simply recommend them through "officers and directors." Any other negotiations with officers of other national organizations were to be undertaken only by officers and directors of the GCA or by a committee appointed by them for that purpose. This was "not meant to preclude meetings with other organizations and zones," but the "head of the relevant national committee should be invited to be present."[1]

The edict seemed to some arbitrary. Clubs in the "northeastern zone" were particularly restless with it, so Harriet Pratt invited their representatives to meet with her at her house. Alice Lockwood, never one to hold back, joined the others in protesting that the arrangement "curbed their freedom." Mrs. Pratt insisted, without explanation, that indeed it did not: discussion would not be restricted, nor was "initiative" to be "discouraged." This discussion did not go far. The five original zones were increased to eight by the close of 1932. For all the limitations seemingly imposed on the zones, the system was a stunning success. Most zones met at the annual meetings. Their ideas and observations were taken very seriously by the officers and board.[2]

Mrs. Pratt's objection to Mrs. Crowninshield's Washington campaign against the nurserymen's lobby was not the first example but an early one of the strong attention the board gave to matters of policy. Even earlier was the resistance to the proposed reorganization in 1919 in Lake Forest, which led to the return to Ernestine Goodman's original mission statement of 1913. That statement, regularly reprinted in the *Bulletin*, was deemed to be the description of what the Garden Club of America was about. An example of the stronger adherence to the mission statement was illustrated in the Executive Committee's reaction in 1925 to a request from the Amawalk Nurseries to include the name of the GCA as a cosponsor of the first national Christmas tree, to be set up before the White House and lighted by President Coolidge. Although Amawalk was on the GCA list of preferred nurseries, the Executive Committee declined. Many another organization would have found the honor, and the accompanying publicity, irresistible.

Reporters from the *Delineator,* a stylish women's fashion magazine that published features on houses and gardens as well, called at GCA Headquarters in 1922 for an interview. After declining emphatically, the Executive Committee explained to the membership, "No officer members [were] permitted to give such an interview."[3] The argument was that in giving interviews or permitting the use of its name, the GCA was "selling prestige." And selling for what purpose? Personal publicity for individuals, perhaps? Popular notice, which the organization did not want or need?

Some members of the Executive Committee felt that the organization's prestige, if cultivated, might translate into political power that would be useful to the club's objectives in such campaigns as the bill-board wars. Why give this prestige away simply to fill pages in a commercial publication? The subject was debated, and the board's decision not to advertise was confirmed by the former presidents at their "president's meeting" at the 1924 annual meeting. The strong and effective stand taken by this group, which began simply as a forum and advisory that met at annual meetings, recommended the group as a permanent advisory of ex-presidents, to be called when advice was needed. While the word *policy* would not be used much at the GCA until later, the Council of Presidents eventually became the Policy Committee. It was vigilant in trapping and debating nuances of action that might lead to major and unwanted changes.[4]

Along the same line of thinking, the by-laws were questioned. Stricter rules of cooperation from the clubs and membership in the GCA came from tightening the existing rules. In 1928 it was decided to slow the pace of admitting new clubs. Failure to send delegates to an annual meeting, heretofore permitted for two years, was reduced to one year, and even that had to be justified before the Admissions Committee— "the committee of nine"—for acceptance or rejection, and in the latter case the club was dropped from the rolls of the GCA. In 1931 a more complete set of rules further curbed the traffic of admissions, which was at least in part an effort to lighten the workload that was overwhelming the New York headquarters. Now a club had to be at least five years old to qualify for consideration.

It was desirable that club members have "gardens of distinction," meaning not necessarily splendid gardens but ones of exceptional horticultural interest. Last, men were acceptable as members, but the GCA had to judge them as outstanding in some unspecified profession, gardening, or botany.[5] This was not the first time the subject of men had come up, but 1928 was the first time a defining rule was applied to it. In an early election Dr. Edward L. Partridge was proposed for president, but the nominating committee dropped his name, with one member insisting that the GCA was a women's club. The idea seems to have been in her head alone. There have always been men in the club rosters of the GCA. Men were very active in a few clubs. As early as the 1920s, for example, men had been elected regularly to membership in Des Moines and St. Louis. As a general practice, however, from a policy established in 1914, men, such as the landscape architect Fletcher Steele, were distinguished by being made members-at-large, a special category of national GCA recognition, which also included women of distinction in areas of GCA interest.[6] It should be noted, however, that even after the 1928 rule, the GCA never referred to itself specifically as a women's club.

What the Garden Club of America went through in the 1920s and '30s was a clarification of its mission and of the means of serving that mission. The strongest hand on the wheel, and probably the sharpest focused eye, belonged to Harriet Pratt. She would not accept the office of president but was often secretary, attending nearly every meeting and usually at the center of discussion. She seems never to have hesitated to intervene when some principle of the GCA might be threatened; she was always strong, always articulate, and her commitment was so admired that she rarely ruffled feathers for long. Harriet Pratt was a formidable individual in any company. Her daughter-in-law remembered that as a bride, one morning in New York she purchased a substantial number of domestic things from Macy's Department Store. No sooner had she returned home than the telephone rang. Mrs. Pratt spoke firmly: "*We* shop at Lord & Taylor."

All the business of the GCA was not administrative or in the area of policy. Unquestionably, for the people of the nation the most visible early achievement of the Garden Club of America was in conservation, foremost in helping preserve the giant redwoods of California. In 1929 a well-known West Coast enthusiast for those forests, Mrs. Philip V. Lansdale, of San Rafael, introduced to the activist organization Save the Redwoods League the idea of encouraging individuals and organizations to purchase tracts of land as memorials. She purchased a grove to honor her late husband, the American naval hero Lieutenant Philip Lansdale, killed in combat at the age of forty-one in 1899 at the Battle of Vailele, in Samoa. The covenant she placed on the grove protected it in perpetuity. Her memorial gift, presented eleven years after the close of World War I, was universally hailed and became a popular means of extending protection of the forests. On the basis of the Lansdale donation and subsequent generosity by others, Save the Redwoods League was able to convince the state legislature, at Sacramento, to match any private funds put up for the purchase of redwood forests.[7]

Mrs. Lansdale, who remained a widow, was socially prominent in the Bay Area and did not hesitate to use her personal connections to assist in the redwood cause. In Santa Barbara she found a rich winter community of easterners who had plenty of time and were eager to talk about conservation. Some were members of the Garden Club of America, journeying west seasonally to escape eastern weather. She formed a close friendship with Mrs. Oakleigh Thorne, a member of Millbrook Garden Club and one of the GCA's most influential members. Helen Thorne and Ethel Lansdale determined to make the GCA a vehicle to spread sympathy for the redwoods all over America. The 1930 annual meeting was to take place in Seattle; why not take the delegates on a tour?

For the Seattle meeting a chain of reserved train cars traveled from New York to the West Coast in what seems to have been one giant, rolling tea party for nearly a hundred GCA members. During the day the travelers stopped now and then to make a brief tour or to refresh themselves at a Harvey House. They met in Seattle for four days. On their return they headed south along the Pacific and stopped first in San Francisco, then Pasadena, where the Pasadena Garden Club, a GCA club, had a strong interest in preserving the redwoods. In the escort of Ethel Lansdale they beheld, awestruck, the solemn beauty of the redwoods.[8]

The travelers' wise hosts had a tour plan. Their guests were taken on foot and by motor deep into the forests, where they walked among the great trees, pushed through lush green expanses of ferns, and softened their steps in the deep, sweet mulch. At one point rain fell and mud deepened, yet the ladies moved on in wonder at everything they saw. At last they were guided to an area where the loggers were at work felling giant redwoods. The strangers awakened to see noble trees tremble and crash to the ground, thousands of years of growth cut into pieces for shipment to sawmills.

Elsewhere GCA visitors were further horrified by "hot dog stands" and other tourist concessions invading the roads that rambled through the trees. How could California let this happen? Be the subject quarantine or redwoods, where government was involved the culprit was naturally politics. With more than a million acres of redwoods still standing, the lumber companies were able to point to "overabundance" in dismissing those who protested stripping the forests away. Pressured by a major industry, the California legislature was unable to do more than curb the logging somewhat, but it stuck fast to matching with public money any private funds given toward saving untouched acreage in the redwoods.[9]

Mrs. John A. Stewart, of Philadelphia, one of the founders of the GCA, had been for some years interested in forestry and thus in the redwoods. A former GCA president, she was seventy on that annual meeting trip in 1930, when she actually saw the trees for the first time, and she was ready to act, returning east determined that the GCA would take up the redwood cause and do its part. Anne Stewart assembled a redwoods committee, with the blessing of the GCA board, consisting of Mrs. Lansdale, Mrs. Thorne, and Mrs. Duncan McDuffie, of San Francisco. Of them all, Helen Thorne was the most fit to go into a conservation war, having for years fought for the preservation of wild plants and against billboard advertising.

Already in the early 1920s that consummate conservationist Henrietta Crosby, during her brief time as GCA president, made an appeal through the *Bulletin* for the clubs to give money to the Save the Redwoods League. Mrs. Stewart's "Redwood Committee" launched the first formal fund-raising campaign for the redwoods, and by the winter of

1931 it had raised ninety-two thousand dollars toward its goal, which she kept pushing up. The GCA had never raised that much money before. That the successful drive took place during the Depression makes it all the more remarkable.

Elizabeth Lockwood, president in 1931, attached the new Redwood Grove Selection Committee to the Horticulture Committee to attend to the details of establishing a GCA-protected redwood forest. The Garden Club of America purchased the so-called Canoe Creek Grove of 2,552 acres, in Northern California, contributing $150,000 to the California State Parks Fund, where it was more than matched by the state. Helen Thorne became the grove's prime patron and, even after much of the money had been raised for the first purchase, encouraged the GCA over many years to buy more and more land. Determined to make certain that the GCA forest was safe, she hired Frederick Law Olmsted Jr. in 1933 to make recommendations for the future. The son of the early conservationist and planner of Central Park and heir, with his brother, Charles, to the family landscape architecture firm in Brookline, Massachusetts, he was at that time probably the busiest landscape architect in America. Under his advice and direction, a beaver dam and a log jam were removed from Canoe Creek, restoring the water's swift flow. Trenching and some moving of roadways created fire lanes. After those labors were accomplished the forest was turned over to the general management of the Save the Redwoods League, with day-to-day care and supervision by the state forestry service.

In May 1934 the first GCA grove was dedicated. Half a century later, with many additions—and a bit of an invoice still claimed by the state—the GCA's patrimony is the largest in the legendary redwood forests of California. Eventually seventeen groves and over five thousand preserved acres would result from the efforts of the Garden Club of America.

The maiden voyage of the GCA into political lobbying was when the delegation led by Elizabeth Martin called on Secretary of Labor Wilson to request official sanction for the Woman's Land Army. A later campaign was halted when Louise Crowninshield's plan to go to Washington to protest the quarantine against imported bulbs, corms, and rhizomes was halted by opposition at the GCA, under the leadership of Harriet Pratt. The story of the GCA and the national capital was merely punctuated by these events, for there was a continuing course of action that led to the committee known today as Legislative Affairs. This committee originated not in New York but in Washington.

Two Washington-oriented GCA members, Mrs. Frank Noyes and Mrs. Fairfax Harrison, were poised to call on Congress and, to give their effort organic meaning in the organization, took to New York the idea of an appeal for a legislative committee. When the formation of the committee came before the board on October 8, 1923, immediate discomfort was expressed over use of the word *legislative*. It seemed too harsh, too bold, too "political." The subject of a name was tabled until the next meeting, on November 12, 1923, when "legislative committee" was changed to Committee for the National Capital.[10]

One cannot be certain that most of the members of the GCA had much desire to lobby the Congress, but Mrs. Noyes, wife of the legendary political commentator, heir, and owner of the flourishing *Washington Evening Star* newspaper, was no stranger to the capital's elected inhabitants, nor was she hesitant to pressure them for favors. Lobbying was as natural to her as breathing. Long interested in the "city beautiful" movement launched in Washington, D.C., during the Theodore Roosevelt administration thirty years earlier, she had admired notable, if slow, changes in the capital in both architecture and landscape. The mighty neoclassical façade of Union Station was now complete, a splendid "city gate" for the great majority who came and went by the railroad. Public improvements of that sort had been called off during the war, and while the Lincoln Memorial had since resumed construction, the rest—both parks and monuments—remained tabled. Janet Noyes had a taste for big ideas and loved Washington.

The McMillan Plan, the grand urban scheme for transforming Washington into a great world capital, seemed by the early 1920s to hearken to another age, a souvenir of prewar aspirations overblown and impractical. Various intrusions stood in open defiance of its dictates: a monumental, misplaced memorial museum to George Washington was in the planning stage; and the U.S. Agriculture Department had built its own intrusive greenhouses, in part for experiment, in part to study quarantined plants. Along the unfinished Mall, which was still interrupted in its sweep by groves of trees, the War Department's temporary buildings, rambling and constructed of stucco over wood frames, lingered as warrens of government offices. Certainly not intended to remain, the barracks-like "tempos" were convenient, so their demolition had been stayed time and again and would continue to be for most of the next half century.[11]

The Washington Committee was approved by the Executive Committee in 1922. Its promoters, including the chair, Janet Noyes, were inspired to see already a revised interest in Congress to return to a program of improvement in the capital. In planning her committee, Mrs. Noyes told the Executive Committee that its members must be "women of influence." Harriet Pratt hesitated. She was not so sure lobbying in Washington was a good idea for the organization. "Trouble in Washington," she said, might make "trouble for the Garden Club of America."[12]

Over three years after 1922, Mrs. Noyes and presumably her committee rather conducted themselves as they pleased in Washington, pressing the politicians and officials for a cleanup of the results of rules relaxed during the war. One of these, for example, was the Tidal Basin, a site developed by landfill that had become a recreation area in 1917, its

banks lined with bath houses used by war workers and people tempo-
rarily in town. Crowds flocked there to relax in good weather, making it
into a minor Coney Island on weekends. This the Army Corps of Engineers cleared away in 1925, reacting to pressures from the Federal City
Planning Commission and agitation from the GCA committee. In the
same year that commission, in an apparent end run, asked the GCA to
appoint its own committee with which it might interact. This was quickly
intercepted by Harriet Pratt, who had it tabled.[13]

There was a bit of cat and mouse between Mrs. Pratt in New York
and Mrs. Noyes in Washington, each woman with ideas of her own and
each accustomed to having her way. Mrs. Pratt's concern was establishing
GCA policy. Mrs. Noyes was fixed upon particular projects. They seem
to have agreed that the nation needed an improved botanical garden in
Washington, one more in step with the great city botanical institutions
in Boston and Brooklyn. But when Mrs. Noyes's committee stepped forward with this, with the blessing of headquarters, they had trouble with
Congress, where in this case they were considered meddlers.

The National Botanic Garden, established by Congress, was housed
for the most part in fancy 1860s greenhouses of wood and glass at the
foot of Capitol Hill. The facility was a great favorite with Congress, and
in the 1920s discussions were underway for extensive improvements.
History sometimes overlooks how devoted the U.S. Congress has been
to gardening. The Botanic Garden greenhouse was originally built in
the 1850s, incorporating abandoned greenhouses, to preserve and study
botanical specimens brought back from the various Pacific expeditions
sponsored by the navy. Congress had declared its exclusive ownership
of the specimens, in defiance of the White House and agencies like the
Patent Office, which also attempted to lay claim, and it had watched over
its ever-increasing collection of plants for some eighty years. A group of
GCA members, alerted to plans underway to change the Botanic Garden, were eager to become involved, but since the lawmakers wanted no

advice, Mrs. Noyes discouraged the board from any intrusion onto this sacred ground until a more favorable climate might exist.

An idea that did seem agreeable between Washington and New York, and perhaps more executable, was for the government to establish a national arboretum. In this the GCA was able to take leadership, assuming armor for a battle that would last for many years but would result in the National Arboretum we know today. The subject had come up before in Washington. In 1922 the Committee for the National Capital pledged itself to support a national arboretum. They assembled in the office of Senator Lewis Heisler Ball, Louise Crowninshield's Delaware cousin, where they found a sympathetic listener, but no arboretum bill resulted. For four years the committee, under Mrs. Noyes, sought in vain for a patron to pull them through. By the fall of 1926 they were trying to find ways to persuade President Coolidge to support a bill. At about that time Senator George Wharton Pepper, of Philadelphia, brother-in-law of Rebecca Willing Pepper, one of the founders of the GCA, righted the dipping battle flag.

Pepper assumed leadership in the cause of a national arboretum. A bill authorizing the planning of such an institution passed on May 4, 1927. The secretary of agriculture, under whom the arboretum was to be developed, was William M. Jardine, who had warmed to the GCA's quarantine issue; for the arboretum project he was all enthusiasm and invited Mrs. Noyes and Mrs. Pratt to represent the GCA on the "proposed advisory" of the Council for the Development of the National Arboretum. The two women met with him in his office. Details of the secretary's placement of the GCA representatives on his council are unknown; he could have seen this as a means of controlling them, or of course he could sincerely have wanted their participation. Suffice to say, Mrs. Noyes and Mrs. Pratt were no innocents to either possibility. They had prestige to offer, apart from being the wives of prominent men. Harriet Pratt was on a committee helping Mrs. Coolidge plan new interior furnishings for the White House. Mrs. Noyes was a civic leader in Washington. To both of them the appointments were at the very least a foot in the door, and they accepted on the spot. As they left Secretary Jardine's office he told them that the money in hand was inadequate, but they could expect a more generous appropriation to come.

Money, however, was not to arrive any time soon. First, Congress passed over a request placed in the general budget of the Department of Agriculture for 1928. The request that followed in 1929 was omitted outright in budget cutting. And by the time the arboretum issue came up in 1930 the Depression had begun. A small appropriation to the Department of Agriculture was diverted to other purposes. The department's request for two hundred thousand dollars in 1931 passed the Senate but failed in the House. Following that, Secretary Jardine left to serve as ambassador to Egypt, and his replacement, Arthur M. Hyde, advised against any effort to raise the money in Congress for 1932.[14]

Mrs. Noyes and Mrs. Pratt worked well together, although when in Washington, Harriet Pratt was overshadowed by Janet Noyes, who was on the scene. Hetty Harrison joined the two in their efforts in 1931, working in Washington with Mrs. Noyes for the arboretum. Wife of the president of the Southern Railroad and, like him, a New Yorker, Hetty Harrison lived during the winter in New York and during the spring on their farm, Belvoir, in Fauquier County, Virginia, which was only about an hour from Washington by motor over gravel roads that crossed the Manassas battlefield.

In the fall of 1932 the three protested against Colonel U. S. Grant's idea of bedding perennials beneath willow trees. The public buildings commissioner under the Army Corps of Engineers, Colonel Grant, grandson of the famous Civil War general and president, was a splendid West Pointer accustomed to command and not inclined to notice unsolicited and unwelcome advice, especially from women. Janet Noyes, even though she knew him socially in Washington, was nevertheless peeved

The first annual meeting was held on May 1, 1913, at Stenton, the Germantown, Pennsylvania, home of James Logan, secretary of state to William Penn. Mrs. C. Stuart Patterson (of the Garden Club of Philadelphia) suggested the venue because the gardens had been restored with traditional colonial plant material. *Courtesy of Rudy Favretti.*

Left: Mrs. J. Willis Martin (of the Garden Club of Philadelphia) formed the Garden Club of America in 1913, serving as its first president until 1920. Mrs. Martin was an energetic and dedicated volunteer associated with almost every committee formed for progressive work in Philadelphia. *Courtesy of GCA Archive.*

Right: Miss Ernestine Abercrombie Goodman (of the Garden Club of Philadelphia), first secretary and treasurer of the GCA, was a neighbor and close friend of Mrs. Martin. Miss Goodman composed the mission statement of the GCA and wrote "The Garden Club of America: History 1913–1938." *Life, May 3, 1948.*

Louisa Yeomans King (of the Garden Club of Michigan, Grosse Point), a founder and vice president of the GCA, organized the Farm and Garden Association, established scholarships in horticulture, and wrote many gardening books. She arranged for her friend Gertrude Jekyll to write articles for the *Bulletin*. Mrs. Martin presented her with the Medal of Honor in 1923. American Horticulturist, *October 1991.*

Mrs. Helena Rutherford Ely (later Mrs. Benjamin Fairchild), a founder and vice president of the GCA, authored *A Woman's Hardy Garden* and many other books. Her garden in Warwick, New York, is still maintained by her club, the Garden Club of Orange and Duchess Counties, Millbrook. *Courtesy of GCA Archive.*

Mrs. Walter S. Brewster represented the Garden Club of Illinois (renamed the Lake Forest Garden Club in 1921) at the founding meeting and was the GCA vice president during 1913–16. She took over the fledging *Bulletin* from Mrs. Martin, becoming editor-in-chief until 1921. *Courtesy of GCA Archive.*

Mrs. J. West Roosevelt served as the first president of the North Country Garden Club of Long Island during 1913–15. She was not above watering her own garden! *Courtesy of North Country Garden Club.*

The first four GCA presidents attended the thirteenth annual meeting, in Santa Barbara, in 1926: (left to right) Mrs. J. Willis Martin (1913–20), Mrs. John A. Stewart Jr. (1925–29), Mrs. Samuel Sloan (1921–25), and Mrs. S. V. R. Crosby (1920–21). *Courtesy of GCA Archive.*

Mrs. Charles H. Stout (of the Short Hills Garden Club, New Jersey) specialized in dahlias. She became known in the 1930s as "Mrs. Dahlia," having hybridized some six hundred varieties and authored *The Amateur's Book of the Dahlia.* She also designed the Emily D. Renwick Achievement Medal. *Courtesy of Short Hills Garden Club.*

Miss Delia West Marble (of the Bedford Garden Club, Bedford Hills), first chairman of the Conservation Committee (formerly the Wild Flower Preservation Committee), helped form the Woman's Land Army during World War I and established a nature trail and museum near her home in Bedford, New York. *Courtesy of GCA Archive.*

During World War I, GCA clubs focused on growing and canning to preserve food. The Garden Club of Lawrence, New York, canceled its summer meetings in 1918 to assist in the Community Canning Kitchen. *Courtesy of Garden Club of Lawrence.*

Edith Tunis Sale (of the James River Garden Club, Richmond, Virginia), seated next to her club president, Mrs. Thomas S. Wheelwright (in black), edited *The Historic Gardens of Virginia,* never dreaming that it would go into five printings. She presented the first edition at the tenth annual meeting, in Newport, Rhode Island, in 1923. *Courtesy of GCA Archive.*

Miss Jane Righter (of the Greenwich Garden Club, Connecticut) was passionate about roses. A graduate of Bryn Mawr College, Jane studied at the Women's School of Horticulture in Ambler, Pennsylvania, and later became its president. Her club established a national award for rose cultivation in her honor. *Courtesy of Greenwich Garden Club.*

Mrs. Frank B. Noyes, member-at-large (center), headed the Committee for the National Capital during 1923–34. The committee worked to beautify Washington, D.C., by removing billboards from the roads leading into the city, planting trees and shrubs around the national memorials, and advocating for the establishment of a national arboretum. *Courtesy of GCA Archive.*

Mrs. William A. Lockwood (Garden Club of East Hampton, New York), sitting in her office at headquarters, served as chairman of the Flower Show Committee for the International Flower Show during 1923–25 and as GCA president during 1929–32. She developed the very successful Miniature Model classes on suburban planting at the IFS. *Courtesy of GCA Archive.*

Sixty GCA members visited England in 1929 at the invitation of the English Speaking Union. Leaving Sulgrave Manor, the ancestral home of George Washington, Mrs. Lockwood planted a clipped boxwood peacock by the entrance gate. *Courtesy of GCA Archive.*

Miss Eloise Payne Luquer (of the Bedford Garden Club, Bedford Hills, New York), an avid wildflower conservationist and botanical artist, served as chairman of the Conservation Committee during 1929–32. She painted endangered wildflowers and used her illustrations for public lectures. Two hundred of her original botanical watercolors are owned by the Brooklyn Botanic Garden. *Courtesy of GCA Archive.*

Mrs. Frank A. Bourne, founder and first president of the Beacon Hill Garden Club, Boston, waters her geraniums in 1929. Her home is said to have contained an eccentric collection of statues among the greenery and a pet cockatoo known for his unpleasant demeanor. *Courtesy of GCA Archive.*

Mrs. Minerva Hoyt (of the Pasadena Garden Club, California), known as "Apostle of the Cacti," was passionate about the desert. She created dioramas of living desert plant material for exhibition at the IFS in New York, as well as in Boston and London. In the 1930s she helped establish a ten thousand–acre desert park near Tehuacán, Mexico, and the Joshua Tree National Monument in California. *Courtesy of Joe Zarki, Joshua Tree National Park.*

Mrs. Oakleigh Thorne (of the Millbrook Garden Club, New York, and the Garden Club of Santa Barbara, California), GCA honorary vice president during 1923–53 and Visiting Gardens chairman for almost twenty years, was a great promoter of the redwoods and was honored at the dedication of the Garden Club of America Grove in 1934. Mrs. Thorne also encouraged the landscaping of memorials to honor war veterans. *Courtesy of the Millbrook Garden Club.*

In 1932 members of the Pasadena Garden Club, in California, held a plant sale to benefit La Casita del Arroyo, a public meeting place constructed almost entirely with natural or recycled materials: stone boulders, fallen trees, and lumber from the 1932 Olympic bicycle trail. The building became a cultural heritage landmark in 1976. *Courtesy of the Pasadena Garden Club.*

Judges were often sequestered at the annual International Flower Show, shown here at the Grand Central Palace, New York City, in March 1933. The GCA first participated in the IFS in 1921. The GCA's exhibits grew in breadth and influence over the decades. *Courtesy of GCA Archive.*

At the IFS in 1931, a conservation exhibit by the GCA featured a swarm of billboards defacing the countryside. Twenty thousand pieces of literature were distributed, and seven thousand people signed a petition against billboards on the public highways. *Courtesy of GCA Archive.*

In 1933 a life-size model of a gas station, designed by the Wildflower Committee for the IFS, promoted a clean-looking edifice with simple plantings of disease- and pest-resistant material, replacing the customary commercial signs. *Courtesy of GCA Archive.*

I think that I shall never see
A billboard lovely as a tree.
Perhaps, unless the billboards fall,
I'll never see a tree at all.

To heighten the anti-billboard sentiment, this widely popular postcard, enhanced with a poem by Ogden Nash, was sold for a penny. *Courtesy of GCA Archive.*

In 1939 this miniature model of a garden center, created by Mrs. Jonathan Butler (of The Little Garden Club of Rye, New York), won first prize at the IFS. Thirty thousand people attended the opening. The crush of viewers made it necessary to protect the exhibits with a fence. *Courtesy of GCA Archive.*

In May 1934 the twenty-five-hundred-acre Garden Club of America Redwood Grove was dedicated by Dr. A. H. Reinhardt, president of Mills College, and presented to the State of California. Mrs. Oakleigh Thorne is credited with this major undertaking that expanded the reach of the GCA to the West Coast. *Courtesy of GCA Archive.*

At the invitation of the America-Japan Society and the Society for International Cultural Relations, ninety GCA members visited Japan in 1935. The group, including President Mrs. Jonathan Bulkley (of the Ridgefield Garden Club, Connecticut), 1932–35, and her husband, toured the gardens of Ryuanji, Daitokuji Monastery, and other sites. *Courtesy of GCA Archive.*

Mrs. Robert H. Fife (of the Middletown Garden Club, Connecticut), elected incoming president at the twenty-second annual meeting, held in Northern California in 1935, participated in the GCA pilgrimage to Hawaii, where she and other members were greeted with Hawaiian leis, and then traveled to Japan. *Courtesy of GCA Archive.*

Fletcher Steele (member-at-large) designed over five hundred gardens. He is best known for his work at Lisburne Grange, New York, and for the master landscape at Naumkeag, New York, which he created over a span of thirty years for Miss Mabel Choate. He wrote a user-friendly book on small gardens and articles for the *Bulletin*, in which he advocated use of the color chart for more vibrant plantings. *Courtesy of the Franklin Moon Library, at SUNY College of Environmental Science and Forestry.*

by his arrogance and turned to the GCA Executive Committee for support. This was declined.

Mrs. Noyes returned to Colonel Grant, her approach softer. He liked her already and warmed up by turning the tables and tossing one of his own problems to her. Under his jurisdiction were eight historic sandstone columns, then stored in a shed and believed to have stood on the front of the U.S. War Department Building until the 1870s, when a new headquarters was built. They were in fact from the old State Department built during 1816–18, which stood northeast of the White House. No one wanted them dumped into the Potomac, the usual fate of such discarded federal building material in the capital, but what might be done with them? Perhaps as a favor to win his goodwill, Mrs. Noyes took on the columns as a challenge. She came up with the design of placing pairs of them at the four major automobile entrances to Washington.

Improving the entrances to the city had been initiated when automobiles began to rival trains as a means of traveling to Washington. Nothing had come of the project, because it became tangled in the issues of highway landscaping and billboard removal and others that federal officials looked upon as politically threatening. Colonel Grant, however, believed it a worthy idea, and he erected two sets according to Janet Noyes's design, with the intention of building more, had the Fine Arts Commission not called his plans to a halt. The GCA treasury was out four thousand dollars for the effort, which became one of those episodes the less spoken about the better.[15] But it was not the last encounter the GCA would have with stone columns from the early federal period in the capital.[16]

Toward the close of 1933 the government's District of Columbia Committee suffered from serious budget cutting by a belt-tightening Congress. Proponents of reviving the McMillan Plan were heartsick. The committee chair, Frederick Delano, cousin of the new president, ordered the envisioned city plan printed on handkerchiefs in an effort to popularize it. Yet troubled times had outrun the city beautiful. All work meant to implement the McMillan Plan was stopped just before Christmas; the construction sites were wintered in, to be left until better times. At the same time the GCA discontinued its own Committee for the National Capital. This seems to have been as much the wish of Janet Noyes as the directors. She and Hetty Harrison told the board that their work could be better accomplished as "special agents" of the GCA in Washington. The board agreed to this self-appointment only because it did not wish to abandon the arboretum project and may also have felt that having a liaison on hand would keep it alive.[17]

The new arrangement of "agents" in Washington was not successful. For all the efforts of Mrs. Noyes and Mrs. Harrison, their only point of entry in a government preoccupied with the Depression was the Department of Agriculture. President Hoover's Secretary of Agriculture, Arthur Hyde, was encouraging, as was his successor under Roosevelt, Henry A. Wallace, but when in October 1934 Mrs. Noyes and Mrs. Harrison again took up the sensitive subject of the National Botanic Garden, trying to have the neglected glass houses near the Capitol transferred to the Department of Agriculture, they once again put their fingers into the mousetrap of a possessive Congress. The trap snapped, and they withdrew quickly. On December 12, 1934, Janet Noyes wrote her resignation to the GCA, concluding her Washington work for the GCA. Her energy and devotion, however, were not to be shelved for long.

The educational efforts of the Garden Club of America suffered no such setback. Its symbol was the library, and its roots were for all time deep in that most honored GCA facility. On its shelves were books by GCA members: Louisa Yeomans King's 1915 classic, *The Well-Considered Gardener;* Helena Rutherford Ely's 1903 *A Woman's Hardy Garden;* Kate Brewster's 1926 *The Little Garden for Little Money.* Also, the GCA's Library Committee had encouraged the reprinting of Andrew Jackson

Downing's 1850 classic, *Landscape Gardening,* praising it as the "first American book on gardening."

The documentary records indicate that the GCA's first love after gardening itself was books about gardens. So numerous were the books sent to them that in 1934 the Library Committee determined to accept from that time on only books about garden design. Already for a decade they had been accumulating rare books. The vitrine exhibits of the old cherished volumes were changed from time to time. There is no question that some members of the Library Committee were connoisseurs of fine books, loving the design and production, the luxury of the paper, the placement of the printing on the pages. The library had over a hundred sixteenth-, seventeenth-, and eighteenth-century volumes. When the board wished to recognize Harriet Pratt in 1928 for "all her work in GCA," they presented her with the two-volume *Theater de la Grande Bretagne* (1708), a richly illustrated presentation of palatial gardens and houses in England. Mrs. Pratt was touched and said, "All the hard work has been rewarded by friendship and inspiration." She put the books in the GCA library, where they may be seen today.[18]

The Library Committee was not focused upon books alone. In addition to functioning as a very active educational branch of the GCA to keep and distribute the popular slide shows, it originated educational exhibits at headquarters in New York. The committee's exhibits at the office in the 1930s rose so high in public favor that they practically crowded out all other business at headquarters. In the winter of 1934, for example, books about sixteenth-century gardens were gathered into an exhibit accompanied by a lecture series. The speaker might be a professor from a university or a botanical garden or a GCA member who had traveled abroad studying horticulture. Lithographs, other types of prints, and sometimes watercolors of flowers and gardens typically varied the headquarters' exhibitions.

Few of the exhibits were limited entirely to books, although tight headquarters space prohibited exhibits of much more extensive content there. Larger exhibits were usually held at the fashionable Ferargil Gallery, on East Sixty-third Street. There the rooms were large, the walls draped, and the lighting theatrical. In addition to books, such a show might feature pottery, flower arrangements both fresh and dried, antique and modern containers, gardening tools, and even floral textiles on one occasion. Miniature arrangements of cut flowers, enjoying a period of popularity with GCA members at about this time, became one of the club's most popular classes in the International Flower Show.

While it is difficult to be exact about the initial academic involvement of the organization, the many private educational connections of GCA members indicate that associations with educational institutions probably began with Ernestine Goodman and Ellen Patterson's founding of a horticulture department at Ambler College, near Philadelphia, in 1910, three years before the GCA's founding. Called the Pennsylvania School of Horticulture, it became the second women's landscape school in the United States, the first being Lowthorpe School, in Massachusetts, founded in 1901. Through scholarships, the GCA participated to an extent in both schools but somewhat erratically until the later 1920s, when, encouraged by Beatrix Farrand and Ellen Biddle Shipman, both practicing landscape architects and members of the GCA, it concentrated more on Lowthorpe.

The Ambler program, however, remained close to the GCA through the Garden Club of Philadelphia. Landscape architecture was considered an appropriate profession for a lady, and the character and tone of the professional roles available to them were of great concern to women throughout the 1910s and 1920s. Opinions varied among women, just as they did about the vote. From a distance, one wonders whether some of those who supported the landscape programs for women were trying to educate gardeners for their own gardens or actually create places for women in a competitive profession usually occupied by men. Perhaps there was motivation in both directions; in any case, that the idea itself was a good one could not be denied.

The interest in gardening as a creative pastime for women was widespread. Among its significant promoters was Mariana Griswold Van Rensselaer, the first and grandest of American female art critics. Also, Ellen Biddle Shipman was the perfect model of a successful woman landscape designer as well as a serious inspiration to gardeners.

No one personally illustrated the ideal of a woman professional more enviably than the soignée Beatrix Jones Farrand, who was chauffeured to her jobs in a Pierce-Arrow car, made her plans surrounded by assistants—unrolling drawings, making changes with very emphatic strokes of her pen—and was always asked to lunch. Privately she never seemed so different from everyone else, but she packaged herself very carefully in public. She was proud to be a member of a club that belonged to the GCA. Her projects were many: summer homes, city gardens, and not least the East Garden of the White House, which she designed in neo-Victorian style at the invitation of the first Mrs. Woodrow Wilson.

Yet the GCA was not feminist in the public way that early twentieth-century feminism is depicted in text books. There naturally is no tally of each GCA woman's personal viewpoint on women's rights, and of course they varied. Elizabeth Martin was not a suffragette but sympathized with granting the franchise to women. In the era there were women who stood by without participation in the protests but supported the cause; others scorned the suffragettes as a narrow interest group, destructive to the already steady advance of women in American life. The GCA, judged as an organization, seems best described by the former, broader viewpoint. The women of the GCA left no recorded objection whatsoever to feminist political agendas. When the suffragettes' quest was over and women had the vote, the GCA continued as it had all along, a union of clubs composed of women pursuing serious interests outside their homes. Even in venturing beyond their own thresholds, they expressed a form of feminism.

In 1925 there were fifty-six GCA clubs scattered across the map. Their members were amateurs dedicated to self-improvement. The thirst to learn and to better their horticultural efforts led the clubs to seek knowledge from professionals and experts. Their hopes to promote and improve the general appreciation of nature and the field of horticulture in its various facets led to an early interest in sponsoring scholarships.[19]

The first major scholarship program of the GCA was a joint arrangement with the American Academy in Rome. This distinguished institution was conceived by American architects such as Charles McKim and William Rutherford Mead, of McKim, Mead & White, and intellectuals like William Dean Howells and Edith Wharton as a "School of Contact and Research (not of design)." There in Rome, Americans would study the enduring monuments of the past and, inspired, would create modern architecture equally timeless. As one of the most successful students later wrote, paraphrasing McKim, "The Academy was the surest way to a cultural appreciation of great classical things as a foundation for big conceptions."[20]

An era of soaring idealism stretched seamlessly from the academy's opening in January 1895 to May 1, 1913, when the Garden Club of America joined its forward march. The academy had supporters among the early members of the GCA, notably, Kate Brewster, of Lake Forest, who, we have seen, was an accomplished landscape designer in her own right. Her choice of articles and her own essays as editor of the *Bulletin* reflected her knowledge and abilities as a gardener. Mrs. Brewster believed that as the architects studied the monuments of the past in Europe, so should landscape architects study historic European gardens. In 1913 she established a fellowship in her name at the American Academy. Her influence led to the first GCA grant of a Rome fellowship in 1917.

World War I interrupted further participation. In early May 1925, Hetty Harrison, a GCA director, met with James Leal Greenleaf, a New York–based landscape architect, and Gorham Phillips Stevens, director of the American Academy in Rome, over tea in the garden of her farm, Belvoir, in Virginia. All parties remembered that it was a glorious day, with the meadows green, the trees in flower, and the white of the big house dappled by shade trees. The subject was the possibility of establishing an ongoing GCA-funded scholarship for one American student a year at the academy. Moreover, the arrangement, as she envisioned it, would be so structured as to facilitate club members, students, and alumni to tour the fine gardens of America and Italy.[21]

While the tour part was relegated to other agencies, the fellowship was funded with the enthusiastic blessing of the board of directors of the GCA. In the fall of the following year, 1926, Richard K. Webel sailed for Europe to begin his studies as the GCA's first fellow at the American Academy in Rome. Marie Prentice, who styled herself the committee's "sometimes chair," took the lead in raising money from the member clubs. She traveled to Rome to better understand the academy; back home, she crossed the country by rail, speaking before GCA clubs about the academy and the need for money to fund it. At the time of Webel's appointment, the academy fund was $8,000. By two years later, thanks largely to Mrs. Prentice's speaking tours, the GCA had collected $56,256 in donations. The academy had requested $50,000 to fund the scholarship. The GCA retained the balance for its own costs in promoting and setting up the program. Webel, back in the United States and based in New York in the 1930s, proved a rewarding investment for the GCA, rising to the top as a leading American landscape architect.

The educational objectives of the GCA were also seen early in the Visiting Gardens program. It is not clear whether the first committee, formed in 1920, was intended to manage only a tour to England or whether its purpose was more permanent. Whatever the case, preparations were as nearly comprehensive as Helen Thorne, the chair, could make them. An active and opinionated landscapist, Mrs. Thorne had designed and cultivated large and dramatic gardens at her home, Thorndale, near Millbrook, New York, and at her winter residence in Montecito, California. She was as handy with a hoe and shovel as she was with a T-square and a draftsman's pencil. A traveler herself, she believed one learned and grew through touring. She was to remain active in instigating many tours, and after 1923 took a special interest in domestic travel.

Helen Thorne and her committee, to be called the Visiting Gardens Committee, sent out some six hundred invitations while planning the trip to England, which took several years. Ninety made the tour, crossing by liner in September 1929, and returning at the end of October. During the planning, the GCA found welcoming helpers in the lengthy planning and genial hosts for the tour in the English Speaking Union. Thus began a long association between the GCA and the ESU.

Stimulated by the success of the English tour, the Visiting Gardens Committee became a permanent fixture in the GCA, a popular feature of the organization's educational mission. Trips to France were set in motion with the assistance of Edme Sommier, whose restored gardens at the seventeenth-century Vaux le Vicomte reflected the great interest France was taking at the time in its gardening heritage. Work commenced on an Italian tour, but its planners admitted, "Italian gardens are most difficult of access."[22]

Hetty Harrison, traveling in Italy, pressed the American Academy in Rome to help out. At last the director, Gorham Stevens, was able to write to her: "I take pleasure in informing you that the Italy American Society of Rome and the Ministry of Fine Arts of the Italian Government have about prepared a scheme whereby Americans, who are lovers of Italian villas, may visit the best gardens throughout Italy." For the cost of a five-dollar ticket, some four hundred villas in Italy would be available to see. "Many of the villas have never been published or photographed." Stevens noted that members of the GCA had called at the American Academy in recent years "in ever-increasing numbers." Why not open American gardens to academy students and alumni?[23]

Under the continuing chairmanship of Helen Thorne, the Visiting Gardens Committee scheduled annual trips and requested permission to tour private gardens in the United States as well as Europe. Sometimes the rush to get on the tours was so great as to justify a second tour, to accommodate everyone. In December 1925, the committee published the *Locator*, listing gardens in Europe and America that could be visited. Names and addresses were all current. Garden visitors were to request from headquarters a "card of introduction," which had to accompany them to the desired garden. The book was a big hit: 450 were printed in 1925; 5,000 in 1927.[24]

Visiting Gardens tours held regularly both at home and abroad in the 1920s and '30s. Records suggest not a single cancellation in those years between the world wars. Mrs. Thorne wrote in 1930 that she saw a purpose to the tours as important as any other horticultural education: "Faraway clubs need our help and inspiration, or they feel out of touch with the central organization." The Visiting Gardens program thus helped build a stronger GCA.[25]

An organization such as the GCA, committed to excellence in its field, naturally saw the need for awards as a means of stimulating the urge to perfection. The first GCA award was created in 1917, the year America entered the European war. It honored Emily D. Renwick, of the Short Hills Garden Club, who was one of the original GCA founders and had died that year, and was designed by fellow club member Henrietta Maria Stout. The second and third awards, long in planning, were approved in 1920 and 1921, while the Executive Committee was still meeting in the Pratt apartment. These other two awards were the Medal of Honor for horticulture and the GCA Medal or the GCA Achievement Medal, a rather open award for outstanding achievement within the GCA organization by members and member clubs. In 1921 Emily Renwick's club, the Short Hills Garden Club (originally called the Nine of Spades for its nine members), commissioned a silver medal, which became the Renwick Medal until the medals ran out and the award was discontinued in 1931.

Many awards have been established by the GCA, and many have run their courses and, like the Renwick Medal, vanished. Both the Medal of Honor and the GCA Achievement Medal were to survive. The first Medal of Honor—which would soon be called the Gold Medal—was awarded in 1920 to Professor Charles Sprague Sargent, director of the Arnold Arboretum at Harvard University since 1873 and a committed celebrant of the GCA and its mission.

A discussion of awards was held in 1921 at the January board meeting. The two awards were defined. Within a short time, without explanation, the board dissolved the Awards Committee. The Gold Medal was given a second time in 1923, to Louisa Yeomans King. But the Gold Medal was discussed very little at the GCA and was awarded very sparingly over the next decade. By 1936 it had been awarded only four times. One or more clubs or an individual or group of people had to nominate a candidate for the Gold Medal.

The GCA Achievement Medal lagged behind the Gold Medal in coming to definition. The new Awards Committee, established in 1927, assigned a subcommittee to develop this in-club award. The subcommittee had seven members, with four set apart as a "screening committee," a sort of "senate." In the raw documents the arrangement seems to be at the least controlling, if not peremptory. When the Achievement Medal was first envisioned, it was called the Achievement Medallion. The idea, dating back to 1921, was to produce three types of medallions: gold for flower shows of the highest quality; silver for plant society shows; and last, bronze for flower shows in high standing among member clubs. Clubs wishing to be considered were to apply for achievement awards with full written justification, which was to be reviewed by the subcommittee.

On February 11, 1931, the Awards Committee announced to the board that the sculptor Paul Manship had agreed to design the Achievement Medallion. Manship, at the peak of his fame, was at the time working to complete his golden Prometheus, which would overlook Rockefeller Center. The committee chair, Mrs. Henry Osborn Saylor, expressed the committee's delight at having Manship design their medal.

In fact, their excitement was such that it was called the Manship Medal of Achievement then and for at least a generation after its completion.

The Executive Committee's only specification had been that the reverse of the medal show the logo or "insignia" of the organization. This insignia, like the Renwick Medal, had been designed by Henrietta Maria Stout, of Short Hills, New Jersey, and had been approved on February 14, 1921. It consisted of a "lamp of enlightenment," standing for education, surrounded by oak leaves and twelve acorns, representing horticulture and the twelve original clubs, respectively. Before special designs were made, the medal awards had only the insignia as ornament. The character of Dr. Sargent's award in 1920 is unknown, for it predated the appearance of the insignia. Manship's design was approved on February 10, 1932, one year after it had been commissioned, and it prevails today. The present insignia is a simplified version of the original created in 2002, by the artist Marilyn Worseldine, both to modernize the appearance and to make the logo more easily printed and used by computers.[26]

Already in January 1932 the Pennsylvania Horticultural Society, admiring Manship's model, asked for permission to use the silver casting of the Achievement Medallion for the "Sweepstakes Prize" at the flower show. This was denied by the board of directors. At the same time the board elected to "enlarge the scope of the prize" to be more inclusive. They presented the Achievement Medallion for the first time later, in April, posthumously to Elizabeth Martin, who had died only two weeks before. Losing her brought a transition to the GCA everywhere, for while running the national organization had gone largely to others, Mrs. Martin had persevered as a beloved symbol of the founding. But the GCA was not her only mourner, for on the day of her funeral, flags in Philadelphia hung at half mast honoring her as one of the greatest civic workers in the city's history.

Manship's handsome medal, with the face showing a draped female figure and the insignia on the back, sparked an interest in medals for the GCA. Two years after the debut of the Achievement Medallion,

Mrs. John H. Gibbons presented the Gibbons Medal, which she commissioned from the Philadelphia sculptor Harriet Whitney Frishmuth, a former student of Rodin and apprentice to a leading American sculptor, Karl Bitter. The Gibbons Medal honored "the use and arrangement of plant material," or, in simpler, less familiar terms at the time, flower arranging. In 1934 the Gibbons Medal, which the donor never intended to be named for her, was renamed the Fenwick Medal.

With the Gold Medal no longer exclusively a horticultural award, a new horticultural award was proposed by Mrs. Edgar A. Knapp, of Elizabeth, New Jersey. As the result of what may or may not have been a design competition, contract for the design and production of the new medal went to Walter Hancock, a sculptor well known for his portrait statuary at the National Cathedral and for the presidential busts in the Senate of the United States Capitol. The resulting handsome bronze disk was called the Garden Club of America Horticultural Medal.

The year 1933 saw a rain of GCA medals awarded by the individual clubs and zones. Clubs proposed candidates for medals to the national Awards Committee, whose recommendations went to the board for approval. Headquarters in New York did a thriving business selling, packing, and sending the heavy medals in their velvet boxes. There were club awards, zone awards, and national awards. Individual clubs often had their own awards, judged by themselves. The Awards Committee duly processed the requests and made its recommendations to the Executive Committee. Not for more than another sixty years would the GCA in one year present so many awards.[27]

On April 10, 1935, Harriet Pratt presented her concept for the Founders Fund, which has been a cherished and useful GCA institution ever since. To most board members it appears to have been a surprise, the idea of a fund actively collecting donations and distributing annual grants. Mrs. Pratt already had honed her plan in private discussions with the

Executive Committee. The fund was to honor Elizabeth Martin, a memorial to not only a founder and a major inspiration of the GCA but also a remarkable American who was the very essence of selfless public service. The Executive Committee attached the following to the proposal: "We cannot expect that the income from this fund, even though our most extravagant dreams are realized, can establish an arboretum, can wipe out a pest, or accomplish mighty tasks; but we can expect that we can follow the traditions of the Garden Club of America in lighting a torch, in encouraging a standard bearer for some object which comes with the definition of the purpose of the GCA and through the Founders Fund can commemorate the name of Elizabeth Price Martin."[28]

The Founders Fund was approved. In the process a debate had continued over the idea of whether to spend money as soon as it came in or to let it accumulate before making grants. Mrs. Pratt, having what she wanted in the approval, set out to raise money. By form letter she contacted all ninety-nine member clubs; ninety-nine clubs responded with donations, which were in the one hundred to two hundred dollar range. The 1930s were somewhat in advance of the era of corporate largesse to organizations like the GCA, so the kitty was filled by individual donations. November 13, 1935, seven months after her intitial presentation of the idea, Harriet Pratt reported having raised $25,377.

In the following January the minutes said of her: "In spite of the depression she felt that the clubs had responded spontaneously and that when member clubs realized that they would have a share in the Founders Fund, there will be much more interest in the fund." One year later, January 12, 1937, Mrs. Pratt announced that her committee had raised thirty-seven thousand dollars and had elevated the goal to fifty thousand dollars, which they hoped to secure by the annual meeting in the coming year. She promoted the fund with contagious enthusiasm. The clubs took up the challenge, raising money by publishing cookbooks, holding plant sales, and sponsoring luncheons, teas, lectures, and garden tours; they opened thrift shops and produced flower shows and auctions, to which they sold tickets and took a cut of the profits. One club complained, "We don't know Mrs. Martin." Mrs. Pratt shot back, "Well, neither did you know George Washington, but you honor him for what he did for his country."[29]

Representing her committee at the board meeting on April 13, 1938, Harriet Pratt rose in victory when she announced having received a total of seventy thousand dollars in donations for the Founders Fund. With emotion she said she "extended deep gratitude to the members of the Garden Club of America for their generosity and their patience in the task of raising so large a sum in these difficult times."[30]

The first grants were made in 1938 to fund publication of an Aztec herbal, the Badianus Manuscript, a medical notebook written and illustrated in 1552. It had been brought to the Smithsonian Institution on loan from the Vatican Library and translated for publication by Emily Walcott Emmart. The notebook is one of the most significant documents surviving from pre-Columbian America, and the translated facsimile, published for the sponsors in a small edition by the Johns Hopkins University Press, was true to the original.

In the same year, 1938, thousand-dollar grants went to Bartram's Garden, in Philadelphia; to the preservation movement to save the Hudson River Highlands; and to research in the genus *Acanthus* at the Blakley Botanic Garden, in Santa Barbara. In 1939 ninety applications were received at headquarters. On March 15 at the Waldorf-Astoria Hotel, six awards were made, four of them to historic houses: Monticello; Gore Place, in Waltham, Massachusetts; Hammond-Harwood House, in Annapolis; and the garden of Abraham Lincoln's house in Springfield. Another research grant was made to Joseph Gable, of Swarthmore, Pennsylvania, for work with azaleas and rhododendrons, and the sixth was a renewal grant for the Blakley Botanic Garden, long of interest to the GCA. The recipients were—and remain—as varied as the member clubs' interests and always reflective of the inclinations of the times.

It was good, available money in a not-so-easy time. Some board members with projects of their own saw the growing fund shimmering brightly and questioned the committee's authority over it. If the money was collected by the GCA, then was it not the board's prerogative to decide how it was spent? Looking over the scant transcripts related to this apparently very heated debate, one can wonder whether the Founders Fund would have survived the storm had Harriet Pratt not been there to protect it. But the lady took no prisoners in her defense of the fund, and the Founders Fund remains today dedicated to its original purpose, and its awards are voted on by the entire membership.

The dark presence of the Depression was rarely mentioned or alluded to in official proceedings of the GCA. There was virtually total silence on the subject, yet the economic stress cannot have been overlooked, for the 1930s were agitated by it on many levels. Even those who appear to have suffered no drastic setback were sometimes beset by a kind of preoccupation with an unseen axe that might at any instant cut them down, taking away the life they knew. In 1933 the Executive Committee asked the midwestern clubs of Zone XI in a circular letter whether they thought that "the serious financial condition throughout the country" made it advisable to cancel the Chicago annual meeting they were at that time planning. No responses survive, but within a month Zone XI reported that the annual meeting was half booked-up.

Nor was the work of the Visiting Gardens Committee in the least lightened by hard times. Helen Thorne, always generous with her time and checkbook, had with other members pressed for trips to Europe and Britain. All the trips sold to capacity with waiting lists—England, France, the Netherlands, Mexico. Tour groups were large—150 in Mexico—and required careful management. The ships upon which GCA tours sailed were the best, the hotels were all first class, and a host of foreign titles spiced the receptions and dinners.

The grandest trip yet was that to Japan in 1935. While the Visiting Gardens Committee's invitation was issued to all the clubs, the members in proximity to Manhattan were the best served. For the tour to Japan the Japan Society in New York graciously consented to present weekly "evenings" in the big drawing room at the Cosmopolitan Club. Those signed up as thinking about going on the trip paid a small fee and enjoyed cocktails, tea, perhaps some traditional Japanese cooking, and a lecture on gardens, costume, history, or Japanese social customs. The program was a big success and contributed to stretching the waiting list for the tour.[31]

The tour, which cost a thousand dollars per participant, began in Los Angeles. Max and Beatrix Farrand welcomed participants to the Huntington Library, where he was director and she, although nominally retired, was involved with developing the library's extensive gardens. Tour participants were also entertained by the Pasadena Garden Club, where the inspiration to help save the redwoods had first come to the GCA. From the port of Los Angeles the party of one hundred sailed to Honolulu for that year's GCA annual meeting. Sailing on from there northwesterly to Japan they joined gracious Japanese hosts, who beguiled them with the loveliness of the gardens, houses, temples, and landscapes.

Six years later, the United States was at war with Japan. After Pearl Harbor the Topographical Division of the War Department in Washington contacted the GCA travelers of 1935 to study the candid snapshots of places they had visited on that unforgettable voyage.[32]

Chapter Four
COMING OF AGE

The brilliant decade of the 1920s did not dim the tragedy of World War I or the fear that another such conflict might come. Americans built memorials and sought reassuring symbols of peace. On November 13, 1929, the board of directors voted to help create a "peace garden" at Niagara Falls, dedicated to America's friendship with Canada. The committee in charge consulted Pierre S. du Pont, who had welcomed GCA members to his then-private garden and greenhouses at Kennett Square, Pennsylvania, just over the line from Delaware.

The original idea for the peace garden was that of Dr. Henry J. Moore, a well-known horticulturist of Islington, Ontario, who thought it time to commemorate the uninterrupted peace enjoyed historically between Canada and the neighboring United States. If Moore's history was a little fuzzy, his belief in his project was clear. He had lectured to the GCA Horticulture Committee in New York and made successful contacts with clubs in the New York and Boston areas. Matters went well until, on reconsideration of the site, he decided that Niagara Falls was too powerful and the river too divisive for what he had in mind. He moved his dream west, to a more placid setting, Manitoba at the North Dakota border; his peace garden was to include land from both countries. The GCA lost interest.

Through the records of the GCA in the 1930s the theme of war appears in many ways: in landscaping war memorials and monuments, in raising money for postwar causes; and at times in a sort of nervous anticipation of future war. In 1932 the Executive Committee sent a delegation to Washington to ascertain how the GCA might make a plan of action in case a war should come. After meeting at the Capitol with Jesse Paine Wolcott, the famous World War I veteran machine gunner, lawyer, jurist, and more recently a congressman from Michigan, they were assured by his best Unitarian rationale that there was to be no more war. With that the pressure seems to have relaxed, and for the time the GCA had little more to say on the subject.[1]

Eight years later, in 1940, the Great War lay only twenty-one years in the past, and another European war had begun. England's plight was fearful. From its headquarters the GCA sent out a "war letter" to every club, urging support for Britain in its trial, "to which all clubs . . . responded generously."[2] Leading the way was the Garden Club of Wilmington, Delaware, with an immediate donation of a thousand dollars for British relief.

By November 1940 the clubs of the GCA were deep into the aid of England. Letters of thanks poured across the Atlantic, very discreetly recognizing donations of seeds from neutral America. The gift seeds had many uses, providing for both British gardens and Royal Air Force bases, where pilots who flew out at night sometimes tended gardens to relieve daytime boredom and tension. The GCA Archive has preserved some of these letters. All over the United States GCA clubs were involved in the Red Cross, Allied Relief, the British War Relief Society, and of course their old friend the English Speaking Union.

On January 9, 1941, the entire board of directors attended the British War Relief Society's illustrated lecture at the Waldorf-Astoria to hear Hugh Findlay, Columbia University's distinguished professor of horticulture and agriculture. The professor, although noted most for his work with ornamental plants, now turned to vegetables in his speech

"Gardens to Live With." Time had come again, he said, for women to garden in preparedness for what might lie ahead. At the next month's board meeting, Robert Appleby, an officer in the War Society, reported on his organization's mission to attract women in Boston and America to war work. The War Society "started in a small way with the idea of having things knitted for the troops," rather than focusing on gardens, because, as he explained, "England's food supply will not come to shortage until later."[3]

Other needs were pressing: "Cigarettes are not essential yet were welcomed in parcels received by prisoners of war. The Germans are most meticulous in seeing that prisoners receive packages mailed to them. Clothing arrives in good condition and clothes are the most urgent need at the moment." On the home front it was seeds the Americans could most usefully supply. By that January meeting six tons of seeds had been sent from the United States. Seed supply programs were in place for Finland as well as Britain, and American seeds were germinating in fields surrounding Royal Air Force bases.[4]

There was to be no American declaration of war until the year's end. Already the GCA was making a commendable record. Each board member headed a war committee in her zone, to guide the zone's club members in useful war work. When the report on contributions returned from the war letter, it was impressive: to the care of European children, $2,165; to the ambulance corps, $13,816, including the actual purchase of ambulances; in "rolling kitchens" both in America and Europe, movable to sites where troops were numerous, $6,700; to the American Red Cross, $32,210; to the nascent American Seeds for Britain, already $305; and to "other British relief," $3,648.[5]

In GCA clubs all over America the spring and summer were filled with house and garden tours to raise money. The clubs of the Garden Club of Virginia, some of which were also GCA clubs, pledged profits from their annual garden week of tours "to lend all possible aid to the stricken people of England." Opening gardens was different from flower shows, in that part of the public's attraction was seeing how their fellow citizens lived, especially if the occupants were famous or notably rich. The successful tour of Mary Riker's boxwood garden at her New Jersey seaside home, Linden Crest, in early May encouraged the sponsors to open it a second time the next week. For the two tours the Rumson Garden Club tallied three thousand paying visitors. Explaining the appeal of touring fine gardens, the GCA offered a gently dubious, slightly condescending reason other than mere curiosity: the visits "show people how to take care of their own little city home gardens in an attractive manner."[6]

At headquarters the question of what to do to help Britain remained current. Kate Fox, of the Fairfield Garden Club in Southport, Connecticut, a GCA worker appearing first in the GCA in the late 1930s, was appointed chair of the War Committee. She was single, which was rare among those most frequently seen on national projects, and was thus able to enter her duties full-time. In preparing for the work ahead, she pulled a fragmented set of good intentions together to create a well-organized whole, which she laid before her and began to plan. The officers and directors seem to have looked on this explosively energetic woman in increasing wonder. She persuaded the Executive Committee to adopt one "unified defense project" instead of trying to conduct many. Her idea was to have the GCA build Red Cross recreation centers in the various army camps. The project was presented at a board meeting on January 8, 1941, which the zone chairs had been urged to attend but made a sparse showing.

Disregarding the weighty approval the Executive Committee had already granted, a number of club members appeared strongly opposed to Miss Fox's plan. Meeting a few days after the attack on Pearl Harbor, the board was in some disarray. Harriet Pratt was by no means alone in saying that the GCA should get full and direct credit for its own good works and not share glory with the Red Cross or any other organization. One wing of the opposition objected to the apparent abandonment of traditional GCA pursuits in favor of war work. Mrs. William B. Mather, the Central Zone chair, was absent but sent word that three of her clubs said they were now "too busy with war work to do anything about gardens." Edith Kohlsaat, of the Central Western Zone, expressed her zone's conclusion to all the discussion: "We needed the peace and comfort of gardens [more] than ever before to keep us normal in these distressed times . . . garden clubs should retain their former identity, conserving beauty and doing everything along conservation lines and . . . war relief work should be done individually."[7]

Rebecca Pepper, a founder of the GCA and the Garden Club of Philadelphia and the director most interested in the brewing controversy, now spoke:

> I wish we would think this over very seriously about the Garden Club's connection with our lives today. It seems to me that we need most tremendously all the inspiration that we had out of our gardens. We are all doing war work in some form or another. . . . I hope very much that the Garden Club of America will remain the Garden Club of America and not start some sort of war work. . . . If there is some definite job that should be done in this country for Conservation along the lines of raising vegetables, necessary herbs—all very well—but let us consider very carefully any plan. I hope the Garden Club of America will keep its head as well as its heart.[8]

In support of this, Violetta Delafield produced the current issue of the British magazine *Horticulture* and said, "There may be a lesson for the people of this country," and then she quoted: "No apology is needed to draw attention to the invaluable aid that flowers and plants can give in the keeping up of our spirits—and morale. The family leaving its dugout in the early hours of the morning is cheered by the fugitive perfume of the rose bed. If the garden had been given over wholly to the culture of vegetables, some of the peace and inspiration one draws from a garden of flowers would have been lacking."[9]

Kate Fox and the Executive Committee saw their idea for a single GCA project fade away before the board's desire to keep the GCA focused on its original objectives and proceeding alone. One had only to stand apart from the prevailing opinion to see why a total turn to war work failed, that gardening had an almost spiritual place in these women's lives. The maintenance of the organization as it had been was their expression of optimism that peace would return and things would be as they had been.

Before the war, the last significant public expression of the Garden Club of America's devotion to tranquility and beauty was in a sense the finale of an era for them: participation in the New York World's Fair of 1939–40, which welcomed forty-four million visitors to the city. It was a splendid event indeed, to be so nearly forgotten today. The "futuristic" architecture represented some of the most famous architects in the world. Invention and technology were featured. Not the least of the 1939 fair's historic high points was the introduction of television to the public for the first time.

In retrospect the event seems detached from reality, a midsummer night's dream in the midst of turmoil. Built in Queens, the fair, with its flamboyant art moderne and art deco design, was a historical commemoration of the Constitution and George Washington's inauguration, but more, it was the herald of an imagined age to come, a monumental tribute to modern technology and the promise of the future. The GCA was involved in the horticultural exhibition, "Gardens on Parade," a five-acre setting of what the *New York Herald Tribune* called "the Most Stupendous, Most Magnificent, Most Gorgeous exhibition of flowers, shrubs, and horticultural beauties ever assembled." In studying the event years later and leafing through old documents, Margaret Anne Tockarshewsky found that the fair showed amazing invention that "struck a thrilling cord in a population stirring from the depths of the Depression." Yet looking back once again, we can now see that it was not the Depression but the war that made this event seem so bizarre.[10]

The GCA's exhibit was Harriet Pratt's challenge, and she and "several thousand individuals" under her direction created the horticultural show, under the auspices of Hortus, Inc., a nonprofit organization she personally seeded with money and in which she served as president. It was an ambitious show from the outset, needing such a spirit as hers to make it happen. She assembled her committee, mostly of men, from among the GCA's admirers and husbands; they became generous donors. Organizations quickly fell into line, including the Society of American Florists, the New York Florists Club, the Horticultural Society of New York, the New York Botanical Garden, and the Brooklyn Botanic Garden. Not omitted from the advisory was the GCA's proven friend Robert Moses, recipient of the GCA's 1938 Medal of Honor and head of the parks system for the city.

At her side was the often-unpaid creative genius of all her other volunteer projects, the architect William Adams Delano, a member of the fair's advisory board and designer of the elaborate entrance gates. He had built two houses for Mrs. Pratt, and they had worked together decorating some of the state rooms of the White House; few friends were closer to Harriet Pratt than Billy Delano. Garden clubs designed and planted fifty-two gardens for the fair under her direction, varying from actual "Woodland gardens," with living trees, to "Gardens of Today," with hedges and turf. A quaint cottage, complete with interiors and thatched roof, was designed by Delano. Educational displays, carefully planned, featured horticulture, including flowers, and conservation. GCA club members from across the country flocked to join the exhibitors. They found at the fair every convenience, not least air-conditioned niches for their flower arrangements, which were changed daily, to include as many exhibitors as possible.

In spite of what seems to us in retrospect precarious timing so close to the outbreak of war, the New York World's Fair was a super show and a great success. The GCA exhibitors, exhausted by their task master, nevertheless felt rewarded for their work, and many from far away lingered in New York to exhibit again and again. In the late spring of 1940 Mrs. Pratt welcomed Mrs. Franklin D. Roosevelt to the fair and joined "all the other ladies connected with gardens"—as Mrs. Roosevelt put it afterward in her syndicated column—in charming the first lady with "a sweet little corsage of carnations, which gave off the most delicate perfume all the way back to Washington."[11]

The Garden Club of America had positioned itself to survive as it was, no matter what might lie ahead. But this did not preclude a strong participation in war efforts on the home front. Kate Fox's wish to centralize war work had failed, but war work itself flourished in all the clubs, giving them a new sense of power in the national GCA.[12]

In the lapse of time between World War I and the beginning of World War II in Europe, much was said but little done to prepare the people of the United States. In September 1939, however, when Hitler's Germany invaded Poland, wheels heretofore grinding along began to spin. The spotty attention given to the war by the GCA fairly well reflects the average citizen's rambling thinking in the two years before the war actually involved the United States. Change came all at once on December 7, 1941, with the attack on Pearl Harbor.

Nine months after that event, when the nation had been transformed by war, a letter from Marion Rivinus, of Four Counties Garden Club, in Philadelphia, appeared in the *Bulletin*. Speaking from her own perspective, she observed that only a year before, "this country was a peaceful conglomeration of super prosperous, luxury-relaxed, many-nationed peoples" with "an active dislike of war and all things pertaining to it." She recalled how the Philadelphia Symphony Orchestra, in 1941, preparing for an outdoor summer concert in Fairmount Park, needed to find cannon to fire for Tchaikovsky's 1812 Overture. The National Guard had cannon enough, but only five shells could be found "in the entire state of Pennsylvania," and "one misfired and the others made a sickly popping noise."[13]

This would not have been the case after news of Pearl Harbor swept the United States and at last motivated the country to join the Allies in Europe. We have seen that the military buildup had already brought GCA clubs into action. The board met at headquarters three days after Pearl Harbor, two days after Congress had declared war on Japan. During the next day came the expected declaration of war on America by Germany and Italy, even as the women were having their lectures, committee meetings, and other events after the board had met.

Kate Fox was now president. She was sixty-one, a woman who attended to business. She had met with the Policy Committee—former presidents and former members of the Executive Committee—to discuss the position of the GCA in "the war emergency." When the board assembled after that, she echoed Lizzie Martin twenty-four years earlier: "America is at war and the Garden Club of America must assume the responsibility its name implies." The GCA had a membership of about eight thousand. "We are a strong body," said Miss Fox. "England has shown that in the midst of war people must garden. We shall follow her example . . . until such time as we are called on for other work."[14]

An annual meeting had been scheduled, to be held in St. Paul, even though the leaders realized that restrictions on public transportation might preclude it. If this was the case, a business meeting would be called at "some central city," hoping those who attended would compose a quorum. The St. Paul representative, Katharine Ordway, expressed her hope that the meeting might be canceled, to be held in St. Paul in better times, when the dinners, tours, and exhibits typical of annual meetings of the GCA might be experienced more fully. Discussion centered rather nostalgically in the pleasures of annual meetings that would now be lost—the private train cars, for example. Helen Thorne said that a private train could cross the continent without being in the "public eye" but rather changed gears in saying they should deny themselves such pleasure and do the work that lay before them.[15]

Kate Fox ran a tight meeting, yet everyone who wished to be heard seems to have been. The president had been an activist in one pursuit or another for the past thirty years at least, showing some preference previously for patriotic and historical organizations. Her venturing into national activities did not begin with the GCA but was greatly extended during her tenure. Her mobility was reminiscent of that of some of the founders, who seemed everywhere at once. It was said at the time that she lived on the train between New York and Washington. Added to travel by train was the more limited availability of commercial airplanes, which she used when she could. In addition to her journeys to GCA zone meetings and club projects, she served on various boards and advisories, such as the War Department's Women's Administrative Bureau.

Even at the December 1941 meeting a telegram arrived for her from the Defense Department, conveying an invitation from the secretary of agriculture, Claude R. Wickard: "We shall much appreciate your attendance at the National Defense Garden Conference here December 1941 to assist in working out a National Defense Gardening program and coordinated plans for carrying such a program into action." Said Miss Fox, "Of course we are attending," and named two GCA colleagues to accompany her.[16]

The GCA's war work in the zones had already taken the general form that would carry it through the forty months of the nation's participation in World War II. While all member clubs did not take part or at least failed to report what they did, three-quarters of them had war projects, and all zones were represented. Projects varied in scale. The primary effort was in building the landscapes of the numerous army camps. When the war began, the interest of the conservationists in the GCA was centered in soil, its protection and improvement. Naturally this subject gained their attention in work on the army camps. At Camp Upton, for example, then being built on Long Island, in the GCA's Northeastern

Zone, the army was offered landscaping plants for a small area, then for the entire camp. In the interim, during construction, when GCA grass seed was brought to the camp, the issue of poor soil arose. Mrs. Montgomery Hare, zone chair of the North Suffolk Garden Club, took the train to Watertown and went by taxi to the camp, to find that "shifting sands" were the big issue there. Builders were finding their framework and foundations slipping in the fickle sand, and they told their visitor, "Soil stabilization is our problem here."

She waded through eight inches of dry sand to the car of the officer in charge, who drove her on a windshield tour of the camp. "After a strong wind," he said, "the snow plow had to be used to move the sand back from off the cement roads." She saw long wavering snow fences, and "around post Headquarters were a few square feet of sod." A small stand of pine trees offered the little shade available. The officers in charge sat with her and spread their plans. She questioned and advised, all the while making notes of the desired trees and plans to take back to her clubs. She asked for compost, which might bind the sand. In parting she requested "immediate grading around the Headquarters building. The work was completed in three days, while she went home to study sand binders and plants that were hardy enough to survive the bitter Atlantic storms and hold to the soil."[17]

In Arizona, Mrs. Walter Douglas, a member-at-large, said that in her home state there were "practically no members of the Garden Club of America." Yet GCA volunteers, in cooperation with members of the Federation of Garden Clubs, were working on four military camps, had acquired five hundred orange trees, and were collecting fertilizer. Recreation areas were being planned for the four Arizona camps. Their achievements with the Camp Lands Corp were commendable, and they, like club participants in all the other zones, were making Christmas wreaths and garlands for the camps. Margaret Douglas was one of 106 members-at-large during the war, all of whom reported enthusiastic involvement in some aspect of war work.[18]

Headquarters was perhaps the most active of all. Already in the winter of 1942 the offices proved too small to hold the many functions the suite served. The Red Cross held classes most afternoons and every evening in GCA headquarters. Lectures held regularly by the GCA had to be moved to the East Seventy-first Street office of the National Society of the Colonial Dames of America. Presentations were topical, related to soil, plants, and the war. Sometimes the subject was nutrition, such as the talk given by Georgia O'Keeffe on that subject at headquarters on June 12, 1943. The painter, an outspoken proselyte of vegetarianism, however, did not attract a notable GCA crowd. Most of the lectures were more popular, because the speaker committee better identified the interests of its audience. Admission was charged, and the tone of these events paralleled that of the Waldorf's wartime cooking classes by the Broadway actor Alfred Lunt and the films shown at the Metropolitan Museum of Art on farming, poultry raising, and vegetable gardening.

An exception to presentations held at East Seventy-first Street was an exhibition on trees, which was deemed so important that it should be held at headquarters. It opened on November 11, 1942, under the direction of the Library Committee, with expert consultation. Most of the furniture had to be moved out to make room. Violetta Delafield chaired the show, which was about trees necessary for war production. Details of the show were fascinating, with examples of wood such as beech, used for making airplanes, and even willow, used for some other machinery parts. The show was so widely acclaimed that it was held over well into 1943, until the space could no longer be sacrificed. Portions of the show were shipped to other locations in the United States. For all the popularity and acclaim the show enjoyed, the needs of the Red Cross instructors prevailed, so the trees exhibit was the only large show to be held at GCA Headquarters during the war.[19]

Smaller shows on other subjects were also held at headquarters. The Executive Committee and the board were involved in projects supported by some other clubs, and one of the most successful of these led to the highly satisfactory Seeds for Britain exhibition at headquarters. While it occupied space only in the glass vitrines and disrupted little, it brought good press and spread the news about the GCA in a way that delighted the club officers. The GCA had joined the Seeds for Britain project in 1940, well before the United States entered the war. By summer's beginning in 1942, American seeds had been distributed to an estimated 1.2 million people in Britain, supplying 85 to 90 percent of the successful British gardens in that year. The effort was still underway until well after the war was over. At headquarters in 1942, seeds were displayed in ornamental patterns and accompanied by illustrations of fruits and vegetables from seed companies that had served as suppliers. Seeds, including those of flowers, also came from private gardens. The British government was strict about what could be sent. The GCA likewise pressed the seed companies to send prime stock and blacklisted those who performed otherwise.[20]

Also in the summer of 1942 Kate Fox returned exhausted from a meeting with the Department of Agriculture in Washington to announce that a shortage of food loomed ahead for Americans. It had been an interesting meeting, in which all participants "worked very hard." At one of Fox's later sessions, General George C. Marshall spoke, commending the women's efforts, while urging them to involve military wives, who were "often living uncomfortably" and were lonely. Various clubs did honor the general's request, but the greater efforts they made were with victory gardens.[21]

The big projects—landscaping army posts, collecting seeds, sponsoring high-level lectures, and collecting admission fees—were not typical of all the member clubs of the GCA. Yet the war involved them all in projects of one kind or another, some great, most small, and the large majority centering on the personal efforts of club members with the idea that they were, in their work, a contributing part of the GCA. Opportunities to join with larger groups abounded. Dating back to World War I, the Woman's Land Army, it will be remembered, had been widespread in

England and America. Never entirely disbanded, the WLA was revived in World War II and thrived to a greater extent than ever but with little official GCA participation. The GCA worked with the Red Cross but no other organizations to any extent. Member clubs had the freedom to vary in their participation locally, and many did. The Executive Committee and the board were inclined to suggest worthy organizations and projects, to give clubs opportunities to partner with others, but this tendency had vague motivations. It was either a control tactic or a means of urging some foot-dragging clubs into action.

The formal list of suggested activities was assembled by Mrs. Samuel Seabury, a prominent member in the national organization and a member of the Garden Club of East Hampton. It was a rather odd list of possible wartime endeavors, which the Executive Committee approved as a sort of guide for all clubs:[22]

1. Study plants used in medicine
2. Study plants used in war production, shipbuilding, airplanes
3. Study the relative nutritive value of foods
4. Encourage crop rotation for the preservation of soil
5. Encourage the planting of green crops for fertilizer
6. Study and develop food concentrates
7. Participate in conservation projects related to the war
8. Develop food substitutes
9. Engage in home canning, including dehydration and pressure cooking
10. Select the best varieties of vegetables and store them for winter use

Maud Seabury provided a bibliography of useful government publications that supported every proposed endeavor. The list was too ambitious for most clubs, to say the least, and there is no available record of who adopted what, but the supposition is that little of the list was put

into effect apart from canning—which was already widely practiced—
and some conservation, as well as some ventures into modern farming.
The overwhelmingly favorite war work of GCA clubs was in planting and
promoting home gardens. Called "victory," "war," or "defense" gardens at
the outset, by mid-1942 they were all known as victory gardens. Angela
Place addressed the board in 1942: "Garden clubs are made up of growers, and their knowledge should be turned now to producing food in
the most efficient and economical way. . . . In the spring a tremendous
drive for Victory Gardens will be under way, and every member can participate in this. Clubs can direct the canning efforts of the community,
either in canneries or in demonstrations to help the individual homes."[23]

The Victory Garden movement was far larger than just the involvement of the GCA, although it was warmly embraced by the clubs as a
reasonable task for the members to undertake. Many women may have
gone out to work in the war industry, but without statistics, it is probably safe to say that far more planted victory gardens. A vegetable garden
outside their door, where flowers had been, was a possibility for women
in the suburbs. Americans produced an estimated half million victory
gardens during World War II, and that figure is probably low.

Just as the federal government encouraged victory gardens, so did
the states. Marion Tallman Warner, of the Garden Club of Wilmington,
was chair of the Delaware Victory Gardens Committee, stirring an early
and successful movement. A garden center was set up in Wilmington
to dispense seed, information, tools, and food. Staffed by volunteers, it
became a regular center of activity, particularly on Saturdays, when new
gardeners convened there. This committee, like those overseeing most
other state victory gardens, was under the direction of Civil Defense.
Mary Ramsay Phelps, in reporting to the *Bulletin,* imported some of
the flavor of the movement. Gardening classes were attended by young
wives, country dwellers, all types: "Some were planting their first gardens, some much larger ones with the idea of canning and having fall
vegetables." The New Castle County Victory Gardens Harvest Show had

an unmistakable GCA stamp: "Along one wall were niches for artistic arrangements suggesting victory. The Garden Club of Wilmington did a most original one, with vegetables piled high at one side, the background a water color of Victory Cargo ships coming home, in shades of soft green and orange-red, the vegetables complementing these colors exquisitely."[24]

Victory garden harvest shows raised money for the Navy Relief Movement and the Army Corps of Engineers, ironic, perhaps, for GCA conservationists were having disagreements with the corps that would multiply in years to come. One garden club member in each state represented the GCA and reported to the Horticulture Committee by way of eight horticultural districts, which were represented by a "district horticultural adviser."

Twenty thousand harvest shows were held in the United States during World War II. It can be assumed that most of them were involved with GCA clubs, although the records that survive are few and not specific. The shows appear as one herculean task when seen only in the statistical numbers, but in fact they were the result of thousands of tasks, shouldered by those who made the victory gardens. Few wartime civilian movements have been so popular. As one of the nation's outstanding landscape architects, Ellen Biddle Shipman drew crowds when she toured and mounted the platform, telling the whys and hows of the "ideal" victory garden. Sophisticated luncheons in Chicago, San Francisco, Houston, and Boston featured speakers on canning and other preservation techniques of fruits. They heard about "freezing machines" that offered an alternate to traditional canning. When jars and lids became unavailable, old jars were refitted with wax and cork.

Success with the army camps and related military projects came early and was gratifying. During the war, in speaking to the Garden Club of Philadelphia, Dorothy Falcon Pratt, a gifted artist and very active member of the GCA, expressed her prediction that horticultural works in wartime would make a difference afterward: "The most hard-boiled of the Military have come to recognize the healing quality of flowers is an interesting fact. . . . After the War, some of these new gardeners will lay down their tools—of course—but by far the greater number, who have felt the joy of 'creating their earth and seeing it is good' as Kipling said, will carry on and I vision an America where the cottage gardens of England may someday have their counterpart."[25]

At headquarters, and nearly everywhere else, Kate Fox was a constant presence. She made herself well-known in Washington, on her own, after the sad news of the death of Janet Noyes early in the war. Another powerhouse left during the war when Sarah Bulkley, of the Ridgefield Garden Club, in Connecticut, passed from the scene. For these and other losses, Miss Fox had to find replacement sources. This she did with remarkable energy, always thinking of the GCA as a national organization greater than its individual clubs. Officials in Washington received her, and she was increasingly invited to briefings and other Washington meetings, usually those with agricultural or botanical subjects. A charming woman, she had benefited sufficiently from the patronage of Mrs. Sherman Hoyt to be remembered on many invitation lists that placed her in informal contact with officials who were of use to her organization. When farming interests denounced home gardening for being in competition with them, she explained effectively that her members were gardening for their own private tables, "thus releasing available stores for Allies and the armed forces."[26]

She always returned from her official meetings fired up with a message for the GCA. Early in the war she announced, "The War Department again urges you to take an active part in the Salvage Campaign. . . . Now, the Office of Price Administration suggests that you further Fuel Conservation." When the army called for donated supplies, the GCA sent one of the office typewriters. Kate Fox's passion for her work rings through every document she wrote or speech she made to the board.

"Mold ideas," she said, "to help win the war." Many of those who helped were her workers. Harriet Pratt, for one, was chairman of the women's division of the USO.[27]

Realizing the power of recognition, Miss Fox established the Public Relations and Information Committee and called out Elizabeth Lockwood to chair it. She created the GCA war service pin, an oval, silver-gilt brooch with the GCA insignia on the front and the name of the recipient engraved on the back, and distributed them widely to recognize good work at victory gardens and harvest shows and to acknowledge lecturers, demonstrators, and those who assisted in creating gardens around barracks and schools. She flirted with allying the GCA with the restored Woman's Land Army, even with restoring the insignia that had been designed by Elizabeth Martin in 1917. An exchange membership policy was adopted, in which GCA members transferred by war to another town were automatically eligible for membership in a GCA club in the new town. When she tried to reduce dues for servicemen's wives, the board balked. The GCA operated "too close to a margin" to be so generous.[28]

Slide shows on vegetable gardening were available for only the cost of postage, and the traffic for these was very heavy. Officers who might be considered lieutenants of Kate Fox journeyed coast to coast. Mrs. Robert H. Fife, of the Middletown Garden Club, in Connecticut, was in charge of relief. This took the form of holiday functions and presents for the troops, including those at home, those overseas, and those who were prisoners of war. It is difficult to say exactly how many men or posts were served in this process, but they certainly numbered in the tens of thousands. Cigarettes, candy, and small games, sometimes stuffed into home-knitted socks, were tyical of the gifts sent to the posts. Materials sent overseas were boxed. At times headquarters was filled with this activity, but more typically the assembly and packing took place in the member clubs. Sarah Fife reported on January 10, 1945, that her committee had sent "100 boxes, 8,500 Christmas ornaments, 350 stockings made and filled, also 9,000 cookies, 100 Christmas trees, 500 Christmas cards stamped for patients to send out." Of all the clubs her committee dealt with, the Winchester-Clarke Garden Club, in Virginia, was the most active for the soldiers at Christmastime, even sending boxes to the prisoner-of-war camp holding Germans nearby. She took to that camp "40 bags of candy, boxes of cookies," noting, however, that they were "for *our* soldiers who are guards at the camp," not the Germans incarcerated there.[29]

At times Kate Fox heard criticism of an apparent abandonment of the purposes of the GCA in favor of war work. She did not hesitate to respond: "I remind you," she said at the close of 1942, when the wheels of her administration were just beginning to spin furiously, "that we do not forget the progress we have already made in the preservation of our trees, and natural beauty, and the creation of interest in corn planting, nor do we neglect these interests in spite of the absorbing war work in which garden club members are engaged." The opposition usually ceased, and as for Miss Fox herself, she could hardly wait to begin postwar planning.[30]

The Garden Club of America held only business meetings as annual meetings during World War II. Rochester, New York, had welcomed the last grand annual meeting in 1941 before America entered the war. It was a fine event, indeed, with dinners and tours, underwritten almost entirely by Eastman Kodak. The next year members strongly felt the need to conserve fuel, paper, and rubber for the war and supported a stark wartime occasion with one formal dinner. That was the annual meeting of 1942. The next year was about the same. For 1944 the veil was lifted a bit, with the annual meeting, though still pared down, held in the romantic setting of the Cloisters, at the northern end of Manhattan. The ladies met in the lovely concoction of twelfth- and thirteenth-century architectural parts, filling the ledges and corners with flower arrangements, rather a parody of annual meeting festivities of the past. In the last year of the war the federal government prohibited gatherings of more than fifty people, so another unornamented daytime assembly gathered in New York.

Although everything was on hold, the deep affection many members had for their club and its past was not. Many were the expressions of friendship among members who did not know one another but had shown hospitality to the GI son of another or visited some wounded friend in a military hospital. David Swain, a young soldier stationed in Iowa, wrote to his GCA mother: "You and Mrs. [William?] Taylor deserve some sort of prize for your marvelous date-getting ability. Your letters to Mrs. Charles Howard, president of the Des Moines Founders Garden Club, have had the most amazing results. . . . My Christmas week isn't going to be lonely after all."[31]

Between the lines in the onslaught of war work, personal moments appear. Mrs. Roland Tileston, of the Diggers Garden Club, in Pasadena, was driving with her husband in California. Wishing to see the GCA redwood grove, they took side roads and arrived at sunset.

> Ignoring the fact that we did not know where we could find a place to sleep . . . we stopped and walked far into that quiet, wonderful place. I wish each Garden Club member might have shared my experience. All the women who have said "goodbye" to sons or husbands and those who have undertaken work beyond their strength would have found peace for a time and spiritual power in those calm, strong and stately trees. They seemed to have become a cathedral guarding America's gifts . . . and inspiration and faith for all of us.[32]

Although the war ended in the summer of 1945, the following autumn found Sarah Fife and Margaret Douglas still planning Christmas decorations for military hospitals and camps. Also that fall the International Flower Show announced its next title, "Four Centuries of Furniture and Flowers." A victory clothing drive was being planned at GCA Heaquarters for the destitute Allied seamen who had lost their papers and were housed on Ellis Island. From everywhere announcements of war memorials appeared, so numerous that Harriet Pratt, now a widow, came in from Long Island to a board meeting, where she made a little speech saying that the GCA must take a stand on these memorials and "express our tastes to prevent anything unattractive."[33]

Alice and Elizabeth Lockwood, who were two of the organization's most venerable and active members and were dear friends but no kin whatsoever, were also still much in evidence when they wished to be. A historical garden chronicler, Alice stood before the board in 1946, proudly recalling what the Garden Club of America had achieved in its recent service to the nation. She proposed that a book be written to set it all down, before memories dimmed. Everyone liked the idea, but no one had time to pursue it.

Vigorous wartime civic and patriotic activities had inspired the far-reaching clubs of the GCA to special pride in being united through their distinguished national organization. The clubs had shown independence during the war, but rather than weaken the national GCA, this strengthened it. Wartime's sort of energy did not fade but continued after peace had come. Clubs and members united as never before according to mutual interests and, in the process of communication and activity, strengthened the GCA. Conservation activity on the West Coast early on had counterbalanced the influence of New York, which might otherwise have been so overwhelming a presence as to preclude any national scope for the organization. As it happened the leveling of the "seesaw" allowed for a building membership of clubs across the continent.

Many other volunteer organizations did not survive the war. But the enthusiasm that had led the GCA to expand so rapidly from its founding was merely rekindled by it. The firm foundation built over the thirty-two years since 1913 had established a strong superstructure for the changes the postwar generation brought. By the middle 1950s the three essential interests of the GCA—horticulture, flower arranging, and conservation—became focused as never before. For all the occasional overlapping that might occur, a singular place was carved out for each pursuit, and the three were to compose future directions of the GCA.

Chapter Five
THE HORTICULTURISTS

For all the effort made to return to life as it had been before World War II, the country had changed irrevocably. It was not that people found themselves in a strange new place. Everything looked about the same, for the time. Most of the far-reaching changes were as yet largely unseen. The pace of living never slowed to what it had been before the war.

Deep in debt from the Depression and the war, the government put heavy pressure on the taxpayer in trying to lift the giant burden of national debt while spreading abroad huge outlays of money demanded of it as the principal world power. American society shifted. Altered circumstances naturally varied with individuals. Even though in its isolation the United States escaped the postwar extremes suffered by Europe and Asia—the principal battlegrounds—it was clear that even in America a new time had come. Americans either challenged or hurried to protect familiar contexts that they once believed might always remain the same.

Change was felt already during the war. At a GCA event in 1943, a comic skit was performed that reflected some of the changes. This is an excerpt from one speech:[1]

Once we had days of leisure—to read, play bridge and golf,
And life was just a round of teas and fun,
Our children all were married, their babies little dears,
All smiling there a-kicking in the sun,
Yes life was very pleasant but Oh the change today,
Our daughters are at factories, camps, on planes—
And who's baby's nurse? Who feeds and spanks and burps?
It is Grandma.

The era of building new private gardens on a scale with Kitty Sloan's Lisburne Grange pretty much ended with World War II, but in fact very few GCA members had ever had such gardens in the first place. The majority of members seem to have had what fell under the usual American platitude, "yards." Subsequently GCA horticultural shows often featured designs and plantings for suburban yards, with driveways and garages. The *Bulletin's* pages regularly offered hints and advice on subjects related to residential landscaping. If, as one suspects, these articles were what GCA members read with the most interest, this focus indicates their enthusiasm for domestic horticulture. One of the qualifications for club membership in the GCA was that a club's members have "gardens of distinction," which was never meant to imply magnificence but rather a sincere interest in growing things.

The primary focus of the founders had been horticulture. They loved their flower gardens, and most of them had fine ones upon which to shower their affection and attention. In a public way the interest in gardening in Philadelphia was perhaps even a little stronger than anywhere else in the country, because it had been stimulated forty years prior to the GCA's founding in the success of the world's fair known as the Centennial International Exhibition of 1876. Taking place in Philadelphia's Fairmount Park, the celebration commemorated the hundredth anniversary of the Declaration of Independence. Though open for only half a year, the Centennial's influence continued over many years.

Horticulture Hall was the most popular of all the exhibition buildings in the fairground and the most enduring. The building itself could be likened to an immense fanciful greenhouse, although not as large as its predecessors at the Crystal Palace Exhibitions of 1851 in London and of 1853 in New York. The glass house, which was small even relative to the other main buildings of the fair, was to stand for many years after the Centennial was over, containing a wonderland of palm groves, orchids, ferns, fruit trees, and flowers, amid spraying fountains.[2]

Not overlooked in the Centennial's broadcast of a century of American achievements was the betterment of life for women. Modern times for women were glorified in comparison to their much-described historical home drudgery, represented at the Centennial by a re-created colonial kitchen. How somberly the heavy iron pots and tin buckets illustrated a woman's former tedium; how brightly the floral art in Horticulture Hall demonstrated the happy lot of a woman freed by technology to express herself with flowers she grew herself. Horticulture Hall made the point more subtly than other exhibits. It immersed the visitor in beauty through flowers enhanced by the wonderful work of women's hands in arranging them. For many years even after the last gaslight of the Centennial had died and strands of electric lightbulbs illuminated the glass spaces, women came to Horticulture Hall to display their homegrown plant specimens and floral art. More than a mere botanical garden, Horticulture Hall was a gathering place and a symbol in the women's movement, as one might title that great wave of women who were not impatient like the suffragettes and protest marchers but progressed in their way just the same.[3]

Certainly many future GCA members could have been found in the crowds that patronized Horticulture Hall during the Centennial, tagging along with their mothers to events or playing among the parterres of bright summer flowers inset in the close-clipped lawn that spread carpetlike around the shimmering hall of glass. Horticulture Hall influenced both those who saw it new in 1876 and those of a generation or two afterward who knew and loved it through the many years it stood. Later largely forgotten, it burned down in 1954 and was not rebuilt. Horticulture Hall helped define the GCA as horticultural long before the organization's interests subdivided to include flower arranging and conservation as well.

Horticulture was the umbrella beneath which the GCA was born and lived for more than forty years. The other interests of the individual clubs grew and branched off as time went by.

The GCA kept its organizational structure stable, if minimized, during the war. The last GCA annual meeting held during World War II was at headquarters on May 7, 1945, just as the war neared its end. Flags still hung at half-mast for President Franklin D. Roosevelt. Black crepe to mourn him remained in windows along the streets. In the early morning hours of that same day, German forces surrendered to the Allies, and the news trickled in from Europe as the ladies seated themselves around the headquarters table. It was a business meeting exclusively. They first opened the proxies that had been solicited from the 131 clubs. Two had been requested from each. The room was tense; it was as though a roll call was being made to see if the GCA still existed. One hundred nineteen clubs responded with two proxies; one proxy came from each of eight clubs; and only four clubs did not respond at all. A very relieved board elected the slate of new officers and directors made by the Nominating Committee the previous December. The war was over, and the GCA stood as solid as a rock in its wake, with every reason to anticipate a productive future.

After four years of pared-down annual meetings the organization was ready for an old-style annual meeting the next year, in 1946, with business, yes, but also plenty to see and eat. The last full meeting had been in Rochester in 1941. Having decreed this, the board went out to join in the celebrations of a city joyous with victory. Word spread among the clubs about the annual meeting to come. In hand in January 1946, an invitation from the Garden Clubs of Massachusetts—the Chestnut Hill, Cohasset, Milton, North Shore, and Worcester garden clubs, the Fox Hill Garden Club, in Dover, and the Garden Club of Buzzards Bay—met with a unanimous acceptance for May 14–16. This was to be remembered justifiably as the most widely anticipated annual meeting ever to have been held up to that point by the Garden Club of America.

The event took place at the New Ocean House, a renovated seaside summer hotel of the 1880s at Swampscott, about twelve miles from Boston. The hotel had deep old-fashioned porches lined with chintz-seated rocking chairs, windows with billowing gauze curtains, and a complex wooden architecture painted white and green, all evoking memories of ways of life that were in a past that seemed to be slipping quickly away. Five hundred very modern 1940s women attended. On May 16, convening in the hotel ballroom, the GCA held the first fully attended business meeting since 1941, before America's entry into the war. It was brief, seeming a mere episode at the end of two days of horticultural and conservation meetings, speakers, luncheons, teas, conversation, dinners, and tours, which, for all the froth a mere listing may imply, served a valuable purpose in the mingling and reacquaintance of the nationwide attendance of delegates, after four years.

The board met separately, as was customary, after the general business meeting and before the final dinner. Twenty-seven out of twenty-eight officers and directors attended, with Mrs. Harry I. Peters, president, presiding. They did not linger. Kate Fox, representing the Policy Committee, reported on "great criticism" from the membership on the number of vice presidents and their longevity in office. Many saw this as a log jam slowing the flow of change in the GCA. She endorsed the suggestion, then current, that officers be rotated so that one-third were replaced each year. Natalie Peters quickly postponed this, asking the directors to "come prepared to discuss it at the June meeting."

Another thorny issue was the use of the word *founder*. Mabel Choate, chair of the Founders Fund Committee, asked the board to direct all clubs that used *founder* in their name to drop the word. This was directed primarily at Dallas, Sarasota, and Des Moines, none of the three easily described as passive. Angela Place interposed that the twelve original clubs had a sort of entitlement where that word was concerned; even so, it seemed unfair to ask other clubs to change their names. Someone puckishly suggested the alternative of changing the name of the Founders Fund to the Elizabeth Price Martin Memorial Fund. This might have passed easily had its few opponents not had it tabled.[4]

Turning to other subjects, the board heard Fannie Cooper of the Horticulture Committee make a plea for the GCA to send a telegram to "the proper authorities in Washington" saying that the attendees at the annual meeting supported a movement to force food stores "all over the United States of America and Hawaii" to withdraw "all food supplies needed to aid famine-stricken countries of the world." The idea was that the currently espoused self-denial of certain foods was not working, and the government should adopt a more stringent program. Some discussion followed. Clearly the board wanted no part of this, insisting that the system devised by former president Herbert Hoover for President Truman was "working very well." A last-minute resolution postponed discussion until June. Meanwhile the Executive Committee, following the prescribed process, had voted to recommend funds for the 1946 Founders Fund project, which were to be used to contribute to the purchase of Bartholomew's Cobble, the picturesque, hilly site near Ashley Falls, Massachusetts, where over five hundred varieties of wildflowers grew in summer riot. By that donation, the annual meeting of ocean breezes and postponed issues helped Massachusetts preserve a jewel in its natural landscape.

The GCA was committed early to horticultural education, but from this core idea, other objectives were to be pursued. Education about plants and trees, agriculture, and the related arts was the foundation of the horticultural program. The nourishment of the original idea has never ceased. From it soon sprang a determination on the part of some committee members to conserve plants in the wild, specifically native holly trees, which were being "ravaged" for Christmas decorations. Within this same group, an old battle stirred in defiance of strict federal quarantine laws, a problem for gardeners after World War II, as it had been after World War I.[5]

The Conservation Committee was first established by the board well before World War II, in the winter of 1924–25, followed in 1933 by a revised, more specifically focused committee retaining the same name. The reason the two separate versions of this committee were created was the nuance of difference in direction that had developed within the committee through the later 1920s. In its original purpose, the actual work of the Conservation Committee was didactics, not politics. It called on Americans to appreciate and protect native plants. But through the 1920s, *preservation* yielded increasingly to a newer word, *conservation*. By 1930 the two words bore different meanings. The first called for retention through appreciation and cultivation; the second, for rescue and protection by law.

Seen a century since its initiation, the rescue of holly trees along the roads and in the forests might seem a simple enough matter of enforcement by the authorities. There was, however, no consensus of opinion that the trees should be saved or that the authorities had any legal right to meddle in the issue. A group within the GCA challenged the idea that protection could not come through laws. The idea grew into a moral quest that loomed over the Conservation Committee, to the dismay of many of its members. And quarantine was somewhat the same in effect.

There had always been quarantines of one kind or another established by the federal government to protect American health and well-being. After World War II, the quarantine of imported plants seemed to horticulturists to have outlived its usefulness. Voices cried out for resolution, but their victories were few and hard-earned. For twenty years a member of the Conservation Committee and one of its strongest voices,

Louise Crowninshield discovered an opportunity to win some territory in removing quarantines upon plants, and she got to work. She and several colleagues from the GCA met a more understanding Department of Agriculture than had been the case back in the 1920s. In fact the department was tired of bearing the administrative burden of quarantines that seemed no longer necessary. The bill finally written was an amendment to the original Plant Quarantine Act of 1922 (itself a revision of an act passed ten years earlier). Mrs. Crowninshield visited the lawmakers, claiming, without board authority, that she had the GCA and its eight thousand members solidly behind her. The bill was signed into law late in the spring of 1947. For the first time in years bulbs could be shipped from the Netherlands. The victory was Louise Crowninshield's, but only one of many in a long life of advocacy.

A third effort of this active committee became a small private war sparked by pressuring nurserymen to stand behind the quality of their merchandise. This was a touchy subject, challenging businessmen who were not so discerning. Ethel du Pont and Edith Scott, both hard-working colleagues in the Horticulture Committee, helped write the standards that they felt nurserymen should follow, encouraging them to import and propagate better plants "as stock." The two women faced unflinchingly the angry accusations of unfairness by nurserymen throughout the United States. Mrs. Scott, a gardener of note in her own right, had founded the Arthur Hoyt Scott Arboretum, at Swarthmore College, in memory of her late husband, president of the Scott Paper Company. Mrs. du Pont, wife of William K. du Pont of Delaware and herself a well-known experimental gardener and one the few internationally recognized experts on orchids, had no use for second-rate plant material.[6]

The two women decided that it would be a good idea for the GCA to supply select nurseries with seed to plant for exclusive sale to GCA clubs. When presented with a proposed two hundred dollar per year cost, the board said no. But the money was not hard to raise otherwise, and the effort did not go unnoticed. The project advanced anyway. When the nurserymen network tightened up and declined to be involved, GCA club members began to experiment at home. Information and advice were supplied on request. Swapping seeds became a characteristic of GCA board meetings and annual meetings. Horticulture Committee members usually took seeds home to try in their gardens. An enthusiastic supporter of seed distribution in the GCA was Mrs. Alfred B. Thatcher. In February 1939 Emma Thatcher brought to headquarters a big flour sack full of Chinese holly seeds, into which committee members dipped for samples to take home and plant.[7]

Through the 1920s the Horticulture Committee, intended originally as an education and study branch of the GCA, developed a split mission. Those interested in education were more numerous, and while they gave their support to the different quests, they were not happy with their committee. On May 10, 1933, with a refocus in mind, the board and committee reaffirmed the educational purpose and reconstituted the Horticulture Committee into what was to be considered a new committee but of the same name. It was never called the "second horticulture committee," but in fact it was that. The battle to save holly trees and curb the quarantines did not die but was carried on by others, like Mrs. Crowninshield, who took her battles to the conservation branch of the GCA, and Helen Kathleen Meserve, a noted hybridizer of holly trees and an activist whose bronze bust can be seen today in the GCA Headquarters.

Individual clubs did not take an immediate interest in the newly formed committee. For all the enthusiasm the committee enjoyed, after its first year had passed, not a one of the 103 GCA clubs had official horticultural representatives. Fifteen club members were on the advisory to the Horticulture Committee, however, and horticultural activities were ever-spirited in some clubs, with regular exchanges of plant material, seeds, and bulbs. Also, the national committee did interact with the clubs, especially in locating, evaluating, and recommending nurseries.

This important effort, not new to the GCA, continued to incur the anger of the nurserymen the committee refused to recommend.

The first horticulture committee had actively addressed itself to horticultural education all along, in publication, broadcast, flower shows, touring, and scholarships. In 1924 the committee released its first publication, a pamphlet titled *Oecology of Plants*. In the next year, GCA horticulturists took part in WEAF Radio's *Better Homes in America* show. Participating in public media was a giant step for the GCA, which was not certain it even wanted to be mentioned in newspapers, but in discussion the Horticulture Committee decided radio might well serve their educational objectives. The show was a gratifying success. The GCA's script, which was written with the able help of WEAF Radio's staff, concentrated upon landscaping suburban homes. Care was taken to make the recommendations attainable to as large an audience as possible. No grand allées or boxwood mazes.

The interest of the Horticulture Committee in promoting good garden design found a venue in the *Bulletin*. Fletcher Steele really got his start in GCA activities writing for the *Bulletin*. His articles on garden design almost certainly influenced thousands of GCA members in their own gardens at home. His early involvement with the GCA exposed him to some of the most ambitious gardeners in the United States and helped him build a long and successful career. Well traveled and exposed to the latest European trends, Steele had brought to American gardens a flavoring of the art deco that he had observed in the most fashionable modern gardens in France. His gardens were meant to beckon the viewer into them rather than simply pleasing the eye. Notable among his early gardens was that of the GCA member Mabel Choate, whose artistic "summer gardens" at her retreat, Naumkeag, in western Massachusetts, were unlike anything seen before in the United States. Steele lectured and published and spread his ideas. In the GCA he found a willing forum and rich clients, whose gardens are to architects and landscape architects the artist's canvas and paints, the poet's pen and paper. In 1929 he was made a member-at-large in the GCA.

Steele's entry to real intimacy with the GCA occurred when he was asked to help the Horticulture Committee with a long-desired publication called *The GCA Color Chart*. The object was to establish a set of definitive standards for colors and color combinations in flower arranging and distributing plants in gardens. After several years of committee discussions and plant comparisons to published U.S. color standards, the project had not moved far, but the enterprising Steele brought the color chart to publication in 1930. Selling for three dollars, *The GCA Color Chart* was a classic the day it appeared, and with modifications it can still be found today in the organization's operational Bible, *The Yellow Book*.

The Horticulture Committee worked with specialists, inviting them to lecture and provide articles to the *Bulletin*. One of many leading botanists of the 1920s who worked closely with GCA education projects was Andrew Burdette Stout, who was at the top of his field in hybridizing, with a specialty in daylilies. For their beauty and hardiness, daylilies were among the favorite garden flowers of the day. As the head of the New York Botanical Garden, Stout received encouragement and donations from the GCA for his work on diseases that threatened his subject plant. In 1931 the committee held a flower show in New York, where the luncheon speaker was Dr. Stout, and his subject was lilies. The lily show was a small affair the first time, but over successive years it was moved to different club sponsorship, and when held by the Garden Club of Alexandria, in Virginia, in 1935, it attracted more than six hundred visitors, proving the far-reaching educational objectives of the horticulturists of the GCA.

The work of the horticulturists did not always take the form of written words and lectures. A member of the Horticulture Committee, Emma Thatcher brought Europe's plight in 1940 to the committee's attention and began the GCA's participation in sending seeds to Finland, sending the first shipments in the late summer of that year. While the program for Britain was vastly larger, with the committee's blessing she asked her fellow GCA members to send any seeds "that can be sown directly in the open ground," including flowers. "The Fins are a flower-loving people," she assured her donors. "Anything that will grow in New England will grow in Finland."[8]

Nor did her efforts end or remain on a single track after the war began. During the war years Mrs. Thatcher seemed everywhere at once. With her GCA colleagues Edith Scott and Brooks Barnes, she led a busy life during the war, centered in and around New York City. Harriet Pratt called them the Three Musketeers and singled them out for special praise for the way they lighted up dark wartime days with the fund-raising lectures they organized and especially the chrysanthemum show they staged in October 1944. For this show GCA horticulturists brought specimens from twenty-two states, joining others in the Lexington Avenue Armory. It became what might be described as a New York moment. Best in show was Max Schling, the fashionable Fifth Avenue florist, who had begun his career with a flower stall in the Fifty-sixth Street Market. The show's cheerful success lay as much in the good feelings its beauty brought to the city as anything else, and the public attended by the thousands.[9]

Most of the GCA's attempts at forming associations with other organizations proved frustrating, a truth that the Horticulture Committee learned soon enough. The power and numbers that the GCA represented naturally made it appealing as a graft for other organizations of like or similar objectives. Alas, the fit was very rarely satisfactory to the GCA. For example, before the war, in the 1930s, the mutual interests of a group of men and women motivated their founding of a new national horticultural organization, United Horticulture, with the stated purpose of education. This seemed a good idea for the GCA to promote in the interest of outreach, and several members of the Horticulture Committee did so. After the idea of association with this new group came before the GCA board, war intervened, so the association was not approved even in concept until the last meeting in 1946, two weeks before Christmas.

United Horticuture had as its patron the eighty-nine-year-old horticultural giant Liberty Hyde Bailey, botanist and founder both of the Cornell University Department of Experimental Plant Biology and of the American Society for Horticultural Science. The founders of United Horticulture knew that Professor Bailey, a poet, naturalist, and scientist, would attract the desired "representations from science, landscape, commercial and amateur" horticulturists, such as those in the Garden Club of America. Bailey's long friendship with the GCA dated back to the club's beginning, and he often lectured to the GCA and enjoyed a continuing association with individual members.[10]

Mrs. E. Page Allinson, who presented the idea of the association to the GCA board, assured her fellow members, "It is far from commercial. . . . Growing plants is a feat of engineering." Also, the proposed headquarters of United Horticulture was to be in Cleveland, so the GCA's Garden Club of Cleveland could be heavily involved with the new group. Even so, the board hesitated at the association, which is not surprising, for the GCA has traditionally hesitated officially joining with others— although at times it has done so, and this was one of those times. When Mrs. Allinson returned home from her meeting with United Horticulture, she said the event was like the "first session of the United Nations." The magic, however, did not last long. United Horticulture, once it had the GCA in hand, never called upon it much. Apart from related activities generated by the very active Garden Club of Cleveland, the association of the two organizations amounted to very little. The GCA withdrew entirely when United Horticulture merged with the American Horticultural Society in 1959. Spanning not even a decade, the relationship was often held up at the GCA as a warning when similar offers appeared.[11]

Another relationship that proved unsuccessful was with the United Horticultural Congress, formed in October 1947. The GCA can be called a major player with United Horticulture at the time, although it had nothing to do with the creation of the congress that carried United Horticulture's name. The congress itself, was managed by seven federally appointed "commissioners." Six groups, including the GCA, were sent out by the congress to "mobilize all activities connected with international problems," largely meaning the feeding of war victims. The plight of starving people in war-torn lands became a household topic in the United States in the postwar years. Forty percent of American wartime food had come from victory gardens. The United Horticultural Congress set out to keep the effort going and did so for several years, with the blessings of many, including President Truman and Generals Eisenhower and Marshall.[12] The GCA did not last long in the program, but it remained current in the general effort to feed war's victims through Seeds for Europe, in which the GCA had been a major player since early on. Joining in an informal partnership with the National Council of Garden Clubs, the GCA helped set up a center at the New York Historical Society, where the public could call and sign up to sponsor a package of seeds for $3.95, to be sent to Greece, Italy, or France.[13]

The experiences with United Horticulture and the United Horticultural Congress resulted in disappointment and lessons learned. While the GCA would often join in other campaigns it deemed worthy, it was convinced by the mid-twentieth century that it must follow its own drumbeats and avoid entangling associations.

The main interest of the horticulturists in the GCA remained in education. They did not entirely shy away from associations of similar purpose. An example is the Williamsburg Garden Symposium, which made its debut in the spring of 1936 and by 1949 was intimately attached to the Horticulture Committee through Alden Hopkins, the director of landscape at Colonial Williamsburg. Hopkins had held the GCA's Interchange Fellowship in 1938 for study in England. He returned to America to take a position in Williamsburg as assistant to the landscape architect

Arthur Shurcliff. In 1941, he became Shurcliff's successor as Williamsburg's resident landscape architect, a distinguished position in his field,
with apparently limitless opportunity.

Lessons in gardening at the Williamsburg Gardening Symposium
were pursued in comfort, with morning lectures and afternoon garden
tours; evenings were crowned with "great dinners" in the Williamsburg
Inn, where Hopkins spoke on some subject in eighteenth-century horticulture or garden design. A dapper Arthur Shurcliff stood by with an
archive of witty remarks to lighten Hopkins's serious discourses. In the
late 1920s Shurcliff had begun assembling masses of original research
on Virginia's colonial gardens and reigned unchallenged as the expert
on the subject.

The captivation of GCA horticulturists by Williamsburg was entirely predictable. In 1924 thirteen hundred members took the train
from the annual meeting in Richmond to see Williamsburg and its historic sites. The patronage of John D. Rockefeller Jr. was still a few years
away, but thanks to a little group of antiquarians, one could read in local "historical" efforts an emerging grassroots pride that predated the
famous restoration. The landscape architect Charles Gillette, the Richmond practitioner who had given a national signature to the "Virginia
garden" with boxwood-lined paths and lawns, was along as a guide. At
the time, he was designing a landscape for Louise Crowninshield's pet
project, Kenmore, the historic eighteenth-century house in Fredericks-
burg, Virginia.

At the College of William & Mary, another of his projects, he asked
the ladies if they would be interested in helping fund a piece of his campus plan. Their response was to pass the hat, which paid in full for rows
of *Magnolia grandiflora* that eventually outlined the historic part of the
original campus.[14] GCA visitors subsequently flocked to Williamsburg,
sharing the general delight in the restoration, which began just before
the Depression. In constant touch with Hopkins later on, they relished
the "green garden rooms" of Williamsburg as he planted them, laying

out their brick paths, placing boxwood and seasonal flowers, and using picket fencing, split rails, or bricks to frame each garden like a picture. The long shadow of this genre fell upon the gardens of many a member of the GCA.

Furthering its educational work, the Horticulture Committee kept the *Bulletin* abreast of the latest in gardening and the clubs aware of the best speakers. Fletcher Steele always headed the list, but there were many more, including amateurs with expertise. At headquarters the slide programs were reviewed, purged, and redesigned to be sent out for use at club programs. Also, many new ones were made, the subjects being practical gardening—how to move a tree, how to plant bulbs, the latest means of keeping deer away from the garden. Roses were an ever-popular topic with the horticulturists. Even vegetable subjects sometimes challenged the ornamental dignity of formal meetings. Horticulture was represented in more books in the library than any other endeavor of the GCA, even flower arranging.

GCA scholarships related directly to horticultural study, and this has largely remained the case. Apart from random club scholarships and what might be called grants from individual GCA members, the first scholarship of the national organization was given to the American Academy in Rome in 1917. In 1913 the academy had merged with the American School of Classical Studies, resulting in an institution with two facets, one for research and one for design. The two were bedded down uncomfortably in crumbling palazzos when the GCA presented its first scholarship.

After virtually shutting down during World War I, in 1921 the American Academy resumed granting its major prize and accompanying scholarship, the Prix de Rome. At this point landscape architecture was part of the academy's curriculum, and this attracted the interest of the Horticulture Committee, which gave its full support to the GCA's American Academy in Rome Committee. After the GCA endowment of fifty thousand dollars was established in 1928, the GCA scholarship, usually awarded annually, helped sustain the "Rome Academy" in its position of influence in the study of landscape architecture.[15]

When the first negotiations were underway with the American Academy in 1925, there was as yet no Horticulture Committee. Being the lubricant of the GCA machinery, committees were created for almost every activity and interest of the organization. Duties of some new projects were assigned to existing committees. The Rome Academy Fellowship Committee cooperated with the Lowthorpe School Committee in providing scholarship grants for women in landscape design and horticulture. It was natural that once the GCA showed interest in funding college scholarships, the organization would be courted warmly. It was, but apart from its support of the Rome Academy, the GCA supported scholarships in only limited ways. Even the grants to the Lowthorpe School, in Groton, Massachusetts, and to Philadelphia's Ambler College were not as generous as those to Rome.

The Interchange Fellowship, mentioned earlier as having been held by Alden Hopkins, is another scholarship that was spawned by the GCA's interest in horticultural education. It is a horticultural scholarship that funds a British student's studies at an American college and, in exchange, an American student's year—sometimes two—at a British college. The scholarship has deep roots in the history of the GCA, beginning in 1922, when the English Speaking Union asked the GCA to help organize and participate in a tour of American gardens. American hospitality was overwhelming, with trips to estates and public gardens around New York, especially on Long Island's Gold Coast; a cruise up the Hudson climaxed a full and elegant event. Two years later the English Speaking Union invited the GCA to London for the ESU's 1925 annual meeting. This invitation of June 11, 1924, caused excitement, and reservations poured into headquarters. Ninety-five filled the trip to capacity, sailing from New York to Southhampton and remaining a month in Britain. The two friendly handshakes over the ocean generated a number of other visits and wartime programs, but the warm relationship was consummated after World War II with the Interchange Fellowship.

Two decades after the reciprocal garden tours, the dangers befalling everyday British life prompted a movement to send British children to America to live in safety with private families until the war was over. The young visitors attended school, played baseball, and celebrated holidays with their American surrogate parents, who watched them grow as their own. When time came for the children to return home, so wrenching was the parting to the American hosts that some of them began asking what might be created to commemorate the bonds between the two nations through young people. Soon enough the spark of an idea found its kindling in a garden club.[16]

In 1948, after attending a meeting of the United Nations Educational, Scientific and Cultural Organization (UNESCO) in San Francisco, several members of the Hillsborough Garden Club proposed that a grant be established whereby a British student could come to America to study horticulture. The idea took hold. Money was raised through donations, house and garden tours, and plant sales. Negotiations with the University of California and the London branches of the English Speaking Union formulated a framework. Two years later, in 1950, the ESU offered a reciprocal scholarship for an American student to the GCA Woodside-Atherton and the Piedmont garden clubs and in the next year added the Hillsborough Garden Club. Praise for this exchange was universal throughout the GCA, leading to the Interchange Fellowship of the national organization, approved at the 1952 annual meeting, in Santa Barbara.

The original idea that this was a horticultural fellowship was soon modified in a new mission with high ideals. Now the exchange was "not only to promote horticultural studies and exchange information in the horticultural field, but also to foster British-American relations and the understanding of each other's cultures." Notwithstanding the additional focus, the scholarships were still horticultural scholarships. Through the decades since it was founded, the Interchange Fellowship has sailed some stormy financial seas. Zones were asked to rotate in sponsorships of students; GCA members underwrote trips and welcomed British students into their homes. The generosity of Nancy McLaren in memory of her husband, Martin McLaren, funded the American student in England for years. In 1948, she established a permanent fund, the Martin McLaren Horticultural Scholarship, at the Royal Horticultural Society. In Britain the English Speaking Union funded an American scholarship for a British student until 1972. When the RHS could no longer afford it, funding for the British student was provided by the Stanley Smith Horticultural Trust, administered in California.[17]

Flower shows have provided the GCA from the outset with one of the most intense and enduring venues for horticultural education. Although today they are thought of as flower-arranging events, before the 1960s nearly every flower show had horticulture as the main feature, with classes (categories of competition) of plants, vegetables, trees, and flowers. Lily and rose shows and other specialized competitions and exhibits were entirely horticultural. *The Yellow Book,* which through its many editions presents the prevailing rules for GCA shows, specifies several levels of classes: junior classes; classes that require written context; challenge classes, which are flower-arranging competitions in which all the entrants are provided with the same plant material and identical containers; small garden classes; potted plant classes; miniature or dwarf plant classes; and "par classes," in which entries are judged on their own merits, not competitively. (A par class, for example, can award several blue ribbons instead of the usual one.)

Containers are regulated as to appropriate size. Classes are provided for cut specimens displayed in various ways for judging. After the 1960s, the rules gained specificity, and the flower shows came to have the same familiar tables with rows of matching bottles holding specimens of plants. Only now and then does one see the diorama or miniature of a landscape with paths and hedges that recall GCA shows of the 1920s. Altogether, a GCA show's display makes a memorable sight. And up close, to those who are aware of the process, ever-sharper rules of showing hone the exhibitors' abilities while leveling the playing field.

The plant exchange, one of the most popular horticultural programs at flower shows, first took place in 1973 at the annual meeting in Lake Placid, New York. Julia Fifield and Sally Reath conceived the idea of a national plant exchange, patterned on a practice already somewhat familiar in club shows and a longtime American market-day tradition among gardeners in the past. The plant exchange soon became a staple at all shows, including over thirty years of annual meetings. In the plant exchange's heyday, the most popular one ever held was in Cincinnati in 1981 at a "major show" that featured trees. The underlying theme was to feature "plant material tolerant of environmental stress." This show received such a gratifying press response that even those members of the GCA who generally disapproved of the organization's being in the papers were pleased.[18]

Soon endangered species became a staple of flower shows. The most significant instance of this, associated with the Philadelphia Flower Show, was a group study called "Plants That Merit Attention." This addressed vanishing plant life and was supervised by two subcommittees of the Horticulture Committee, the Rare and Endangered Plants and the Seed Exchange. The demise of the plant exchange came first as the result of individual state quarantines, especially in California, and later as the result of an ecological reevaluation of taking plants from their native habitat and inadvertently introducing them where they could become unwanted, perhaps even invasive, plants.

In 1981 the Horticulture Committee began work with the Smithsonian Institution on a multivolume series of books, the first volume carrying the signature name *Plants That Merit Attention: Trees.* Nancy

Peterson Brewster was the author; and Janet Meakin Poor, the editor. National support was overwhelming, with every zone sending nominees for inclusion in the book. By 1983 volume 1 was ready for the press. Published by the GCA and the Smithsonian Institution in cooperation with the Timber Press, it was an expensive edition of only 450 books, yet it stimulated lectures, other books, and films, and the Conservation Committee itself published a series of postcards—horticultural "baseball" cards—of endangered species. Negotiation for a companion issue of postage stamps for volume 1 was successfully completed by Gina Bissell and Jan Pratt. Selected plates from the horticultural book were adapted for the stamps. The limited edition of books, together with the popular issue of horticultural stamps, marks a signal success for the Garden Club of America. Both products, which have become objects of interest to collectors worldwide, continue to be models in their fields.

While at a glance *Plants That Merit Attention* might appear to be a set of conservation books, the approach taken is academic. No overt appeal is made for the preservation of the threatened native species of trees. Janet Poor described admirably the educational purpose it serves: "So important are plants in the web of life that it is estimated that each plant that becomes extinct causes the extinction of 10 to 30 dependent species of insects, higher animals and other plants."[19] Volume 2 of *Plants That Merit Attention* was published in 1996.

Yet the great concern of Mrs. Poor and her GCA colleagues was that Congress would either decline to pass the Endangered Species Act or pass it and riddle it to meaninglessness with amendments. By the early 1980s, as will be seen in a subsequent chapter, a strong conservation branch of the GCA stood by to take up the cause. Horticulture turned to the Legislation and Conservation committees for support. The result was mixed but victorious at least in part. Meanwhile the Horticulture Committee and its satellites in zones and individual clubs scattered more of their 1997 booklet, *Choices to Gardeners,* encouraging the use of native plants rather than "exotics," which, like the mimosa tree, an ornamental, and the kudzu vine, imported for soil stabilization, have become invasive pests.[20]

As the Garden Club of America passed into the fourth quarter of the twentieth century, the horticultural work of the organization really came into its own. It was a time, it will be seen, of many changes but more so a period of increased activity in public projects. In 1960 horticulture was represented in fifty projects out of 160 clubs, all of the projects of a major character and a visibility beyond the activities of GCA: there were parks, roadside improvements, historical gardens, scholarship on particular plants, and experimental plantings. Scholarships were given in clubs and zones alike, apart from the national scholarships. In 1958 and 1959 the Horticulture Committee began sponsoring classes at some women's prisons, a program that is ongoing today. Pupils have proved eager and interested.

At the same time, the universal fear of garden poisons led the Horticulture Committee to join with the Conservation Committee and the Committee for the National Capital to follow Sweden's lead in banning DDT. The GCA's indomitable voice in the battle was that of Mrs. Thomas M. Waller, of the Bedford Garden Club, in New York. Wilhelmina "Willie" Waller's passionate oratory roused congressional committee and lecture hall alike. When both houses of Congress referred the DDT issue to a new "pesticides committee," the combined GCA committees stepped aside and let the others carry the fight. Not that they were silent; they simply had made their point.

The Horticulture Committee turned its energies to its more traditional educational approach. Members looked to the quality of plant material, proclaiming through the individual clubs their opposition to seed catalogs that advertised threatened material that ordinarily would not germinate. The Horticulture Committee chair, Mrs. Wyllys Terry, suggested they try to get the nurserymen to stamp "untreated seeds" across such materials when they sent them out. Some nurserymen agreed and were designated "honest ones" by the committee. As for the others, they made quite a noise, thinking mistakenly that their critics would back down. The GCA had made lists of preferred nurseries before World War II, but to continue that after the war was considered a risk of bad publicity and an invitation to a lawsuit. Nevertheless, in 1986, under the chairmanship of Louise Wrinkle, the Horticulture Committee published a list, "Nurseries That Grow Their Own Material." It has been updated year after year.[21]

In 1950 horticulture lost one of its most devoted adherents with the death of Kitty Sloan. She left the GCA five thousand dollars as the Katharine Colt Sloan Fund, the interest of which was to go to the Founders Fund. Also, Ethel du Pont died suddenly while in Singapore studying and teaching about orchids at the Singapore Botanical Garden. It was said at the time, if she had written her last scene she wouldn't have changed it a bit. Of the most visible builders of GCA horticulture in the 1920s and '30s only Helen Thorne remained. In the 1950s, younger women, such as Betty Corning and Sally Brown, were fast appearing to take up their work.

The horticulturists' educational work in the Garden Club of America climaxed in 1952 with the establishment of the Fellowship in Horticulture. The Horticulture Committee described the fellowship as "the best to use as a means to stimulate the knowledge and love of gardening." Its roster in years to come would include promising biologists, botanists, horticulturists, and landscape architects. Attention was given to educational work as never before, embracing all the clubs. Educational programs broadened through flower shows, to which participants were attracted in order to enter large central competitions and exhibits, hear outstanding featured speakers, attend propagating panels, and join in seminars on landscape design held by leading regional specialists.[22]

When the board met in 1952 in New York, the Horticulture Committee opened to the public the lectures it had always presented heretofore to only the GCA. This was tried for the first time on June 10 later that year. The lecture was presented in the Metropolitan Museum of Art before a packed house, with standing room filled well beyond what the New York City Fire Department allowed. On the roster the Horticulture Committee had engaged was the landscape architect Alice Recknagel Ires, of the Brooklyn Botanical Garden. At the Brooklyn Botanical Garden she had electrified the horticultural scene with a fragrance garden, one of the first in America. The *New York Times* has called her "one of the remaining links to a golden age of landscape architecture as a profession for women." Among the most celebrated professionals in her field, Alice Ires's objective was to build "a bridge between the 19th century tradition of gracious landscaping for grand estates and elegant modern designs for post war suburban houses." Her goal could not have been more on target for the late twentieth-century GCA.[23]

By the 1960s the Horticulture Committee was overseeing projects in horticulture that rivaled the best efforts of professionals. At all the major flower shows and some smaller ones as well, inspired horticulturists created full-scale or sometimes two-thirds-scale settings of gardens with actual flower beds, summer houses, fish ponds, statuary, and massed pots of blossoming plants. This practice, which began with miniatures, had grown into larger-scale exhibits beginning with the house exhibit at the Philadelphia Sesquicentennial, of 1926. Rose gardens were popular, created with potted roses and elevated turf floors to suggest planted gardens.

The GCA's "ivy garden" created by the horticulturists for the 1962 International Flower Show is surely the most popular exhibit ever shown there, a wonderful garden with green grass, ivy borders, and garden shelters. So well received was this exhibit that it remained open and in place for three weeks after the rest of the show had been closed down and carried off. It was paid the greatest compliment of all when the famous Judith Garden, whose florist shop on East Fifty-seventh Street was the peak of fashion in Manhattan, came forward and paid the GCA a handsome price for the entire ivy garden and took it to her shop.

While it was more typically the Committee for the National Capital and the Conservation Committee that conducted business in Washington, D.C., the horticulturists suddenly found themselves in the national capital.[24] In the year 2000, to celebrate the millennium, the GCA undertook to create the Butterfly Habitat Garden on the Mall and launched what was to be a generously rewarded nationwide campaign to pay for it and thereby realize the designs of Alice Ires. A gratifying success from the start, the Butterfly Habitat Garden has basked in popular appeal. Some GCA horticulturists were quick to observe that in addition to the garden's obvious charm and beauty is the scientific purpose it has to "demonstrate host and nectar plants for butterfly habitats." Along the crowded walk on summer days are those who come to admire and those who come to study.[25]

Also in 2000, the Maryland-based Casey Foundation presented GCA horticulturists with the opportunity to direct a project to adorn the capital city with trees. This news—what Nan King, the director for the Washington and Baltimore area, Zone VI, called the "newest news" for the Horticulture Committee that year, after the butterfly garden—came very suddenly. Betty Brown Casey, the widow of Eugene B. Casey, asked Jenny Karr, of Baltimore, to arrange a luncheon at the Four Seasons in Georgetown, to include the two of them and Bobbie Hansen, the GCA president, Nan King, and the Casey Foundation lawyer Barbara S. B. Sullivan. While these women lunched, Mrs. Casey explained her idea of embellishing the District of Columbia with trees, with the project to be under the management of the Garden Club of America.

In the course of the meeting, Mrs. Casey presented Mrs. Hansen with a check for two million dollars, saying more was to come. Hansen, then president of the GCA, still tells of her momentary sense of suspension: "What could I say? My first reaction was to be afraid I'd lose the check." Within two months, fifty million was added to the first gift.[26]

Mrs. Casey's specifications were few but emphatic. The money was to be spent in Washington for tree planting and protection of the "urban canopy." About a century before, the "city of trees" had fallen before the axe of the city beautiful movement's concept of open spaces and monuments. Mrs. Casey proposed no return to the designs of that previous time, only the redevelopment of a city of trees within the context of the present. She granted Mrs. King and cochairman Barbara Shea full authority to establish policy and arrange for the office and staff, and they were to have final say in every other aspect of the program as well.

Bobbie Hansen's successor as president, Ann Frierson, became concerned that in managing the Casey project directly, the GCA could expose itself to dangerous liabilities. In council, the board of the GCA and its lawyers worked out a new arrangement that separated the GCA from the foundation and made it the head of what the Internal Revenue Service called a "support organization" to help govern the foundation.

Hardly had a few years passed when Mrs. Casey added to the foundation's assets her 750-acre farm on the Shenandoah River near Berryville, Virginia. The idyllic Springsburg Farm was to become a tree farm, encouraging research and supplying trees to Washington. Along with her farm and its eighteenth-century house she gave another fifty million dollars, bringing her gift to the Casey Trees Foundation to over a hundred million. In making the GCA the vehicle for her ambitious dream of a more beautiful capital, Betty Brown Casey paid a high compliment by recognizing the volunteer organization's ability to get big jobs accomplished.[27]

Meanwhile, on the club level, the Horticulture Committee strengthened its outreach. Through the 1980s and 1990s, with an eye to practicality, the committee designed programs tailored to club use. They sought, and still seek, proven expert speakers within short distances of

Mrs. Harold I. Pratt (of the North Country Garden Club of Long Island, Oyster Bay, New York) stands at the entrance to the "Gardens on Parade," a five-and-a-half-acre space of fifty-two gardens at the 1939 World's Fair in Queens, New York. Mrs. Pratt was the sole female member of Hortus, Inc., the organization that sponsored this popular exhibit. *Courtesy of GCA Archive.*

The Cohassett Garden Club, in Massachusetts, donated this mobile canteen to the local Red Cross during World War II. Over a two-year period the canteen served two thousand suppers to troops who were transported from Boston for weekend outings. *Courtesy of GCA Archive.*

Miss Aline Kate Fox (of the Fairfield Garden Club, Connecticut), GCA president during World War II, served on numerous government committees in the nation's capital. Her friends described her as "living on the train" between New York and Washington, D.C. *Courtesy of GCA Archive.*

Mrs. Harry T. Peters (of the South Side Garden Club of Long Island, Islip, New York), GCA president during 1944–47, and Mrs. Harold J. Seaman (of the Green Tree Garden Club of Milwaukee) attend a meeting in 1944 of the American Red Cross Camp and Hospital Council, the group directing garden clubs' camp planting and hospital services. *Courtesy of GCA Archive.*

Ladies of the Green Fingers Garden Club, in Greenwich, Connecticut, model hats created by husbands at their flower show in 1940. The hats, featuring fresh fruits, vegetables, and flowers, were later auctioned to benefit war relief. The winning entry (center right), worn by Mrs. William Gould, displays "green fingers" of asparagus. *Courtesy of the Green Fingers Garden Club.*

Mesdames Seabury, Colie, and Rennell staged a display depicting a small home vegetable garden in the 1941 International Flower Show. This exhibit was awarded the GCA Silver Medal. *Courtesy of GCA Archive.*

Mrs. Luis J. Francke (of the North Country Garden Club of Long Island, Oyster Bay, New York), the GCA's Conservation Committee chairman during 1942–45, appears with her friends, Louis Bromfield (left), chief of Agriculture Soil Conservation and director of the Tennessee Valley Authority, and Hugh Bennett (right), an avid conservationist. All three were members of Friends of the Land, founded by the two men. *Courtesy of GCA Archive.*

Junior Flower League

Because I love my country, America, and my state _____ and want them to be beautiful, and because I know that grass, flowers, bushes, trees, and birds help to make them so, I shall try never to harm them, and and I shall try to enjoy them without injuring them.

Signed_____

Address_____

The Wild Flower Preservation Society of America

I Promise,

To protect our native plants,
Not to destroy rare flowers and ferns,
Not to injure any shrub or tree and
Not to set fire to the fields or woods.

Name...

Address...

Date...

Mrs. Luis J. Francke (of the North Country Garden Club of Long Island, Oyster Bay, New York) loved young people and started the Junior Flower League to encourage their interest in conservation. The pledge cards for both the league and the Wild Flower Preservation Society of America express a commitment to protect all beautiful, rare, and native plants. *Courtesy of GCA Archive.*

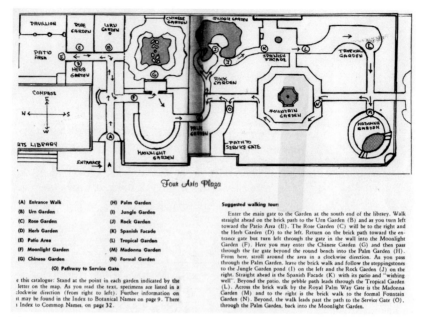

This plan was developed after World War II to restore the small demonstration gardens at the Society of Four Arts in Palm Beach, Florida. Four Arts Plaza was intended to help new homeowners choose plant material for their landscapes. The Garden Club of Palm Beach continues to support these gardens. *Courtesy of the Garden Club of Palm Beach.*

Mrs. Jerome K. Doolan (of the Pasadena Garden Club, California), the first GCA president from the West Coast, advocated for conservation issues and was a trustee of Keep America Beautiful. During her term, 1968–71, a GCA conservation education packet for fifth and sixth graders, titled "The World around Us," was published and distributed nationally. *Courtesy of Emily Keyes Belt.*

In 1972 the Akron Garden Club, in Ohio, bought and equipped a scientific trailer to serve as a mobile experimental lab for the Akron public schools. It was still in operation in the late 1980s. *Courtesy of GCA Archive.*

Mrs. George P. Bissell Jr. (of the Garden Club of Wilmington, Delaware), GCA president during 1975–77, stands next to the winning entry in the Bicentennial Miniature Room Exhibit at the 1977 annual meeting in Washington, D.C. Clubs depicted historical period rooms with appropriate flower arrangements. The Greenwich Garden Club, of Connecticut, created the winning room from the Bush Holly House. *Courtesy of Emily Keyes Belt.*

May, 2, 1975

Dear Mrs. Bissell, and the Garden Club of America,

I thank you, and the Garden Club of America for making this trip possible for us. This trip was alot of fun I will never forgot this trip to Washington DC. I thank the Garden Club, and I thank you Mrs. Bissell, because you have been so nice to us Now you will remember that here was a class that made trees live a little longer.

Thank You, Yours truly,

HILDA REYES

Mrs. George P. Bissell Jr. (of the Garden Club of Wilmington, Delaware) received thank–you letters from fifth-grade students invited to attend the Council of Presidents in Washington, D.C., in 1975. The students presented a program, "Preserving Our Trees," inspired by "The World around Us" environmental education packet developed by Mrs. Avery Rockefeller and Anne Bucknall (of the Greenwich Garden Club, Connecticut). *Courtesy of GCA Archive.*

The Bay City Garden Club, in Michigan, celebrated its fiftieth anniversary in 1977 by establishing the Kantzler Memorial Arboretum. The club transformed an unsightly riverfront into a beautiful educational park that now includes hundreds of trees, shrubs, and flowers. *Courtesy of the Bay City Garden Club.*

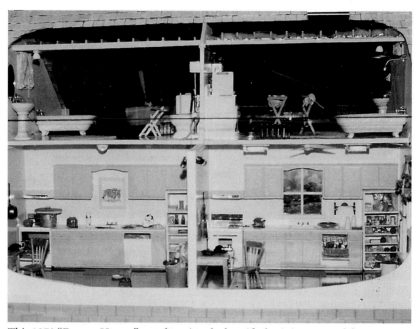

This 1978 "Energy House," an educational, electrified miniature model, was a conservation project of Hortulus, a garden club in Greenwich, Connecticut. Brainchild of Anne Bucknall, it was built and furnished by Mesdames Hagen, Cragin, Jennings, and Platt. It traveled to eleven states, was viewed by over a hundred thousand people, and received the Zone II Conservation Award. *Courtesy of Hortulus.*

Elise Deans, member of the North Country Garden Club of Long Island, Oyster Bay, New York, and cochairman of the New York Area Committee, works with local school children in the Central Park Conservatory Garden, at Fifth Avenue and 105th Street. This restoration project extended from 1977 to 1985 and involved twenty-five clubs from Zones II, III, and IV. *Courtesy of GCA Archive.*

Marjory Stoneman Douglas received the Margaret Douglas Medal for service to conservation education at the annual meeting in 1990, in her hundredth year of life. Mrs. Douglas wrote *The Everglades, River of Grass*. Her effective lobbying resulted in the creation of the Everglades National Park in 1947. *Courtesy of GCA Archive.*

Judges (from left to right) Nancy D'Oench, Anita Salembier, and Marilyn Walzer evaluate an entry at the 1990 annual meeting flower show held at PepsiCo Corporation in Purchase, New York. The PepsiCo property includes the Donald M. Kendall Sculpture Gardens, originally laid out by E. D. Stone Jr. and extended by Russell Page. *Courtesy of GCA Archive.*

Nancy Murray (of the Garden Club of Palm Beach, Florida), chairman of the Book Committee, assisted with this centennial history of the Garden Club of America. *Courtesy of Garden Club of Palm Beach.*

Past GCA presidents wear their finest for the awards dinner at the 1995 annual meeting in Boston.

Left to right, standing: Chris Frietag (of the Akron Garden Club, Ohio), Sadie Gwen Blackburn (of the River Oaks Garden Club, Houston), Nancy Thomas (of the Garden Club of Houston), Jane Ward (of the Providence Garden Club of Pennsylvania, , Wallingford), Kay Donahue (of the Little Garden Club of Rye, New York), Catherine Beattie (of the Carolina Foothills Garden Club, Greenville, South Carolina), Gina Bissell (of the Garden Club of Wilmington, Delaware), and Elizabeth Norweb (of the Garden Club of Cleveland).

Seated: Nancy Belcher (of the Millbrook Garden Club, New York), and Etheldreda Reid (of the Piscataqua Garden Club, York Harbor, Maine). *Courtesy of GCA Archive.*

For its millennium project, the Garden Club of the Oranges, in South Orange, planted two thousand daffodil bulbs on Interstate 280 in New Jersey. *Courtesy of GCA Archive.*

Schoolchildren learn about the ecosystem at the Norfolk Botanical Garden. The Garden Club of Norfolk, in Virginia, won the Founders Fund Award in 2003 to create a unique native plant garden at the Norfolk Botanical Garden. The project consists of four habitats with a boardwalk around the edge of Lake Whitehurst. *Courtesy of GCA Archive.*

"Two and a half" members of the Halten Garden Club, in Baltimore, Mrs. Cristi Barry (left) and Mrs. Kathleen Cecil with baby Lily, plant New York asters at the Sparks Elementary School in Cockeysville, Maryland, in 2002. The club's association with the school, named after a founding member, began during World War I and has continued ever since. *Courtesy of the Halten Garden Club.*

The GCA Conservation and National Affairs and Legislation committees survey invasive species in a swamp during a trip in 2002 to study environmental issues firsthand. *Courtesy of GCA Archive.*

Edie Loening (of the Millbrook Garden Club, New York), archive chairman, and Anne Myers (of the Garden Club of Irvington-on-Hudson, New York), GCA historian, meet with Page Kidder (seated) (of the Garden Club of Englewood, New Jersey) on her last day of serving in that office in 2010, completing nearly twenty years of service. *Courtesy of Munro Bonnell.*

Jane Dwight (center) and other members of the House Committee polish the silver in the kitchen at 589 Madison Avenue, for use when member clubs visit headquarters or when the Executive Committee and national officers are in town. *Courtesy of GCA Archive.*

clubs and shaped the program possibilities to answer zone needs. Excellent prospects have been found in the federal and state agencies, such as the state and federal forest services and wildlife agencies and even the GCA's avowed enemy of other times, the Army Corps of Engineers. Colleges and universities have produced professors and technicians who have presented admirable programs. The most popular programs have been on propagation and garden design. In both cases the Horticulture Committee, as we know, has developed slide shows with texts, which, if all else fails, can be enlisted. Fletcher Steele's 1930s lecture has surely been read hundreds of times, for its slides have been restored and copied a number of times. His principles have remained clear and succinct. More recent programs have featured fruit trees, tropical plants, and gardens that demonstrate established patterns of garden design.

Under the chairmanship of Louise Wrinkle in the 1980s, the Horticulture Committee gave special attention to an issue popularly called the "rape of the bulbs." Narcissus and tulips again came to the fore, threatened this time not by quarantine but with extinction. The bulbs in their native ground were being "scraped up by bulldozers in Spain and Turkey," trucked to dealers in Holland, dried, and sold in lots. Few survived the ordeal. These were the bargain bulbs one found in sacks at some nurseries and grocery store garden centers, while the expensive bulbs were nursery-raised in the United States or the Netherlands and could be found in the bulb bins at better nurseries. Nancy Thomas, of the Horticulture Committee, added, "Trillium grandiflorum and cypripedium could not be propagated early or quickly enough (if at all) to be sold cheap." She headed a 1987 study in the Horticulture Committee "to encourage people to raise their own bulbs."[28]

The Horticulture and Conservation committees soon united in researching the sources the American dealers used for bulbs. Mrs. Michael McIntosh, chair of the National Affairs and Legislation Committee, then joined in, worked quickly through the red tape of the Department of Agriculture, and prompted the implementation of restrictions on imports to settle the "plight of the little bulbs," as she put it. The cooperating committees outlined their efforts to the board, concluding, "To have it all tied up in a neat package by Mrs. McIntosh of the National Affairs and Legislation Committee was too good to be true." The end result in 1991 was that all bulbs from the Netherlands were required by American law to be labeled as "bulbs from a wild source" or "bulbs from cultivated stock." In the fall of that year, Horticulture and Conservation invited prominent bulb dealers to meet with them at headquarters. The result was a sort of standoff, in which the nurserymen ultimately had little choice but to yield."[29] Remembered one: "The ladies used real bullets."

The ever more extensive work of the Horticulture Committee saw some geographic subdivision into state and city committees under the GCA umbrella in the late 1970s and then again in the 1990s. New York City's group was the first, responding in 1977 to the persistent feeling that the city needed a GCA club, yet not wanting an actual club. The resulting New York Area Committee was administered by a board, with an advisory composed of one representative from each of twenty-two clubs near or relatively near New York City. The committee considered many city projects, such as restoration work and planting in Central Park, the cultivation of wildflowers there, and gardening for certain historic houses in the Bronx. Eventually the committee centered on one major project, restoration of the Conservatory Garden at 105th Street. A neglected WPA project from the 1930s, its fountains were dry and cracked, the flower beds empty; under the chairmanship of Jan Pratt the New York Area Committee brought the garden back to life.

The committee raised money by holding both foreign and domestic tours. These trips were quite specific in their objectives and unlike the more general format of the Visiting Gardens tours. Special tours abroad, designed to study particular subjects and areas, were approved in advance by the Executive Committee and drew wide attendance beyond the New York area.

Planned and supervised by Elise Deans, a prominent landscape architect who lived on Long Island, the tours to Europe were a signal success for the New York Area Committee, always leaving a waiting list. Mrs. Deans raised a hundred thousand dollars through the tours and other endeavors to fund a garden planted in the Hudson River Trust Park, a project delayed by the terrorist attack of 9/11 and delayed by Elise Deans's sudden death not long after. In response to many requests to take part, the committee decided to welcome a general membership, which greatly enlarged its numbers. At this writing the GCA is a minority in its roster, but the board is still composed of GCA members.

The 1980s in horticulture saw the joining of neighboring states into informal unions to achieve various goals, usually attendant to horticultural education focused upon local circumstances. New Jersey formed a committee in 1987, when eleven clubs in Zone IV agreed to pool resources in creating the New Jersey Committee "with the objective of cultivating horticulture and providing education of the Garden Club of America purpose within our state." By-laws and articles called for two delegates to represent each club in the zone, along with the usual slate of officers. These became the "reps" and actually "comprised a committee." Headquarters was placed at the Frelinghuysen Arboretum, in Morristown. In 1989 the New Jersey Committee held its first fund-raiser, the Harvest Show and Plant Sale, attended by two thousand. In the committee's 1998 accounting to the GCA, the show had greatly increased in attendance and earned sixty-six thousand dollars, which were donated to worthy causes in the zone.[30]

The Philadelphia Committee was organized in 1965 by Margaret Day Dilks and composed of twelve clubs. By the year 2000 it had ten substantial projects either in process or completed at locations throughout the city, including the perennial favorite, Bartram's Garden; the Children's Crisis Treatment Center; Kearsley, the oldest retirement home in the United States; and the historic houses in Fairmount Park. Funds were raised in addition for the Pennsylvania Horticultural Society and the Schuylkill Center for Environmental Education. The scope of these projects of the Philadelphia Committee well represents the wider focus of the public endeavors of the GCA across the nation.[31]

The Horticulture Committee held the first annual GCA National Horticultural Conference in 2002 in Pasadena, California, where the giant redwoods had been saved several generations earlier. One hundred forty participants met for the Shirley Meneice Workshop in Pasadena and the new botanical center at Huntington Gardens. After two days of lectures, a third day of working with plants among the fine collections of the Huntington completed the conference and sent the carefully screened participants back to their clubs with new ideas. The conference was inspired by a concern of the Horticulture Committee that the horticultural education in the GCA was not "filtering down to the club level."[32]

A plant study project had been launched in 1988 to address this issue. Spoken of as a "national project," or, officially as the Joint Endangered Species Project of 1987, it had been a combined interest of the Center for Plant Conservation and the Conservation Committee since 1981. Clubs were encouraged to adopt an endangered species—not a new idea in the GCA—and each was to take several different thrusts with this: (1) produce a postcard illustrating two or more endangered species of plants in their area; (2) design and make a poster of the species to publicize the danger it faced; (3) provide a high-quality color slide of the species to be incorporated into an educational program; and (4) cultivate the plant in members' gardens, for which if necessary the Center for Plant Conservation would provide the seeds.[33]

The national project met with mixed success. Where a club had an enthusiastic horticultural base in membership, the program flourished and has continued. In a club that favored flower arranging or conservation, the result was less gratifying. A smaller-scale program launched in 1991, Partners for Plants, has been more successful, simply because it is less ambitious. Each club selects one plant family and studies a particular genus or just a single plant within that family. "Hopefully," the committee said at the program's start, "choices will include plant material rare in the Nursery Trade."[34]

With such programs the Horticultural Committee has sought closer communication and participation with individual clubs. The basis of the committee remains educational.

Chapter Six
THE FLOWER ARRANGERS

Flower arranging in the GCA has always had a broad constituency but has been a relatively quiet presence that belies its influence, when called upon, in the endeavors of the organization. Sometimes through the years flower arrangers have joined horticulturists and conservationists on issues and projects that are not related to flower arranging but of mutual philosophical concern.

It is fairly safe to say that whatever other interests they might have, GCA members have nearly all been flower arrangers to one degree or another. Headquarters always displays either fresh greenery or flowers and, when the board meets, usually a plentiful supply, arranged elegantly in vases, called "containers" in the jargon of flower arranging. Many a board meeting in the 1920s and 1930s had arrangements of magnolia blossoms sent up from Savannah on the train or orchids by air or sea from Hawaii or wildflowers brought over from the Upper Peninsula of Michigan. Christmas and other holidays saw the mahogany tables and bookcases made colorful with poinsettias, if not holly, and, after Williamsburg was underway, with wreaths and garlands of boxwood or fresh fruit. Today amaryllis has taken the place of the earlier materials.

The same affection for artistically arranged plant material has always been present at meetings and events involving the GCA across

America. From the early days horticulturists and conservationists vigorously objected to cutting leaves from a landscape or lopping off branches of forest greens. But their flower-arranging colleagues were likely to be culprits of the crime when they needed to perfect a flower arrangement—for example, in the "natural style" with which the Manhattan florist Judith Garden dazzled them from the 1940s to the 1960s.

Flower arranging has a long past, but its development as an art form is not so venerable. That is, until recent history, arrangements were made casually, more to show the flowers than for artistic form. The wall paintings in Pompeii show flowers loosely arranged and lush floral garlands. King Tut's tomb was apparently filled with floral tributes, and his necklace of wildflowers that adorned his mummy is usually credited to the women of his family. Americans have generally considered non-commercial flower arranging almost entirely a women's pastime. Not so in the Middle East and elsewhere in Asia or, historically, in southern Europe. Those marble urns in Renaissance gardens were sometimes arranged with cut flowers by the gentlemen of the household. Fresh flower arrangements were not common in American houses before the mid-nineteenth century, when doctors abandoned their belief that flowers ejected poisonous vapors.

It was in the late 1850s that a craze for real flowers in domestic interiors overtook the earlier custom of arranging flowers made of wax or hair and keeping them dust free beneath glass domes. In 1817, President James Monroe ordered wax flowers from Paris for the White House dinner table and the drawing room mantelpieces. Jessie Benton Fremont, in her memories of the 1830s, notes some progress beyond wax: "stands" of camellias, presumably potted, were brought in from the greenhouse to decorate for parties.[1] Bouquets of cut geraniums were fashionable gifts of affection and greeting during the Civil War, bought from the florist in a wrap of lace made of thin, shiny, gold paper. The library at the GCA Headquarters has rare nineteenth-century books translating the "language" of flowers, each blossom with its own special meaning, the camellia, the rose, the daisy, and so on.

Funerary tributes historically could be quite elaborately floral, as many nineteenth-century photographs portray: crosses made of roses, open Bibles made of carnations, and sprays of long-stem flowers issuing from decorative baskets. Preserved arrangements like these survive from the funerals of Lincoln, Garfield, and McKinley. Floral offerings of the sort were as likely to be made of artificial flowers as real ones, however, and an occasional one was made of feathers—all rivaling the tawdry plastic flowers one sees in some cemeteries today.

Gardeners who had heretofore left flowers outside, intact on their stems, were bringing the blossoms inside by the 1850s and arranging them in water-filled vases. A few photographs, paintings, and prints document early flower arrangements. The rich photographic archive of the George Eastman House, in Rochester, New York, boasts a daguerreotype portrait of a vase of camellias rather casually arranged, less an artistic effort than a horticultural display. The widow of the legendary Wade Hampton of South Carolina, an avid gardener, was photographed around 1859 in her Columbia drawing room, sitting close beside a single daylily in a vase, doubtless from her garden outside. Two years later, Mrs. Lincoln made a wreath of japonicas to decorate the coffin of the heroic young Colonel Elmer Ellsworth, the first Union casualty of note in the Civil War.

Those who work with flowers fall generally into two groups: one, the horticulturist, who loves the flowers because of the plant that produces them and, of course, because of their place in the garden scheme, and the other, the arranger, who appreciates flowers as elements of a work of art. The novice, probably as well as the horticulturist, cringes to see beautiful flowers pulled and twisted and some relegated to the garbage bin in the process of flower arrangement. Yet the result can be magic, born in the eye and gift of the arranger as surely as a statue is first conceived in the mind of the sculptor. A concept is shaped by the artist through materials.

Flower arranging is the creation of a temporary work of art. The generation that founded the GCA was interested in "artistic" arrangements, as had been the generation before them. It would be surprising if they had not. One of the attractions of the Philadelphia Centennial's Horticulture Hall was the changing panorama of floral art displayed there, and the tradition continued there well into the twentieth century. The "gallery" was located at the back of the hall. Arrangements were placed on stepped wooden benches, similar to those in greenhouses of the time.

Besides arranging flowers from their own gardens for their own houses, early GCA flower arrangers were no strangers to flower shows, even though horticulture was the more customary feature of early shows. The shows usually were city shows, and they were spiritual descendants of country fairs. Beauty lay in the eyes of the judges. Personal taste joined vague notions of color combination and form in driving the judging. Design concepts of the painter and sculptor were applied to the most artistic flower arranging. When the GCA established the Flower Show Committee in 1922, it was naturally called the Art Committee, indicating the perspective the organization had on flower arranging.[2] Not for sixty-four years would the word *art* be retired in favor of simply *flower arranging*. The flower shows that involved most GCA members must be considered separate from the International Flower Show, which was a New York activity almost entirely.

In regard to GCA shows early on, separating flower arranging from horticulture is often difficult in the written record. The Flower Show Committee was so named in 1923, because Alice Lockwood declared "art committee" inadequate. She resigned in 1925 to begin editing and writing *The Gardens of Colony and State*. Mrs. Percy Williams, president of the New Canaan Garden Club at the time, then became chair, with Maud Seabury as vice chair. Although the Flower Show Committee members had their own local flower shows, as a committee they also wanted a big, national-scale project. Priscilla Williams and Maud Seabury were very interested in the International Flower Show, so when the invitation came in 1925 to participate the following year, they accepted it and decided to make the IFS the major project the committee had looked for. The show was a success, attracting 81,500 at the gate, which, although 20,000 fewer than the year before, was a fine turn out nevertheless.[3]

Flower arranging thus became part of the International Flower Show, but GCA horticulturists were already involved in the show, and, being the most ambitious and popular of all the exhibitors, they easily swallowed most of the club's annual appropriation of twenty-five hundred dollars to cover costs related to the show. GCA flower arrangers nevertheless were very much a presence, providing studied displays of flowers, which were replaced by new arrangements every other day. The GCA section in the Grand Palace was always filled with vases of flowers and other arrangements made for competition. These were displayed on long tables in applied art classes.[4] Table settings were often the format for flower-arranging classes in the earliest shows. Wedding bouquets and mantel arrangements provided other vehicles for the entries. Little of what appeared was similar to the "pure art of flower arranging" one encounters at GCA shows today. The road to the future started in the artistic classes in the 1920s.

The only written standards were found in current books on flower arranging, and these standards were limited, vague at best, so taste continued to govern judging, guided by common experiences in flower arranging. An ever more important event in the show involved flower decorations at the show's luncheon. This effort probably did more to interest members in flower arranging than all other aspects of the shows taken together. For the luncheon the arrangers took over decorations, bringing containers from their homes and flowers from their gardens and the flower stalls of New York. Little else at the luncheon ever outshone the beauty of the floral decorations.

Begun in 1928 at the Waldorf-Astoria Hotel, the luncheon grew fast in popularity. By the time the three years from 1929 through 1931 had passed and the Waldorf had yielded its Fifth Avenue site to the Empire State Building and built itself anew and ever more opulently on Park Avenue, the annual flower show luncheon had become a major New York social event. Tickets were very hard to come by. After the return to the now-new Waldorf in 1932 the luncheon welcomed over a hundred guests. It was an event that had become too demanding for volunteers to carry alone. With some exceptions the decorations were turned over to florists, while the Flower Show Committee directed the production, and all "pieces" were done to their precise specifications. Even so, a virtuoso arranger might take on the head table or the entrance, making a splendid arrangement representing GCA talent.[5]

In the 1930s American flower shows really came into their own. The New York show was not the only big and prestigious flower show, but it was the most fashionable and received the most notice. Chicago had a "world show" on a large scale; the Philadelphia Flower Show, one day to be called "international," was a major event; and the last big show in the spring season, the New England Flower Show, in Boston, was a mecca for the northeastern states, but most notably in horticulture. Two divisions were basic to them all, horticulture and "artistic," meaning flower arranging, and of the two, horticulture remained by far predominant, even beyond World War II. Of the shows, New York held first place as the top one, with top attendance and notice. However, neither it nor the New England Flower Show was to survive.

Flower exhibitors, like the horticultural exhibitors, sometimes traveled great distances to participate in the International Flower Show. In 1940 a hundred exhibitors in flower arranging came to New York from ninety-five clubs of the GCA. Prizes varied from silver trophies to ribbons and certificates. Flower arranging was upstaged during the war by victory gardens and vegetable exhibits at shows; there was no International Flower Show in 1943, 1944, or 1945. In the last of these years the flower arrangers had a discussion about perhaps having a show of their own at the Museum of the City of New York. They agreed with museum officials that it could be based upon the Chelsea show in London, with which the GCA, through Chicago associations, had a friendly relationship. As an entirely amateur show, the museum show would establish an admirable venue for education in flower arrangement. In the hustle that accompanied the spring of 1945 and the close of the war, the new flower show project seemed too ambitious and was dropped, only to be revisited again in the 1950s. Had horticulture been involved, perhaps it would have revived, but the flower arrangers were as yet still the weaker branch.[6]

In 1946 the International Flower Show opened again, but was not the spectacle it had been in the 1920s and 1930s, nor would it be again. The usual GCA space was cut to one-third of what it had been, over protest from the GCA. The GCA board sent a bulletin to the entire membership urging exhibitors to come to New York, hoping numbers would revive the waning show. To everyone's surprise the return was quite large, and the premise of the competition was especially successful, using flowers to interpret works from the Museum of Modern Art. Several hundred women answered the invitation. The GCA, empowered by its helping hand, demanded and won its space back and entered the show with force and optimism.[7]

The interest in flower arranging increased after World War II. Publications on the subject became more readily available, although they were usually not very specific in rules and forms, unless their emphasis was Asian or "Oriental" flower-arranging traditions, which had stringent rules. The Ikebana school, from Japan, began to realize great popularity in the West in the 1920s and after the war made a strong appearance at the flower shows in the Midwest and Northeast. Mitsu Arai, of the Greenwich Garden Club, in Connecticut, taught ikebana and took her students on study trips to Japan. One of Ikebana's most famous teachers,

Tomoko Yamamoto, was decorated for her work by the emperor of Japan before she became a U.S. citizen. An active member of the Des Moines Founders Garden Club from 1943 until her death in 1966, she was an influence on an entire generation of flower arrangers.[8]

The 1940s and early 1950s were crucial years in the development of GCA flower arranging. By the mid-1950s the how-to of flower arranging centered for the most part in concepts of proper or desirable scale and ratio. For more one had only the books on the Asian arrangements, in which philosophy motivated every technique. Mrs. Yamamoto held classes that are remembered as intellectual experiences as well as instruction in flower arranging. Most flower arrangers worked in a more open field than Asian arrangements, one devoid of guiding rules. They might embrace some aspect of arranging from countries in Europe, although European characteristics were not widely different from one country to another. The strongest influence upon American arrangers was Britain, where form and color, as well as the appropriateness of plant material in combination, all seasoned by personal taste, still governed the artistic filling of containers with flowers, and many of the British arrangements in competition were by today's standards so subjective that they might be better classed as dioramas than artistic flower arrangements.

Flower arranging made its first significant impact, foreshadowing flower arranging to come, at the International Flower Show in 1922. In Manhattan the show became a flower-arranging moment. Proclaimed a headline in the *New York Times*, "Cut Flowers Take a Bow at Show Here," and the article described arrangements of "roses, carnations, tulips" bounding from "standard displays." Floral color and beauty teemed in large "colonial," "French," and "Georgian" bouquets, dazzling the thousands of onlookers who came to admire.[9]

Flower arranging, the quiet face of the GCA, began to gain a public face. The resulting excitement wakened the Flower Show Committee to work that needed to be done and a promising road ahead.

Concern over the quality of judging surfaced within the year, in 1953, although the subject was not entirely unfamiliar. Judging in horticulture was obvious in the quality and condition of the specimens, and in landscape design, in the architectural and horticultural effectiveness of the entry. Flower arranging was more a pure art, and art is not easily bound to rules, except for the familiar standards of form and color. Yet a flood of complaints from the clubs seems to have wakened the committee to a prevailing concern over lax rules or none at all in flower arranging. The force of the objections helped identify that the problem lay in judging. There was need for a "recognized judge list," which of course called for specific qualifications. The Flower Show Committee was stymied and did nothing much to find a solution. Complaints continued to come and by the mid-1950s were sometimes punctuated by the withdrawal of dissatisfied clubs from the GCA. Realizing that it had to avoid the trouble somehow, the Flower Show Committee sent out a frail appeal for "judges and arrangers" of merit. This did not solve the problem.[10]

What was to be known as the Flower Show Judging Committee, a subdivision of the Flower Show Committee, was originally known as the Special Committee on Judging, and it included in its duties all judged classes in flower shows, notably conservation, horticulture, and flower arranging. While horticulture and conservation seemed well in hand, flower arranging cried out for a solution to its problems. In 1956 Elizabeth Reynolds, a noted flower arranger, became chair of this special committee, and she gave both her full attention and that of her committee to improving the judging program for flower arranging. Hardly had she taken office when she presented a report to the board outlining a "vast reorganization" of flower arranging.[11]

This report established steps for the future of GCA judging in flower arranging as well as in horticulture. The flower-arranging part, in the context of a lax past, was radical. Mrs. Reynolds proposed a strong program for arranging that was to be developed through a series of seminars or "judging workshops," a phrase she introduced into the flower show lexicon. Artistic flower show judges were also to be cultivated as teachers. While they might hold workshops or demonstrations themselves, more important they were to teach through judging in flower shows. In this way arrangers would learn by doing and by observing, hearing criticism of their work and that of others.

The Flower Show Judging Committee compiled a list of respected judges from the International Flower Show and invited them to meet and "to suggest a guide by which judges would be selected." The standards then set were published in March 1957 by the GCA. The *Bulletin* reported on the meeting, which took place at headquarters, describing it as "the first time that the judges agreed and disagreed orally before a listening audience." Forums in the zones produced names of possible judges or those interested in the role; these the Flower Show Committee assembled in a prospective list by zone. When the list was all together, the committee said that through it they "personally know all the abilities and caliber of each one of the judges."[12]

The first judging workshop under the new rules met in 1959 in Memphis, at the invitation of Ellie Harwood and Lois Eason, both members of the Memphis Garden Club and major players in GCA flower arranging. It was a two-day workshop at the Brooks Art Gallery, with "line mass and dried arrangement classes." The meeting had a purpose outside being a flower show: it was the first "workshop," filling the educational function its promoters had hoped to achieve in flower arranging. Its white-glove Memphis hospitality was enhanced by mild October days. Coverage of the entertainments filled the society pages of the Memphis *Commercial Appeal*.[13]

Less was printed about the flower-arranging classes for which flower-arranging history will remember the Memphis workshop. Elizabeth Reynolds addressed the opening to explain the new way flower-arranging rules and competitions would be managed. For one thing *flower arranging* was now the official term. *Artistic* and *floral art* were retired, out of style. Then she told with the certainty of an expert, according to Penelope Pepys, society columnist, "just what makes a collection of flowers an 'arrangement.'"[14]

Star participants were judges selected from the International Flower Show. Each judge was assigned to a class, where she taught and observed. Those students or participants who seemed promising as GCA flower show judges were consulted privately, and, if all was in order, their names were submitted to the Flower Show Committee. As a result of observations conducted in Memphis, three judges were selected, the first of sixteen who were to compose the judging staff in the Southern Zone of the Garden Club of America. In 1960, Etheldreda Reid recalled that seven years earlier as a vice president of the GCA she had seen to the creation of a committee "to reorganize judging at GCA. They needed new rules, latitude for creative arrangement, and to settle great discord over standards that were archaic." It took some years to get started full speed, but she was justly proud of what had come to pass.[15]

This relatively simple beginning, established from a pattern begun in the 1950s, is still followed today in the training of GCA flower show judges. Through the late 1950s and early 1960s the popularity of flower arranging became evident at every show, and the GCA's board noted the "upsurge of interest." A flower show forum was held in 1960 at the Metropolitan Museum of Art. Technically a forum could be a competition, workshop, or flower show. This one was a flower show titled "Color in Art" and dealt directly with flower arranging. A similar forum, "Art in Bloom," took place in the same year at the Museum of Fine Arts, in Boston, under the auspices of the GCA and was more a workshop for judging than the one in New York, with thirty "students" and five classes. Members of the Flower Show Judging Committee had worked out a format for teaching judging through participation, rather than exposing students only to lectures, as it had always done before. The winners in each class became in turn judges of the other classes. This mode, if not without shortcomings, brought the Memphis format a little closer to to-day's competitions. Ironing the kinks out would take nearly twenty years, by which time the special committee had become the Committee on Judging.[16]

The International Flower Show began a slow, almost impercep-tible decline after the war. Nevertheless, it retained enormous panache and filled all its classes annually through the 1950s, even though it had seemed it would not survive the move from its midtown location in 1953 to Kingsbridge Armory, in a different part of New York City. Shuttle busses successfully bridged the distance there from the preferred, more convenient location. The 1957 show was considered at the time the best flower show ever held.

Arrangers and horticulturists alike had resented being sent judges from regions other than their own, who did not understand local plant material. The judging program honored their concerns and spread the geographical locations of qualified judges to such an extent that the judges serving any given show could be mixed and their decisions seem even and fair.

GCA judges were in demand. For the World Flower Show in Chi-cago in 1959, Elsie Sutter, of the Kenilworth Garden Club, in Illinois, scheduled Jane Emerson and Catherine Webster, with her husband, Joseph A. Webster, a member-at-large, and Betty Corning, to judge horticulture in the "GCA section." Soon many flower shows had GCA sections, and big shows, like those in Oakland (California), Cleveland, Chicago, Philadelphia, and Boston, as well as elsewhere in New England, were by the 1960s in the hands of GCA judges. In the spring of 1961 the GCA published the *Flower Show and Judging Guide,* which would one day—many editions later—be an insert in *The Yellow Book,* containing rules of GCA shows.

At the December board meeting in 1967 the directors observed a "national demand for flower shows" and were surprised that flower ar-ranging had surpassed horticulture in both participants' and the public's admiration. It was, after all, the flower-arranging classes that now filled up first of all at the International Flower Show. The Executive Committee was so happy with the flower shows and the elevated place of the GCA in them that they voted to donate a hundred dollars to every flower show, to help with expenses as the sponsoring club or clubs saw fit. Excitement and high spirits distracted attention from the account books. Spending on the International Flower Show became rather free.

Soon enough the treasurer's report brought bad news to the Flower Show Committee. After the money had been allocated, debts paid, and receivables counted in May 1968, it was discovered that the International Flower Show costs of the GCA had an overrun of $4,445.59. Elvira Broome Doolan, making every effort to "soften the blow," explained, "We must not overspend, otherwise we cannot survive."[17] After much discussion on how to raise money to close the deficit, the board decided to avoid creating a stir, simply take the money from the general fund, and in the future make sure the reins were drawn more tightly on flower show spending.

In the fall of 1968 the GCA decided to withdraw permanently from the International Flower Show. The eastern flower shows had always been weighted more toward horticulture than flower arranging. The GCA felt the need for attachment to another show, so in 1968 the organization entered New York's Bryant Park Flower Show, a festival-like, open-air event located on Fifth Avenue at Forty-second Street, behind the New York Public Library. The Executive Committee appropriated twenty-five hundred dollars, with a warning to the committee in charge that there would be not a penny more. Where the GCA was concerned, the International Flower Show passed into history.[18]

Held in tents, the Bryant Park show presented security dangers, and the ever-present threat of bad weather complicated nearly everything else, but the GCA took part with good cheer, a civic duty. Members set up a bright yellow marquee as the GCA gathering place for coffee and sandwiches, calling it the "members' terrace," and the yellow tent became the show's signature. In spite of a board member's remark in October 1976, "The Bryant Park Show is the most important contribution to New York City by GCA," it never really was the show the GCA wanted. Still enchanted with memories of the heyday of the International Flower Show, both flower arrangers and their horticultural colleagues looked around for other, more extensive venues.

After two years, Nancy Baldridge, chair of the Flower Show Committee, predicted a short future for the Bryant Park show. She did not like it, and others agreed with her. Was it really serving the GCA's mission? The new trend, she said, was to "bring the flower show to the people rather than the people to the flower show."[19] She spoke of malls, museums, and retirement homes as new and desirable venues. Already her committee had begun to alter show traditions in small ways to serve a broader public. For example, once there had been no visible explanation of why this or that entry won whatever award it won. This was a shortcoming in the educational process, which was part of the purpose of the flower shows. To correct this, exhibit entry cards were redesigned to provide a space on the front to allow the judges' decisions to be written out, so that spectators could clearly read them. A decade later, if the schedule writers wished, they provided a card to allow for comments by the flower arranger as well, to describe what the arrangement was supposed to say. This was a radical, if optional, change. When it was used, it could be said that what poets called the "new criticism," art without accompanying explanation, was out the window.

In 1979 a new flower show called Autumn in the Atrium opened in the Citicorp Center, in midtown Manhattan. One hundred eight entries were registered from twenty-six clubs across the nation. Happy with this success and the great beauty of the show, the GCA considered Autumn in the Atrium its new gift to the city. The show was all the greater in 1980, with many more entries and numerous prizes and awards. Autumn in the Atrium continued to grow. Tens of thousands of people came to see. The show opened with a gala reception with speakers, including the mayor. Tickets were sold to this event, raising substantial money. By then the GCA had twelve zones, and eleven of them were represented with flower arrangements.

The GCA, however, was now giving much more attention to shows across the country than to the one surviving New York show, Autumn in the Atrium. Indeed, at this point GCA members appear to have been far more interested in local and regional shows and the old favorites. The Philadelphia Flower Show, for example, remained the mother of American flower shows, with those in New England and Chicago almost as revered in the GCA. And the Garden Club of America held ever more numerous flower shows of its own. GCA flower shows are defined in *The Yellow Book,* which as of this writing has reappeared in seven editions since it was styled as *The Yellow Book,* in 1961, and nearly as many printings in addition. In the 1960s, a major show was a show sponsored by a club or a "nationally recognized horticultural organization." It was an event that was regularly scheduled for at least every third year, preferably in the same place; open to the public for at least two days, the major show offered a minimum of six competitive classes and received at least one hundred entries, sixty of which had to be in horticulture; it also had to include an educational program to be judged by GCA judges.

"Small flower shows" were those that were sponsored by an individual club or zone, were open to the public, and had a minimum of three competitive classes and fifty entries in horticulture; also at least 51 percent of the entries had to be from members of the GCA, and the shows had to have GCA judges. Zone meeting flower shows, held only at zone meetings, were less "structured" but somewhat followed the pattern of small flower shows. Club flower shows were the least formal of all and were meant to be held in conjunction with club meetings. They were judged by a panel of three GCA judges. Medals and awards could be offered at major and small flower shows. For the most part, certificates and ribbons were the awards at zone and club shows.

By the close of the 1960s the character of Garden Club of America flower shows had been established. There would be changes, more along the line of refinements, as the popularity of shows continued to grow. For example, categories of judges shrank in 1968 with the replacement of GCA conservation and landscape architecture judges by guest professionals working in those fields. In 1970 the Flower Show Committee began actively favoring zone shows that had a decidedly local flavor. The zones, on the other hand, made every effort to introduce and extend GCA days at the great regional non-GCA flower shows that had risen in popularity over the years. The GCA had ignored those shows heretofore, being absorbed in the International Flower Show to the virtual exclusion of everything else. The Flower Show Committee considered these large shows of other sponsorship to be the "national shows," including the ones in Morristown, New Jersey, and Flora Pacifica in Honolulu, along with the shows in Chicago, Boston, other New England sites, and Philadelphia, to which the GCA naturally felt a longtime kinship. GCA members, being among the leaders in flower arranging, had a natural wish to participate in these large shows.[20]

In November 1972 Ann Jones, chairman of the Flower Show Committee, urged the GCA to sponsor more flower shows. Overwhelming public response had proved that "everyone loves flower shows." She called for more workshops, classes, and staging. "GCA is falling short," she warned, because so many new non-GCA garden clubs were appearing and holding shows.[21] The Federation of Garden Clubs, with several hundred thousand members, also held many shows. If the GCA was to remain in the forefront (a position the organization never doubted it held), then its show activities and events that brought people together had to be increased. Flower shows were ideal meeting venues for GCA committees, regardless of the committee's particular discipline.

Not least in making the shows appealing to members were the awards. By 1970 there were many, with even more to come. In categories, the awards recognized national, zone, and club excellence. There were awards for both GCA members and nonmembers. Like the show rules, regulations and procedures that governed GCA awards continually improved as the number of awards grew substantially. There were thirteen "national" medals, beginning with the Medal of Honor and the GCA Achievement Medal, described in chapter 3, and eleven more with specific qualifications. Nominations originated in the clubs and went to the Awards Committee, which met usually in New York in conjunction with board meetings. The Medal of Honor and the Achievement Medal alone had to be approved both by the Executive Committee and the board, whereas all others were within the jurisdiction of the Awards Committee, whose judgments were based upon nominations submitted from the clubs and individual GCA members. A year or more could pass with an award remaining dormant. This was entirely up to the Awards Committee.

For flower arranging, awards often have had a more academic sort of impact than the satisfaction of recognition that accompanies other GCA awards. Flower arranging, although sometimes called the "gentle art," is nevertheless basically competitive when arrangers assemble for a show. On that competitive level, flower arranging came under ever more stringent standards and rules after the turnaround in 1956 and the instigation of the new qualifications for judges that took place in Memphis three years later. Neither horticulture nor conservation has fallen under the same sort of control. The flower arrangers decided that for their purposes the spirit of competition sparked the lamp of learning, and they have not deviated from this belief. Show ribbons are awards made by the judges, whereas trophies may be zone awards or club awards. Yet standing apart from the awards, one of the most memorable achievements for a flower arranger, whatever other awards might be earned, is to be named by the judges "best in show."

Flower arranging, stimulated by the improved judging program, has become a major pursuit among the GCA's clubs throughout the country since the 1950s. What had seemed abstract was now clarified, insofar as it could be. Regulation of flower shows and standards of judging were managed ably by the Flower Show Committee and the Flower Show Judging Committee. Both flower arranging and horticulture were under the Flower Show Committee's supervision. With the numerous shows sponsored by zones and clubs and the interest in flower arranging widespread, need for a general education program became evident. Arabella Dane, attending a flower show at Versailles, was impressed by the many international entries, and it occurred to her that there was "no forum for GCA ladies on the international stage."[22]

Interactions among individuals in the judging program had elevated the judges to a high level of flower arranging ability, but what of everyone else? In wondering how an education program for everyone might be enriched, Mrs. Dane envisioned the Flower Arranging Study Group. The concept of the FASG was that, through a separate organization attached to the Flower Show Committee, the most skilled members would compete internationally and at all the best American flower shows. They in turn would return to teach—*demonstrate* is the term—in zone workshops and shows, as well as for beginners in the clubs. She believed that the FASG would precipitate "levels" of skill from novice to the blue-ribbon arrangers. Education in flower arranging through these levels would broaden the benefits that the judging program had brought to relatively few since the 1950s.

To get started, Arabella Dane collected names of all the arrangers across the country. "I expected perhaps fifteen responses but got nearly fifty at once."[23] When the study group was set up, members began to join in numbers. Cindy Affleck arranged for the founding group to meet at the Franklin Institute Science Museum during the Philadelphia Flower

Show in 1988. The Executive Committee of the GCA was invited; some of its members feared a "take over" when the FASG asked to make itself an adjunct to the Flower Show Committee, protesting that the GCA did not have affiliates. Approval was granted under the presidency of Jane Ward, who remained unconvinced that such a link held any threat, and the arrangement was formalized under her successor, Sadie Gwin Blackburn.

The Flower Arranging Study Group was to be connected to the Flower Show Committee but was to be a separate organization, electing its own officers, keeping its own funds, making its own rules. The chair of the Flower Show Committee was to appoint the chair of the FASG, and the FASG was to file its fiscal records with the committee. Within several years the study group had over a thousand members and produced a regular newsletter. They held week-long workshops in various places, such as the 1995 workshop at the Frank Lloyd Wright fellowship, Taliesin West, near Scottsdale, Arizona. This meeting was so well attended as to require two separate seminars over a period of two weeks. Other workshops met with a similar response, and the back-to-back double sessions have become typical.

The advantage of the Flower Arranging Study Group was to relieve the Flower Show Committee of the heavy burden of education, which by the 1980s had become an obligation almost too big for the committee to fulfill. It will be seen that National Affairs and Legislation, under a wholly different arrangement, came to serve the Conservation Committee in much the same way.

Arabella Dane's vision was realized in more sophisticated entries at flower shows. The change was remarkable. Already the mass arrangements, which had once been predominant, were varied by entries following the Asian schools; this led to inventive flower arrangements in many different forms, from many different sources, with a creative use of containers and materials. The trend was stimulated by top arrangers returning from Europe with new ideas, and it spread through the flower shows and workshops. "A window had been opened to something new," said Penny Horne, "and it was never going to close again."[24]

On March 5, 1997, Bonny Martin, a strong supporter of the FASG and a widely recognized flower arranger, spoke to the board:

> The Southeastern Flower Show in Atlanta opened last week, but the 1997 Flower Show season really started with a Big Bang this week. Philadelphia, Cleveland and Green Fingers will have opened with Boston to follow. Our GCA judges are busy trekking from one to the other. The GCA should be very proud, for these judges will be giving our major awards. Seeing our judges both in Horticulture and Flower Arranging at these shows inspires one with the importance of the flower shows. We learn every time we judge a show and we are inspired by others. We educate the public with our exhibits and although they may not always agree with our decisions, the winners are happy.

In concluding, she reviewed improvements in scheduling: "We have come a long way."[25]

Pursuing the international participation that had substantially marked GCA flower shows in the 1990s, the FASG made a bid to join the World Association of Flower Arrangers. Consisting of thirty member countries at this writing, WAFA represents the highest level of global competition in flower arranging. At the world show in 1990, at Chateau de Bagatelle, in the Bois de Boulogne, the FASG made a bid to join as a separate part of the GCA. This was rejected for the apparent reason that the GCA's membership of fifteen thousand was too small to be considered representative of American flower arrangers. At the World Flower Show in 1996, held in Wellington, New Zealand, the FASG, linked to the National Garden Clubs, Inc., which had over two hundred thousand members; united with these two groups, the FASG reapplied for membership in WAFA and was admitted. Membership in the World Association of Flower Arrangers provided a vehicle for GCA flower arrangers to compete and learn globally, completing Arabella Dane's original idea for the Flower Arranging Study Group.

Membership in WAFA further expanded the educational opportunities of the FASG and thus enlarged the scope of the Flower Show Committee. American arrangers flocked to the world shows, held every three years, and competed with their flower arrangements. A world show attracts some one thousand participants, and thousands more of the public attend once the judging is done and the doors are opened. In 2011 the Tenth World Flower Show of WAFA was held in Boston, the first of the world shows to be held in the United States.

In 1977 the Flower Show Committee took under consideration Mary Jo Garre's presentation on the issue of photography. For some years the "official photographer" of the GCA had been Emily Keyes Belt, who covered many subjects and traveled to photograph in color slides many GCA programs, not only flower shows. Mrs. Garre was more particularly interested in photography as part of the shows. Flower arrangements are ephemeral, die quickly; specimens of horticulture change from their prize-winning forms. The photograph was about the only way to record their existence and perpetuate them. Furthermore, new educational goals required photographs of outstanding flower arrangements for future study, beyond photography as an art form. Nonetheless, photography was embraced as an art in itself, even though the subject matter had to relate to the purposes of the GCA. Thus a coal mine or a mountain ledge belonged as much to GCA photography as a bouquet of flowers or a pot of ferns.[26]

Flower show photography competition and exhibition were nothing new for the GCA as documentation. The beauty of flowers has always attracted the photographer's artistic eye. The first appearance of GCA photography was at a flower show in Chicago in 1916, where wildflowers were shown in a gallery of memorable photos. In addition to documenting shows and gardens, photographic contests took place at times in other shows, notably in the 1920s and '30s at the International Flower Show, with prizes for artistic photographs, judged by such well-known photographers as Ezra Stoller and Ralph Eugene Meatyard. Arrangements were filmed with important guests. Photographs taken at the shows were frequently intended for transfer to lantern slides to be incorporated in the GCA's educational traveling shows. Indeed in 2004 the Archive Committee chair, Marnie Laird, found scrapbooks on the floor of the GCA Headquarters; photographs of flower arrangements made as private endeavors from 1923 to 1969 had been pasted onto their pages. She and her committee cut through the backing paste with dental floss to free the pictures for conservation.

Photography with the GCA counted for documentation but also, at times, for aesthetics, which might include photographs involving any facet of GCA interests. "It is my goal," said Mary Jo Garre, "to present guidelines for schedule writing, staging and judging photography exhibits so that entries in this very popular flower show subdivision will once again be eligible for ribbons." The Executive Committee in December 2002 approved "the establishment of an ad hoc committee to develop a pilot program for studying and teaching photography judging and to set standards for that judging." Finally in 2004 a strong recommendation that the proposal be enacted came from the Flower Show Judging Committee. Thirty-six new candidates stood ready to become flower show photography judges. In 2006 Corliss Engle, who had worked for having photography judged since the 1970s, said, "The photography program is thriving," and further noted that "sixty-four people were seeking approval as judges." She believed that both documentation and aesthetics were important, particularly for flower arrangements, although horticultural and conservation subjects were becoming popular with participants.[27]

Apart from the competitions, nearly all flower shows today are video-recorded or captured in still photographs. Had photography not suffered such a sporadic history in connection with the shows, many earlier GCA shows could have been preserved in pictures. With the exception of the International Flower Show, photography was slow to advance within the GCA, although the interest was always present. Not until the late twentieth century was a competitive photography class automatically included in a GCA flower show.

In the Garden Club of America, flower arranging has had a history quite different from that of horticulture, as we have previously seen, and from that of conservation, whose discussion is yet to come. Since the first efforts in the 1970s to enlarge and simplify—"demystify," as GCA members put it—the GCA flower show has continued the process of refinement without interruption.[28] In 1998 in Williamsburg, Virginia, flower-arranging competitions and exhibitions became for the first time a feature of an annual meeting. A decade later, in November 2007, "templates" for the many essential parts of GCA shows were launched on the GCA Web site. Also in 2007 Debbie Oliver launched a new approach to "thinking green" in judging.

For over a half century the Flower Show Committee and its right hand, the Flower Show Judging Committee, together with the auxiliary Flower Arranging Study Group, had given the American art of flower arranging a basis in order and form. As an organized pillar of the Garden Club of America, flower arranging might be considered only fifty years old, even though flower arranging itself has been present in the GCA from the time of the founding.

Chapter Seven
THE CONSERVATIONISTS

Conservation has been important to the Garden Club of America from the outset, although, early on, it was rarely ever referred to by that name. *Preservation* was the earlier word most typically used to describe conservation, and the spirit it aroused was inclined to be emotional. With time conservation stood out as the noisy voice of the GCA, while horticulture and flower arranging have been less so. But in the beginning, they were all the same, considered "horticulture," with branches. Conservation's seeds, as it were, began to germinate on their own, however, well in advance of flower arranging.

By name and inclination, the Conservation Committee in the GCA originally grew up among those on the Wild Flower Preservation Committee interested in native plant preservation. From the Wild Flower Preservation Committee, the preservationists inherited the energy, independence, and passion to keep natural beauty from exploitation or violation, but they were activists, not scholarly horticulturists like their fellow committee members. They wanted the public to be aware that wildflowers should be respected.

Eloise Payne Luquer, as we saw in chapter 2, and Renee du Pont Donaldson were early promoters of the protection of wildflowers, especially along the highways. Through the Wild Flower Preservation

Committee such preservationists enjoyed an early and visible success in protecting natural plant material, which was being cut down wholesale for Christmas decorations. A significant aspect of the beginning of the GCA's long history of conservation efforts was this group's stance against "roadside vandalism," which they spoke out about, making it part of their promotion of the preservation of plants and wildflowers. Heady with the results of this commendable achievement, they took ascendency in the Wild Flower Preservation Committee and in 1924 renamed it the Conservation Committee.[1]

Fanny Day Farwell, of the Chicago area, had been their Joan of Arc, champion of wildflowers and all wild things wherever they grew on the earth, as we also saw earlier. Her looming presence on the new committee was that of a gifted horticulturist with an inclusive view of the earth. One never knew quite what aspect of her wildflower interest Mrs. Farwell would take up next. An extensive gardener with a staff of gardeners in Lake Forest, she traveled in 1923 to Egypt to see the tomb of Tutankhamen, then being opened by archaeologists in the Valley of Kings. The modern world marveled that the tomb, cut into a solid rock mountain, had stood undisturbed for more than three thousand years. Mrs. Farwell transported home seeds from long-decayed floral tributes scattered over the interior of the tomb and planted them in her Lake Forest greenhouse. The seeds germinated under the care of her gardener. When they bloomed they proved to be sweet peas, noted as *Lathyrus sativus*, whose blossoms were not only electric blue but also smaller than those of the familiar garden variety sweet peas. Botanists cried "impossible," a seed over twenty-five years of age was not going to germinate, much less a seed of three thousand years. Mrs. Farwell stood her ground in a debate that popped up again and again through the duration of her generation and even today appears occasionally when some gardener boasts on the Web of blossoms descended from seeds originally picked up in Tut's tomb.

Mrs. Farwell's jolly persona concealed the shrewd and determined woman she was in her pursuits. She demanded clarification from her colleagues. For example, she asked the committee if by wildflowers they meant roadside flowers? What, then, when "wildflowers" were cultivated? Were they still to be considered wild? The differing answers to this particular question foreshadowed the split between preservationists and conservationists. This would divide once again the purposes of the GCA's Wild Flower Preservation Committee.[2]

The members of the former Wild Flower Preservation Committee remained close to the Conservation Committee when it was formed in 1924, wholly approving the crusade to save hollies, laurel, and pine from Christmas clippers, but remained dedicated to nurturning wildflowers. During a bout of bad health in the autumn of 1925, Fanny Day Farwell resigned from the national committee, after a successful campaign to which she contributed fund-raising paper napkins printed with a slogan of her invention: "How many wild flowers will there be next year? It depends on us. Keep the flowers growing. They do their own sowing." At that point she stepped aside to make way for the more potent Conservation Committee.[3]

The mingling of the two committees was not one made in heaven, for the wildflower group did not turn its eyes from wildflowers, and the preservationists were quick to adopt conservation issues. Appearing in public as the Wild Flower Preservation Committee rather than the Conservation Committee, the champions of wildflowers gained new vigor with the Smithsonian Institution's 1925 publication of Mary Vaux Walcott's *North American Wildflowers*, a study completed in its last stages upon Mrs. Walcott's death by Mrs. Charles Platt, a Philadelphia artist and active GCA participant. This book, with its beauty and expertise, broadened scholarly interest in the subject as well as instigating a widespread cultivation of wildflowers.[4]

Preservation of Christmas greens was not set aside, however, and the committee convinced the New York Flower Show of 1924 to feature the endangered greenery. The show pleased most of its patrons, but baited hooks attract fish sooner or later. Eventually the Reverend R. Reiland, rector of St. George's Church, on East Sixteenth Street, stood up to be counted. Offended by the GCA's policy on Christmas greens, he said that it had "no foundation" and that the greens would still decorate his church "no matter what the ladies said." The GCA responded modestly to his newspaper harangues by saying that it would not back down but would use a "less arbitrary tone" in its pursuit.[5]

Henrietta Crosby succeeded Fanny Farwell as the conservation chairman. A committed conservationist almost before the word was attached to the idea, she had written the GCA leaflet "Helpful Hints in Conserving Wild Flowers."[6] But she had moved beyond wildflowers and identified with the preservationists or conservationists. In accepting chairmanship of the Conservation Committee, she was emphatic that she would serve only until 1929 and that the committee should consider her replacement well in advance. The early achievements of this capable woman are sometimes overshadowed by her occasional unpredictable actions; for example, as president of the GCA she rarely attended any meetings because she was always out of town, and eventually she abruptly resigned the presidency and went for a prolonged stay in Europe with her children. Yet in her four years as conservation chair, from her appointment at the end of January 1924 to her departure in 1929, she gave the committee form and directed it toward conservation to such an extent that the word *preservation* was not used in connection with it again. Yet the Conservation Committee's position was dangerous

By 1928 Henrietta Crosby had negotiated the establishment of conservation committees in thirty-one gardening clubs in all forty-eight states. Mrs. Crosby's work even with clubs that were not members of the GCA was motivated by nothing more than her belief that conservation should be inclusive of all the states. She had presented the idea of expanding the GCA's conservation work to the board, but apparently facing a wall of silence, she enacted, on her own, what became a movement. She stressed organization and communication among the committees, still acknowledging that most of the significant work of conservation came from headquarters meetings in New York, where public inquiry, which poured in, was processed and letters answered. She was exacting in her management.

When Henrietta Crosby resigned, as agreed, in May 1929, committee members were asking how important being in New York really was. Mrs. Crosby had agreed that moving the conservation interests to a club more or less in the center of the country was appealing. Chicago had made an offer that was difficult to refuse, including an office downtown; Connecticut made a bid, also very appealing. Still, Manhattan made the committee seem the vanguard of a "national" movement. Washington was too close to the battleground. Being in New York was being above all that, in a sense, and permitted assistance to everyone equally. Anne Stewart, head of the Redwoods Committee, agreed and urged that the Conservation Committee build on Mrs. Crosby's work and try to achieve a "national policy" on conservation. In what better place than New York might one launch such an effort?[7]

Helen Thorne, in the East, opposed too strong a GCA national identification with conservation activism: "Our province is a very simple one. Our clubs should have Conservation Committees and do the work locally." Clubs could best carry the campaigns to the local papers and decide what to support. They could, of course, submit their projects to the national committee for consideration, like every other club committee. She recognized that the difference between conservation and the other efforts of the GCA was conservation's need for haste, instant reaction, to save this or that. Some of conservation's most important work was thus in public opposition. Did the GCA want to be a protest group or remain an organization dedicated to horticultural study and education? "The time has come," said Mrs. Thorne, "when our clubs should decide what they wish to do."[8]

The debate boiled down to whether the GCA should take a leading part nationally in the American conservation movement or scatter the effort to those member clubs that were located close to where issues arose. Lillian Gustin McEwan, in Seattle, was sure the GCA could have it both ways and was mindful of the value of the organization's national prestige: "We established our conservation work on the Pacific Coast, California, Oregon and Washington on a large scale. In Seattle we have membership consisting of life members, charter and active members, and children pay ten cents. . . . We are working for representation in all the hamlets. . . . We are trying to take the case of everything that is beautiful in the name of the Garden Club of America. If you take that honor away, we would feel it was a great sacrifice."[9]

The question was not answered, nor has it ever really disappeared. Conservation in the GCA grew from work it had already begun. Only the issue of what degree of national involvement remained. As for New York City, after Mrs. Crosby's retirement it was proposed that a separate conservation committee be appointed for the city, for "its situation is different from the rest of New York." This was discussed but received little support, there being no club in New York City, and such a committee would have had to rely upon area clubs that were already giving strong support to the New York headquarters. Another burden they did not want. The issue would not be satisfied until formation of the New York Area Committee in 1977.[10]

Eloise Luquer became conservation chair in 1930. Three years later confusion was at once lessened and increased when Miss Luquer consolidated the Wildflower or Roadside Committee and the Billboard Committee into the Conservation and Roadside Committee. An activist in total agreement with Mrs. Crosby's views and plans, Miss Luquer took to the road, visiting local clubs to drum up interest and find those with the strongest interest in conservation. Her first visit was to the French Broad River Garden Club, in the North Carolina Smoky Mountains. Their enthusiasm for conservation was highly gratifying. In South Carolina she found less interest in conservation but more in ornamental gardening.

And so the various currents went, as Miss Luquer tallied the places of strong and weak interest. Secure in its permanent name by 1936, the Conservation Committee, under her meticulous leadership, had already become a pillar of the Garden Club of America, even though one supposes from the records that the large scale of its presence in the future GCA was not yet even suspected.

It was perhaps inevitable that the Conservation Committee and the GCA in general would become interested in America's national parks. The perpetuation of public lands by the government had begun with forests, which were needed for shipbuilding, notably the Santa Rosa live oak reserve near Pensacola, Florida, established in the 1820s by President John Quincy Adams and placed under the Navy Department. President Ulysses S. Grant had set Yellowstone aside in 1872, and through the late nineteenth century various currents began that finally united at the turn of the century into a full-fledged national parks movement. The National Park Service was established within the Department of the Interior three years after the founding of the GCA. Their paths were to cross often.

The preservation of vast reaches of public land was not entirely altruistic. Commerce had been squandering America's natural resources wantonly from the day the first white man set foot on the continent. Beauty was rarely an issue. The wonderful waterfall in downtown Rochester, New York, was praised originally not for its beauty but for the energy it provided to power mills, thus it became crowded in a setting of warehouses and commercial structures.

The slaughter of the buffalo is a well-known story, but the gluttonous devouring of the natural landscape is less so. Around 1890, after the West was won, American leaders realized that some of the nation's lands must be set aside and protected from the advance of the entrepreneur. It was not that the leaders held any animosity toward the businessman; far from it, for indeed governmental conservation had its business-related objectives. A powerful underlying motivation for saving lands was to conserve natural resources like a savings account that might be called upon for public use at some time in the future. This pragmatic reason, while never so stated as the political justification for designating public lands, was very persuasive with the Congress and the presidency then, as it has remained, and has led to the preservation of vast acreage. But the entrepreneurs did not turn away. As they advanced, the goddess of conservation sometimes met them at the gate with a sword.

The saving of the California redwoods represented conservation entirely for beauty, a god-given patrimony to keep. Sawmills had become the slaughterhouses of the redwoods. As the interest in their preservation rose to an outcry, rescue of the forests from the woodsman's axe became a very delicate California political issue, with the lumber companies standing strong on one side and conservationists protesting on the other. The GCA marched in alongside other private organizations after World War I, giving support to another private organization, the Save the Redwoods League. The ardor of the GCA climaxed in May 1934 with the dedication of the GCA's Canoe Creek Grove of redwoods, as we saw in chapter 3. Numerous members stood in often tearful attendance. The garden club's total of 2,552 acres, deeded to the park system of California, was to be increased over time. The GCA's part in preserving the redwood forests was and remains one of its proudest achievements in conservation. The location of such strong activity on the West Coast drew the GCA ever closer to being a national organization. Pacific coast clubs became outstanding members, drawing wide attention to the GCA in its early years. Notable among these were the Pasadena Garden Club. Athough support for conservation was strong among GCA clubs from the East Coast to Seattle, it was the Pasadena club that was the seed ground.

Minerva Hoyt was a member of the Pasadena Garden Club. She had a deep affection for a part of the landscape few cared about, the "useless barrens" of the desert. Suffering from the deaths of her husband and son, she sought peace and distraction. On camping trips into the harsh land, she grew to love the tough vegetation that overcame natural adversity. Already by the time of World War I, desert campers and plant collectors were damaging the natural scene; cacti were burned to create night light; camp fires left untended burned off hundreds of acres. Invited in 1927 to serve on a commission for new state parks, she began to interact with Frederick Law Olmsted Jr.

"Rick" Olmsted—as he was nicknamed—was contracted by the state as consultant for the California parks system. Minerva Hoyt, inviting him to camp with her in the desert, opened his eyes to its unique beauty. As a result of her tutelage, he included in his master plan for California parks Death Valley, the Anza Borrego Desert, and the Joshua Tree forest, located in an obscure area in the San Bernardino Mountains, near the Sonora and Mojave deserts. Mrs. Hoyt ghostwrote Olmsted's justification to the state for each of the desert parks.[11]

Probably influenced by Olmsted, Mrs. Hoyt came to believe that the deserts would be best protected as national instead of state parks. She was successful with Sonora and Mojave, which culminated in a million-acre preserve, but the Joshua Tree groves, splendid in spring with their creamy white flowers, proved daunting. When President Franklin D. Roosevelt came west on a tour, she pressed him to preserve the spiky Joshua trees in their mountain setting. Dangerously by-passing state officials when necessary, she summoned all the influence the national GCA could muster, inspiring the formation of the Committee for the Preservation of Desert Flora in December 1931. Not until she was able to show Interior Secretary Harold Ickes the Joshua trees in bloom did she succeed, in the summer of 1936, in seeing her admired groves become the Joshua Tree National Monument.

Relations with the National Park Service were usually warm—but not always. Logging in the Ouachita National Forest of Arkansas, an old national forest established in 1907 by Theodore Roosevelt, greatly alarmed conservationists, who lobbied Congress to make the 1.8 million acres in Arkansas and southeastern Oklahoma into a national park. The park service hesitated. Such an idea was politically shaky because of big private contracts for zone cuttings the service regularly made with lumber companies. The park service staff also stated frankly that the land was unworthy of national park status. The GCA entered the fray. Officials were contacted in person and showered with letters. The park service stood pat. Ouachita remained with the U.S. Forest Service.[12]

This encounter turned some GCA conservationists' attention from parks to the national forests. They studied forest fire protection and silviculture. Among the foresters they made good friends. Even though they conflicted over tree cutting, the conservationists understood that an aspect of the role of public lands was as suppliers of raw materials. On March 20, 1935, the Conservation Committee gathered GCA members and foresters at the Waldorf for an all-day seminar. If ever a learning event took place, it was that. Sixty-seven clubs participated from twenty-one states. Nine members-at-large were present, and the principal speaker was Henry Solon Graves, founder of the Yale School of Forestry and former chief, under Taft and Wilson, of the U.S. Forest Service. Like all to follow in his position, he was honored with the lifetime title of "chief." At his meeting, Eloise Luquer, also a well-known lecturer and botanical artist of leaves and wildflowers, spoke personally about her love of American trees and wildflowers. The remaining speakers spoke in a more scientific way about the most modern methods in silviculture.[13]

Through their experience with the California redwoods, GCA conservationists had developed an interest in trees and forestry. Soon they joined with the Arnold Arboretum in raising money to fight forest diseases. Teamed up with William P. Wharton, leader in the rescue campaign, they pressed Congress to fund the Dutch Elm Disease Education Project, which was started in 1936, thanks in part to the GCA.[14]

Even as this was taking place, GCA conservationists elsewhere joined popular writer Sherwood Anderson in an effort to prohibit rock quarrying in the Hudson Highlands, upriver from New York City. A threat to an idyllic scene, the proposed quarries would doom forests of ancient hardwoods. From their battles, which made some of the gentle

GCA gardeners cringe, the conservationists learned that their troops must be well organized and well informed nationwide. To promote organization they financed a speaking tour by the Reverend E. Russell Bourne, of the Lenox Garden Club—one of the few males in the GCA roster—on how to form a conservation campaign. He was vice-chair of the then-named Conservation and Roadside Committee. Twenty clubs signed up immediately, and many others followed.[15]

What was happening through the late 1930s was the identification of conservation as a major part of the GCA mission. The impulse that had begun with billboards and wildflowers in 1913 germinated with the redwoods, then spread to the trash dumping on highways and in cities. The redwoods campaign had led to a splinter group, the National Parks Committee. From midwestern and especially western beginnings, the conservation passion spread to every club in the GCA. The journey was accelerated by Mrs. Crosby's organization plan between 1924 and 1928. By 1940 the Conservation Committee was the most conspicuous national committee of any in the GCA. It fully realized the fears of those who predicted that it would overshadow horticulture and flower arranging. But that sort of monumentality was imagined only from the outside. Within the GCA, conservation was simply one of the three branches of the organization, if sometimes, in contrast to the others, a bit unruly.

As World War II neared, conservationists were fighting harder than ever to protect Christmas greens. In 1941 florists advertised fresh laurel and holly. The Conservation Committee hoped in vain that the GCA would issue a national protest, but as GCA tradition dictated, the board would urge that the clubs alone be heard publicly, not the national organization. Where the Friends of Land was concerned, the Conservation Committee seems to have acted entirely on its own, seeking another venue for a national voice. The short-lived agriculture-based organization Friends of Land set out to protect America's fast-disappearing farms. One of the issues was to urge the government to omit farmworkers from the military draft. Yet the Friends of Land had broader objectives that anticipated the ecology movement to come, which still espouses the organization's principles today. In 1940 GCA conservationists flocked to the founding meeting in Memphis. Jane Bush Francke, Conservation Committee chair, reported fervently to the GCA board that the Memphis meeting was the first national conservation assembly the GCA had.[16]

When the war was over, conservationists resumed their efforts energetically. The board meeting in April 1945 was followed the next day by a Conservation Committee seminar at the Metropolitan Museum of Art. Speakers included Paul Manship, the sculptor and old friend of the GCA. The Philadelphia landscape architect Markley Stevenson was also there, a very visible and active proponent of state and national parks in the United States and Canada and soon to be renowned worldwide for the landscape that surrounded the Omaha Beach Memorial in France. The architect Francis Keally, whose moderne-style Oregon Capitol had recently been opened to wide acclaim for its originality—and a few quips that it looked like a coil-top refrigerator. And last of the special guests was Gilmore Clarke, chair of the Fine Arts Commission in Washington.

Serving as moderator was Jay Norwood Darling; the famous syndicated political cartoonist "Ding" Darling, one of the country's most influential proselytizers of conservation and founder of the National Wildlife Federation, was, not least, a member of the Des Moines Founders Garden Club. It was an impressive program, and the attendance was very large, with the general public admitted in greater numbers than GCA members. The crowd extended throughout the lecture hall and out into the hallway, where loudspeakers conveyed the proceedings.

One year later, to the board's discomfort, the previously soft-spoken National Parks Committee joined with the Seattle Garden Club in initiating legislation to protect threatened evergreen huckleberry and salal (*Gaultheria shallon*), a low evergreen shrub. While in Seattle, representatives of the Conservation Committee learned that the National Park Service intended to permit logging in the Olympic National Park. Sallie Wright, chair of the National Parks Committee, pled with the

Executive Committee to oppose the park service decision. As might be predicted, the Executive Committee hesitated. While its members supported the cause, some of them feared that the political tone of a protest might endanger the GCA's nonprofit status. Nonetheless, Mrs. Wright was given permission to issue "strong protest" in the name of the GCA at her "discretion."[17]

At the same time, Congressman Frank A. Barrett, of Wyoming, introduced a bill to abolish the Jackson Hole National Monument. He was supported by local ranchers whose operations were negatively influenced by the government designation of so large an area. The landowners protesting the loss of grazing rights were assisted by a sympathetic neighbor, the movie star Wallace Beery, who took the ranchers' cause to the front pages. The controversy was pitched as both trespass and light comedy. Opposition became almost overwhelming. The bill passed with only a few of the conservation amendments the National Parks Committee had hoped to attach.

The postwar building boom soon found its way into the redwood forests in a major invasion by loggers. Save the Redwoods League called on its longtime colleague the GCA to raise money to expand the protected zones. Every member club on the West Coast participated. The return from the rest of the country was less than inspiring, although there was no question that all of the GCA was proud of its redwood grove. On the heels of the redwood alarm, privatization of the Tennessee Valley Authority sent the Conservation Committee into legal discussions with fellow conservation organizations about protecting the streams of Tennessee and the flanking states of the TVA from any threatened industrial pollution. Mrs. Leroy Clark, chair of the Conservation Committee, sitting in on the deliberation at the U.S. Capitol, was "frightened by the trend" of privatizing public land.[18]

Conservation grew in the GCA through the 1950s. In the next decade the GCA conservationists began to challenge the club's long-held tradition of avoiding formal connections to other organizations and taking stands in public forums. Conservation's work called for giving opinions pro and con. Political power, the conservationists insisted, came in numbers. So by the 1960s, objections notwithstanding, conservationists began seriously considering partnerships, albeit temporary ones. An individual of note who had urged them to proceed in this for two decades was the dedicated conservationist Dr. Isaiah Bowman. Retired president of the Johns Hopkins University, he liked to say, "In the Bible the land is mentioned more often than love."

Cooperation among diverse conservation groups, which Bowman long promoted, was in fact really nothing new to the GCA. The redwoods had been saved in conjunction with the Save the Redwoods League and the state of California. The tireless efforts for the National Arboretum, in Washington, were helped by association with groups with similar objectives. Formal association, however, was another matter, and the GCA at the national level continued to hesitate and still does. Yet the conservationists pressed on, pursuing what they believed was a necessary course.

The Conservation Committee's work took its members more and more to Washington in the late 1940s and early 1950s. Washington efforts by the GCA had been greatly hampered by the passing of Janet Noyes in 1942. She, who had single-handedly blazed a GCA trail to the Capitol, had set a pace that took a very hardy woman to follow. The GCA did not soon recover the Washington strength it had enjoyed previously, for the organization faced a very new postwar environment in which many demands were made of Congress. Domestic costs and national debt alone made the politicians less welcoming of proposed changes that did not seem to them essential. It was the conservationists' job to change this point of view in their labor to see laws passed that were sympathetic to conserving the natural heritage.

The most notable of Mrs. Noyes's achievements was in 1927, with the creation of the National Arboretum. She did not live to see it develop. It was barely funded, and each year a doubtful Department of

Agriculture was likely to shift elsewhere the funding it did receive. GCA proponents of the arboretum were promised a beginning annual budget of two hundred thousand dollars. The arboretum board was able to rescue enough of this in the late 1930s to start planning and constructing an administrative building. Illness forced Mrs. Noyes to the sidelines, although she continued to have her say. She is remembered at this time as frail and elegant, propped up on cushions among the flowers in her conservatory, greeting the great and powerful who still came to pay court. After her death, her GCA protégés cherished "unforgettable memories of her patrician grace, of her hospitality . . . of her unfailing warmth and gaiety."[19]

Angela Place, a colleague of Janet Noyes on Washington projects, was a National Arboretum board member and stepped forward as the main GCA worker for the fledgling institution. The new administrative building was not the traditional Japanese architecture anticipated, but it was nobly simple and functional. Inside the building and in the sheds outside, plants were accessioned in large number. The Dutch sent hundreds of azaleas, and seedlings of trees came from all over the world. GCA clubs across the country liked to woo newspaper space with news of National Arboretum tree plantings accompanied by ceremonies in honor of someone who might merit being honored. The first such ceremony recorded by the GCA took place in 1949, under sponsorship of the Founders Garden Club of Dallas. Mrs. Place urged conservation committees in all the clubs to get all the news coverage they could get and to pressure their senators and representatives to proceed with the arboretum. From contacts in the U.S. Congress she learned that a dedication of the arboretum might be hoped for in the fall of 1950. She presented President Truman in person with large GCA contributions to the project.

The National Arboretum, authorized in 1927 and begun in 1934, was dedicated at last in 1950. Chartered busses from New York and back cost a special rate of twelve dollars a ticket. The event was a success, the realization of a GCA dream, as well as the dream of other organizations interested in horticulture. But Mrs. Place, reporting to the board, "asked to speak frankly." She called the arboretum "the only project for which the Garden Club of America has given its blessings that has not prospered." In 1951 the arboretum consisted of 415 acres tended by 115 men. In contrast, Kew Gardens employed one man for every two acres.

Ethel Garrett, from Baltimore, applied heavy pressure for additional congressional funding. Assistance from the well-known Everglades author and conservationist Marjory Stoneman Douglas took the form of many telephone calls to senators and congressmen. In 1955 Mrs. Garrett appeared before the congressional advisory council and managed to get the next fiscal year's appropriation of $161,000 raised by $50,000. She pressed for road repair, receiving $300,000 at the same time, half to be funded through the Department of Agriculture and half paid directly by the government to the arboretum.[20]

In the course of her involvement with the National Arboretum through the 1950s, Mrs. Garrett found that the architect of the U.S. Capitol planned to remove the old east front of the Capitol in an expansion, replacing the historical sandstone. She went to the Congress and asked that the Corinthian columns be carried to the arboretum for some use there. But when the columns were taken down, with the rest of the sandstone, they were laid out in a field in Maryland, abandoned, awaiting disposal in the Potomac River. Mrs. Place laid claim to the columns and envisioned them set up at the arboretum, an event that was not actually to take place for another forty years.[21]

The National Arboretum remained the stepchild of the Department of Agriculture. Mrs. Place and Mrs. Garrett politicked for funds from Congress almost as a vocation. They learned to make sure their requests were cleared by the Department of Agriculture, to assure that the funds, when appropriated, would actually go to the arboretum and not to some other project. In 1952 they enlisted the support of Mildred Bliss, whose residence, Dumbarton Oaks, was one of Washington's most famous, set in gardens designed by Beatrix Farrand. Hetty Harrison joined them, with Edith Savin, who was more interested in reviving the early twentieth-century city plan of the capital than building the arboretum. They composed a GCA Washington committee, with a strong ally in Mrs. Bliss, one of the capital's prominent women.

At that time, however, Angela Place was still the best friend the National Arboretum had. By car and train she went back and forth from New York to Washington. One snowy March she headed to Washington to work in Congress for restoration of the $185,000 promised for the arboretum and then cut from the budget. The snow increased until the train stopped, and she was stranded. When she arrived at last at Union Station, she was informed that the funds for her project had again been reappropriated.[22]

In the spring of 1958, wearied by the slow progress of the arboretum, Mrs. Place began promoting the idea of having the arboretum transferred to the province of the Smithsonian Institution. She called on officials in Washington and explained that the arboretum was poorly cared for by the Department of Agriculture and that the department was obviously not interested in it. The landscape architect Perry Wheeler confirmed what she said, calling the arboretum "shabby." Agriculture quickly responded by pledging to apply to Congress for a 1.9-million-dollar appropriation to turn the arboretum into an institution worthy of the nation—and worthy of the Committee for the National Capital of the GCA.

The promise was fulfilled in part. Development of the National Arboretum got underway in earnest. Dr. Henry T. Skinner, its director, suggested that a first-rate "Oriental" garden be planted as well. In 1959 the Fine Arts Commission approved construction of an administrative building, which was to be designed as faithful to traditional Japanese architecture.[23] Construction started in the spring of 1960 was stopped at the foundation stage when funds were suddenly cut off; in the urgency to complete a building the Japanese theme was sacrificed in favor of a plain, utilitarian design, but even it proved too big for the remaining budget.

Mrs. Place and Mrs. Garrett pressured Congress for a million dollars to start up the administrative building and build some greenhouses. While they did not receive the full request, they got basic funding.

The first greenhouse was built before winter, just in time to receive the collection of fine bonsai trees assembled by the late ambassador to Japan, Larz Anderson, in his greenhouses in Brookline, Massachusetts. These were rescued by Boston area GCA clubs, when Anderson's residence and garden houses were demolished by the city of Brookline, to which the estate and its hundred acres of gardens had been bequeathed a decade before for the benefit of the public.

A construction hitch in some of the arboretum's greenhouse designs required that they be rebuilt even before they were completed. Finished at last, they were dedicated in 1962. So that the GCA might leave a visible trace of its long years of work for the arboretum and to celebrate the GCA's fiftieth anniversary, Perry Wheeler designed a gazebo, which he placed high on a bank overlooking a grove of trees. Anglo-Japanese in design, open sided, and painted a Japanese red, the delicate wooden shelter was a vignette borrowed from the orderly residential gardens of Japan, set on a knoll in the developing wilds of the arboretum, which at last had at least a touch of the Japanese garden tradition that the founders had wanted.

Problems continued for the arboretum. It was a big undertaking, for which the big problems were under control; little problems, however, popped up constantly. Congress provided funding for eighteen workers. In 1967 only three suitable men could be found. A new highway system promised very desirable highway access after a long period of messy construction. The light could be seen at the end of the tunnel, in spite of all the problems. The recording secretary at the GCA could write on October 11, 1967, paraphrasing a conservation report, "Arboretum flourishing; at long last there is enough money."

All that remained was the fate of the sandstone columns from the Capitol. Thirty-three were piled up on their sides, catching rain, their

Corinthian capitals half hidden in weeds and vines. Ethel Garrett called forth champions to carry her project forward, enlisting Vice President Hubert Humphrey, who presented a funding bill to Congress. Landscape architect Edward Durell Stone Jr. made a plan that the lawmakers admired. Richard H. Howland of the Smithsonian assisted Mrs. Garrett with design details, as did Perry Wheeler. Yet no provision was made for the columns, and the project dragged on year after year. It would be 1990 before the Capitol columns would be dedicated, embodying Washington's most unusual monument and surveying a sprawl of green turf, the final positioning of the marble shafts determined by Stone's successor, the landscape architect Russell Page.

The founding and realization of the National Arboretum belong to capital beautification enthusiasts for their legislative campaigns and arduous journeys through federal red tape, while the idea of the arboretum itself really belongs to the realm of horticulture. The subject is given to the conservationists here because the conservationists learned from it about Washington. Over thirty years their effort involved joining hands with many different organizations. No permanent connections were made. Nonetheless, the National Arboretum was a training ground, a laboratory for many conservation quests to come for the GCA.

The GCA has always returned to its core objective, education. By midcentury the conservationists found that popular education in conservation was essential to building political support for their projects. While there was no conservation scholarship before the Clara Carter Higgins Award was established in 1964, education for both adults and young people had become an interest of the Conservation Committee even before the 1950s. One of the best ways the committee found to inform the general public was through carefully managed public relations, making use of the press and radio. The "public" part was where the work of the conservationists necessarily departed from the other branches of

the GCA. Both horticulture and flower arranging were deep into education within the clubs of the GCA. The most public contact they made
was through the flower shows and the campaigns against plant diseases
and poison sprays conducted by the Horticulture Committee. Otherwise
they had little need for going public, and it was clear that they did not
think it appropriate for the GCA.

With mild, "soft" publicity the GCA was experienced. Although
comfortable appearing in the society pages of newspapers, the organization had no use for being the focus of hard news, and indeed its members seem rather to have feared becoming involved with it. The formal
coordination of public relations was not to be official in the GCA until
the 1980s, although the organization had endeavored to engage in public projects now and then, as when it exhibited at the world's fairs and
planted magnolia trees on the mall at Independence Hall, in Philadelphia. One of the most public programs was the 1937 campaign against
throwing trash along highways. Mrs. Daniel M. McKeon designed the
program and created its signature, the "litterbug," a play on the name of a
new dance craze, the jitterbug.[24] The goodwill generated by that program
and its general popularity were very beneficial to the GCA. While the
name of the GCA was not up front in the program's ensuing and ongoing
promotion, the GCA's role was as important as anyone else's. Likewise,
during World War II the GCA had assumed a very public profile, but the
organization did not enter into controversies.

Conservation's later interaction with controversy invited coverage in the press. In January 1951 the Conservation Committee member
Caroline Few asked the board to entertain the concept of having a public
relations committee. The proposal was quickly tabled. Newspaper articles mentioning the GCA continued to appear. None has been found
that could be considered derogatory, but it seems that even those members who agreed that public relations needed some accommodation in
the GCA hesitated taking seriously the management of the news. Mass
communication as we know it was dawning. Television was present, if

still young and not as pervasive as today; newspapers were at their high noon. Garden clubs were often in the press locally, but the national organization remained quite a different matter. More than once or twice members of the Conservation Committee stood before the board of directors in defense of or in apology for being mentioned in the press.

Also in 1951 the Conservation Committee launched a committee newsletter, *Conservation Watch,* which appeared quarterly. The publication, both an educational and a public relations document, was nominally for GCA members, but its uses were far more widespread as an informative notice of GCA conservation issues and what the GCA was doing in that field through its local clubs. This approach was radical in the context of GCA tradition. Within the first year demand for the newsletter rose so rapidly that by December the committee was printing twelve hundred copies per quarterly issue and overruns. No question that the news reporters found useful information in this publication and trusted its facts.[25]

The Conservation Committee followed the new newsletter with other publications that knew widespread circulation. Henrietta Crosby's leaflet "Helpful Hints in Conserving Wild Flowers" was reprinted. In 1953 Mrs. Avery Rockefeller designed a chart, "How to Attract Birds to the Garden," which was printed in many editions. Local clubs increased the support for conservation. The Portland Garden Club published a journal, the *Gardeners.* Local activities were numerous, ranging from conservation meetings to rescuing or preserving natural areas as conservation parks for the public benefit.

In response to conservation curricula at both public and private universities, Edna Fisher Edgerton and Anna Rockefeller compiled a study guide packet, "The World around Us," with course outlines, leaflets, and brochures, clearly written and handsomely designed. Published subsequently in many editions over a span of forty years, the packet's distribution numbered in the tens of thousands. Conservation education was ongoing, and the most important continuing constituency was young people. With this in mind and wishing always to participate with the National Park Service, Edna Clark, former chair of the Conservation Committee, visited nearly all of the 160 member clubs in 1957 and 1958, raising money for a project her committee called the Student Conservation Association. The idea for this summer program with student volunteers was conceived by Elizabeth Titus in her Vassar honors thesis in 1955, and Mrs. Titus, a member of the Bennington Garden Club in Vermont, went on to found the program itself two years later.[26]

The generosity of the clubs attracted other donors. Edna Clark's $3,325 nest egg of 1958 grew to substantial annual amounts, and the successive directors of the National Park Service, first Conrad Wirth and later, beginning in 1965, George Hartzog, made every resource of the service available for this highly successful program. Its headquarters was established at Theodore Roosevelt's Sagamore Hill, on Long Island. Eventually the Student Conservation Association was incorporated with a membership program, and the management moved entirely to the National Park Service. Few programs in GCA history can claim greater success than this one.

Conservation's ever more visible public presence slowly changed the Garden Club of America, stepping outside the educational and self-improvement pattern into the more modern realm of public ideals. In a sense, however, the new was not exactly new. On a national scale, the GCA itself had long fought the Army Corps of Engineers in its efforts to block rivers and streams with dams that supposedly served the altruistic purposes of public recreation when the impetus was in fact usually the electrical power business. President Truman's seminal executive order of 1950, reserving air space over wilderness parts of the Superior National Forest, in Minnesota, was celebrated with high praise by the GCA's conservation activists as a beginning of an important trend to protect wild territories more fully in the United States.

Civic idealism had been a GCA interest all along in the clubs' endorsement of countless local parks. The national organization had shown strong support for the city beautiful plan of Washington, D.C., and it stood by the concept in the plan's darkest hours after World War I. Indeed GCA clubs had also supported the city beautiful plan for Chicago. In 1929 the Garden Club of Palm Beach commissioned and paid for a city beautiful plan for Palm Beach. It was approved and accepted by the town fathers in the same year.[27]

But in 1953 when the GCA raised money for flood relief in the Netherlands, its old and close friend, that venture into charity did drift beyond the historical boundaries of the GCA. The conservationists encouraged and designed the program and set aside July 1 as the official GCA day for Netherlands relief fund-raising. Already GCA clubs were extending conservation's scope further, beyond the land and its plants, to include study and political activism in the areas of air and water pollution.

In 1954 Helen Throop Bergh, chair of the Conservation Committee, produced the following mission statement for her committee: "The purpose of the Conservation Committee is to translate the principles of conservation into personal action, and thus encourage others to recognize our responsibility for our National Resources." The brief statement was loaded with implication. It called for communication, but it also called for activism and recognition that authority lay in the committee, which had responsibility for our natural resources. Just what the "our" was supposed to mean was not clear.[28]

The mission statement did not come from the Conservation Committee itself but was produced by a subcommittee appointed by the Executive Committee to study the Conservation Committee's role in the GCA. Conservation's assumption of independence on public issues had been controversial for years and was more frequently questioned in the early 1950s, when other aspects of the GCA were being reconsidered. That the discussions were organized around a subcommittee and apparently supervised by the Executive Committee was a departure. Nothing remotely similar had been imposed upon horticulture and flower arranging. It was conservation, however, that seemed to have a life beyond the GCA. The issue, not really very clear at the time, was of long standing: how necessary was this independence, and how could it be a working part of the GCA mechanism?

As it had developed, the organizational structure of the GCA's conservation activities centered on having a representative for each club responsible to the national committee. Given the volume of work since World War II, this was cumbersome, so the Conservation Committee reduced its advisory membership to include one representative from each zone. Individual clubs were to channel their business through this representative to the national committee. Curiously enough, the subcommittee found no fault with this organizational arrangement. Its deliberations, records of which are lost, seem to have boiled its work down to the mission statement, which apparently clarified any confusion that had existed before, if it did not entirely solve the institutional aspect of the problem. In a sense the mission statement formalized the approach the Conservation Committee had developed over the years since its establishment.

Meanwhile, conservation was becoming more a national subject than it had ever been before. In November 1953, President Eisenhower spoke to a large Washington convocation, Resources for the Future, which had been called by the Department of the Interior. His address served as the introduction to the eight working sessions that followed. Representatives of the GCA were among the twenty women in attendance; the roster listed sixteen thousand men. Discussion continually gravitated to the subject of water. Lewis Mumford had stated again and again his opinion that water would be the great need and issue in the second half of the twentieth century and beyond, as cities swelled in population and rambled ever greater distances from their centers, into suburbs and ancillary towns.

Communication at the working or discussion sessions was difficult because of the contrasting interests among those attending. For example, exchanges between representatives of industry and those of nonprofit organizations sometimes bordered on hostility, the businessmen mocking the ideas of the conservationists as "esoteric," and the conservationists, claiming higher purpose, denouncing the businessmen as callous to mankind's best interests. Very much present and saying little was "the ogre of the Army Engineers with financial resources," wrote a GCA representative, making a "shadowy fugleman in the background of discussion." As lake builders and raisers of dams, they were tarred by the conservationists as enemies.[29]

Impassioned causes can create strange alliances, not least the GCA's warm friendship with Robert Moses, which will be remembered here from the 1939 World's Fair. Moses, the coordinator of construction for the city of New York, was brilliant and ruthless in his use of almost unbelievable political power in his transformation—his supporters called it the salvation—of New York through demolition and construction, and he was one of the most conspicuous public figures in pre- and postwar America.

The billboard restriction bill he wrote in 1950 and promoted through New York congressmen and senators touched the hearts of GCA conservationists, who went to him and promised a deluge of support through letters. How much GCA conservation adherents influenced the idea of the bill in New York State is not clear, but they did draw attention to the bill when it came before Congress. The bill revived the objections to billboards that had simmered for many years. The resulting 1960 congressional amendment to the Highway Act of 1956 restricted billboards on parkways and federal highways. While the law would be broken and its spirit often violated, it was a beginning, a victory long awaited. The GCA took little credit for itself and praised Robert Moses to the sky.

The continued loss of America's wildflowers was an issue as old as that of the billboard. Mrs. Lucien B. Taylor, chair of the Wild Flower Subcommittee of the Conservation Committee, turned the situation entirely around in the 1950s by suggesting that Americans garden with wildflowers. Her efforts, rather than signifying a disinterest in rescuing flowers in the wild, indicated a wish to extend natural beauty. She and her committee endorsed the planting of wildflowers everywhere they might be grown, but in particular along highways. A new and extensive system of highways was being built across the country. The idea of making these beautiful, covering the roadsides and hills with wildflowers, immediately appealed to the press and to the public and proved that the subcommittee had struck a popular chord.

"The cultivation of wild flowers," Mrs. Taylor wrote, has led to new "horticultural activity"; thus horticulture, not conservation, became the category for wildflowers. Mrs. Taylor never said so, but reading between the lines of what she did say, one suspects she thought beautifying the highways would generate definitive public disapproval of billboards. Whatever the case, the subcommittee's idea did succeed brilliantly at increasing the cultivation of wildflowers. Within the GCA, seeds and cuttings were solicited for propagation by zone. Wildflower plant exchanges were sometimes part of the zone and annual meetings.[30]

The records reveal a great variety of conservation projects and interests in the GCA through the 1950s and into the 1960s. In addition to extensive ongoing educational programs, conservation efforts now constantly involved campaigns of opposition. The Conservation Committee, mainly in the zones, fought the building of artificial lakes and accompanying dams ordered up by politicians and developers from the Army Corps of Engineers; the cutting of old forests by timber companies; billboards by every sort of advertiser; and the power companies that made trees along their power lines unsightly or unhealthy by lazy pruning with chain saws. GCA conservationists fought the seemingly careless plotting of pipelines and electric utility lines; they fought outdoorsmen across the nation who hunted from dune buggies, four-wheelers, snowmobiles, or airplanes. Along with animal rights enthusiasts nationwide, they rose to the aid of wild horses in the national domains, protesting that in Nevada alone, by estimate, a hundred thousand had been slaughtered for their meat between the end of World War II and 1960. The accumulation of conservation campaigns waged by GCA clubs, in addition to those endorsed by the Conservation Committee, has an Old Testament monumentality.

For the conservationists the greatest congressional challenge came in 1960 with the Wilderness Bill. This bill, if it passed, was to prohibit grazing or logging in the national parks and permit very limited hunting, under the supervision of game wardens. It was also to limit recreational use of the lands, which proved to be a mistake, for it weakened the bill in the public eye as being too exclusive. As the bill lingered, it encountered dangers. Political motivation picked at it. An unwelcomed modification gave Congress the right, essentially, to issue permits to graze, hunt, or commit any of what conservationists considered severe infringements. Support of the bill heated up as hopes for it shrank. The GCA rose in alarm in 1961 on hearing that Congress was about to allow a six-hundred-room hotel to be built "hanging" on the rim of the Grand Canyon. Always the march of commerce seemed to threaten the wilderness; usually the conservationists were scorned as reactionaries by the opposition.[31]

In the winter of 1963, for the first time, the Conservation Committee gained GCA support for an agreement with the Sierra Club. This agreement was to join their forces in a letter campaign fighting a determined California utility commission's issuance of a permit to build an atomic energy plant on Bodega Bay, on the Pacific coast sixty-four miles north of San Francisco. The battle got big press, Sierra Club style, and while some GCA members may have blushed, the conservationists among them ultimately celebrated a win. It was a victory for the Sierra Club and also a great victory for the GCA.[32] While that particular war did not end in 1963, the terrible Anchorage, Alaska, earthquake of the next year precluded efforts to revive the project for reasons of safety at the proposed site. It was ironic that the GCA, representing in large measure a cross section of upper-class American women, should lobby so furiously against the interests of big business. Yet they did then and were to continue to do so.

The Pacific Gas & Electric Company's wishes for an atomic plant in California had hardly been dashed when the Conservation Committee next recoiled at U.S. Steel's announced intention to support a new major shipping port to link the Great Lakes to the Atlantic for ocean shipping. In the path lay many potential tragedies and none more acute than the Indiana Dunes, a small state park that, since its establishment in 1926, has been part of a magnificent setting of great ecological interest. President Kennedy had approved the port in exchange for creating a national park on Cape Cod. What seemed impossible to prevent was stopped by Indiana state senator Paul A. Douglas (nicknamed "Washington's third senator from Indiana"), who went full force against it with the support of many conservation groups, including a major effort on the scene in Washington and through letters from the GCA.

Officials in government agencies in the 1960s sometimes were openly hostile toward the conservationists. Many conservationists thought that nature's preservation was best served in the private sector, with legal easements and covenants given to nonprofit groups. Dr. George S. Avery, of the Brooklyn Botanic Garden, in speaking at a GCA meeting in New York in 1963 said, "Our great contribution of the mid-twentieth century may be the preservation of small, private holdings by individual gift deeds in perpetuity."[33]

The GCA was party to some of these easements, as when Mrs. Richard Pugh, a GCA member from Houston, along with others, sponsored the preservation of thirty-four hundred acres of Gulf coastal prairies for the Save the Prairie Chicken movement, favoring notably the large, zebra-feathered Attwater species. The GCA had never wanted to be burdened with the ownership of real estate, so the Conservation Committee's interest continued to favor public lands under federal protection, as was the case with what became of the Attwater Prairie Chicken National Wildlife Refuge. Conservation Committee members also labored hard for the Wilderness Bill. At the end of 1963 it was "bottled up" in the House Committee on Internal and Insular Affairs. Amendments that would weaken it were promoted in various quarters, urged on by important business interests. The GCA was publicly accused of "threatening development" and thus America's economic well-being.[34]

The board of directors, although cyclically replenished with new members, was consistently adamant for years in refusing to issue general statements from the GCA. For example, letter-writing campaigns, which were inevitably political, were very rarely authorized by the board of directors itself, although committees, zones, and clubs sponsored them freely. The board set aside its usual hesitation on November 19, 1964, when, after a familial discussion centered in appropriations and implication, the members voted to release a strong statement opposing a hydro-electric plant proposed for the banks of the Hudson River. This was in the Storm King Mountain locale of the Hudson River Highlands, an area long admired by the GCA as a beautiful site for public recreation. Victory came in a court of appeals decision in January 1966. The voice of the national organization had played a powerful role, but that voice was not to be any more easily raised in the future than before. Its significance, however, had been noted within the Conservation Committee and to the conservationist world looking on.

Protest was allowed a wide arena. Mrs. Daniel McKeon, former chair of the Conservation Committee, took up the welfare of wild animals, even as the legions were battling for Stone King Mountain. Animal life was an issue relatively new in the 1960s and as much rooted in what would be called animal rights as in conservation, but the matter was brought to Louise McKeon's familiar turf, the Conservation Committee. It was received by some as being outside the perimeters of the GCA; still there was a push to become involved. Polar bears, seals, tigers, and leopards especially, but other beasts as well, were being killed for their fur pelts, to be made into rugs and coats. Mrs. McKeon hoped that patrons of fashionable furriers would write notes, then threaten cancellation of charge accounts, notably at B. Altman, Bonwit Teller, and Lord & Taylor. The subject of such requests never came up again, but the issue was to resurface.

Mary Louise Saunders represented the Conservation Committee at the White House Conference on Natural Beauty, held May 24–25, 1965. The GCA was not especially enthusiastic about the Johnson administration's beautification program, believing it mostly political show.[35] The Highway Beautification Act of 1965, for example, was part of the overall program, and on that subject Willie Waller testified at the Capitol in 1967 before the House Subcommittee on Roads, of the Committee on Public Works: "The Garden Club of America has never been particularly enthusiastic about the Highway Beautification Act of 1965, as we feel it is an exceedingly difficult piece of legislation to administer and deplore the mandatory compensation" that was proposed as payment to outdoor advertising companies when law forbade their building billboards in certain places. She did not support a repeal of the act, only the removal of some of the amendments.[36]

The GCA remained suspicious of the motives behind some of the Johnson administration's many programs, but its members were admirers of his interior secretary, Stewart L. Udall. A holdover from the same cabinet position in the Kennedy administration, Udall was a handsome and athletic man, vigorous in his forties; he had a poetic sensitivity toward the natural world. With him, GCA conservationists felt at home. They delighted in his stands against developers whose plans for commercial tourism at the Grand Canyon and on other public lands threatened all that had made those places lovely. He stayed in touch with GCA officials, welcoming them cordially to his office in Washington, forwarding letters and materials to them for comment.

The National Trails System, which Udall established in 1968, received unanimous approval from conservationists and addressed America's increasing love of the out-of-doors and public parks. Federal mandates were watched closely by the GCA. For many GCA clubs, the Water

Quality Act of 1965 had motivated a desire to evaluate the standards required by the act in justifying water-related projects. For example, Connecticut GCA conservationists reported to the Conservation Committee that 582 of the state's 8,400 miles of river were too polluted to be designated as wilderness areas. President Johnson's Clean Water Restoration Act of 1966 and the Air Quality Act in the following year addressed such issues and were hailed by GCA conservationists as major steps forward.

Just as the horticulturists and flower arrangers often worked together through flower shows, the Conservation Committee found like purpose at times with the Legislative Affairs Committee. Established in 1968, the Legislative Affairs Committee was to monitor the Congress on matters of interest to the GCA, meaning of course the conservationists in the GCA. This committee became the right arm of the Conservation Committee. Soon the two committees were meeting together in Washington each year.

First called the Washington Committee in 1922, what was to become the National Affairs and Legislation Committee in 1965 was originally established for the express purpose of supporting an effort to revive the city beautiful movement in the national capital. The McMillan Plan had been shelved as a Republican program by the victorious Democrats in 1913, and of course it was further obscured by the more immediate necessities that came with World War I. The city was bedraggled: a shaggy Mall, still blocked by trees, marred by temporary wooden office buildings; the Lincoln Memorial under construction and about the only activity left from the city beautiful days. In 1925 the name of the Washington Committee was changed to the Committee for the National Capital, to suit the new role of that year as adviser to the new National Capital Park Commission. Still called the Washington Committee within the GCA, this gentle group was given an electricity of its own by Janet Noyes, as we have seen, and aggressiveness was her bequest to it when ill health forced her to step down.[37]

Not much was heard from the Conservation Committee through the postwar 1940s, but in the 1950s it began to work frequently with its own legislative subcommittee, which had its roots in the very effective Committee for the National Capital. The subcommittee helped plan legislative conservation strategy and took on issues for which the committee itself lacked national political experience. In the mid-1960s the Conservation Committee was formally entrusted with supervision of all legislative activities in Washington. In 1969 the legislative subcommittee was reorganized into a full committee on its own, eventually to be called the National Affairs and Legislation Committee of the GCA, and Willie Waller, long experienced in interactions with Congress, became the first chair. She had served as chair of the Conservation Committee for three years in the 1950s. The 1960s were years of expansion by the federal government, not only of public parks and lands, but of highways as well. Planned for practicality, with not much regard for scenic beauty, the extensive and elaborate highway system presented numerous challenges to conservationists. Not least was the threat the highways made to private and public open lands.

Issues before Congress were centered not only in roads. An interest in the environment, including water and clean air, which had gained force since the war, inspired President Nixon to create the Environmental Protection Agency in 1970. The EPA, formally launched on December 2, 1970, was assembled from many existing programs in many agencies, but particularly from the National Air Pollution Control Administration, of the Department of Health, Education and Welfare, and the Federal Water Quality Administration, of the Department of the Interior.

Having been heartily endorsed by the Conservation and National Affairs and Legislation Committees, the EPA brought to the GCA an era of notable influence in Washington. Under Willie Waller's chairmanship, the National Affairs and Legislation Committee became bold again in the way it had been in Mrs. Noyes's time. If Mrs. Waller, unlike Mrs. Noyes, had little "insider" status in Washington's political scene, the formidable lady made it quite impossible for a congressman or senator to overlook or bypass either her, as chair, or her committee members. These women were resourceful and tended to be better informed on the issues than either the congressional members or their staffs.

Obtaining restrictions on pesticides was a major objective, which brought a rain of opposition from nurserymen and chemical manufacturers. Notable was the GCA's opposition to DDT (dichlorodiphenyltrichloroethane), the pesticide for which Dr. Paul Herman Muller, its inventor, had received the Nobel Prize in 1948 but which was brought to public attention in the most negative light by Rachel Carson in her 1962 book, *Silent Spring*. The GCA celebrated Rachel Carson and her work, presenting her with a special citation in 1963. Conservation and Legislation joined with other special interest groups and helped carry the opposition along until DDT was banned in the United States in 1972.[38]

During the Johnson and Nixon administrations a more political GCA came into being. Both presidents saw the government as the key to successful conservation and a clean environment. Congress lent support, and the GCA conservationists rode a wave of successes. From 1968 to 1973 the various conservation, environmental, historical, and transportation acts came on so swiftly and seemed such a tangle that the GCA's Legislative Affairs Committee had to pull them apart in setting their targets. The Endangered Species Act of 1973 brought out another group of conservationists to urge the committee toward new goals that had little to do with gardening.[39]

A main interest of the conservationists was the so-called Alaska Wilderness and its millions of unoccupied acres of land. In 1978, during the Carter administration, the Legislative Affairs and Conservation committees allied to support the secretary of the interior Cecil D. Andrus in designating as public land fifty-six million acres of unspecified Alaskan Wilderness, finding justification for this in the Antiquities Act of seventy years earlier. Additional Alaska Wilderness acres were set aside as a wildlife refuge. An impassioned effort to protect even more acreage as forest land resulted in only a ten-year period of protection. Claims were already being staked in the forest that conservationists wished to save, with red flags dropped from planes well before the end of the ten years.

Conservation and Legislative Affairs welcomed Jimmy Carter as a conservationist and reminded him of his campaign promises. Carter assured conservationists of three objectives: he would curb the power of the Army Corps of Engineers over public and private land, tighten controls and limits on timber harvests, and bring strip mining under comprehensive rules. Over the last point, strip mining, the GCA's honeymoon with Carter came to an end. In fact, the glory days of progress in conservation had already begun to wane, with a widely shared belief being that it had come on too fast. In 1980 the Alaska Wilderness legislation was modified with a large amount of the land returned to the State of Alaska. Under President Reagan the conservationists saw darker skies, hearing from the White House "outright objections" to environmental legislation.

Legislative Affairs, in its report to the board on October 14, 1981, observed "a great change in the nation . . . the greatest since the Depression in the economy, defense, social budgeting, resources and environmental politicies." The next month the committee reported that "destruction amendments" were eroding all that had been achieved. In February 1982 the National Affairs and Legislation Committee spoke more softly through Mrs. Robert H. Glore: "Reasonable people can urge modification of the environmental policies of the administration and still be good citizens." She said, "Congress is listening," but she was not happy with Reagan and felt that in fact Congress was listening more to the needs of men in industry than to the appeals of the GCA.[40]

As the weeks passed, Elizabeth Glore began to blame the White House for many ills related to conservation's losses. Some hope appeared in the spring, with the reinstatement of a few pieces of what had been lost. But she was still dismayed that the administration was "systematically destroying laws and programs which protect public health from pollution and preserve publicly-owned resources for public good." She listed over two hundred actions or policies of the Reagan administration she believed were detrimental to the public good. In May she said to the board, "Well, it's almost summer. Our gardens are beginning to bloom. Believe me I would like nothing better than to forget all about Washington for a few months."[41]

In 1983 public reaction to the fears expressed by Mrs. Glore led to a conservation uprising in Congress. The Garden Club of America played a significant, unsung role in convincing the lawmakers to reconsider and at least meet the movement halfway. From the Conservation Committee to the zone chairs and the clubs, letters were generated to all the members of Congress, pleading for an eye opening to conservation and especially attention to the environment. In the fall of that year the National Parks and Conservation Association held a seminar in Washington to prepare its colleague organizations, including the GCA, for the upcoming session of Congress in 1984. They set their goals carefully at this seminar and from that meeting set out to hack away the jungle of amendments that had all but strangled the best efforts in the conservation movement for the past thirty years.

The Conservation Committee carefully laid out its strategy. Each of the five areas of interest—clean air, clean water, toxics, national parks, and public lands—was to be assigned to an individual member of the Conservation Committee. That party was to "fully acquaint herself" with the subject, prepare all official letters regarding it, and serve as a clearinghouse for information; she was to be available to go to the zones to speak on the topic and distribute printed materials; on behalf of the Conservation Committee she was to present to the Executive Committee any issue within the area of her subject that required Executive Committee discussion or approval. By the year's end the Conservation Committee had begun to narrow its focus, abandoning toxics for the time, in favor of clean air and water, national parks, and public lands.[42]

While the Conservation Committee had by no means abandoned the horticultural directions that had given it birth, such as development of the National Arboretum and the preservation of wildflowers, its net over the preceding sixty years had been cast far more widely than what most people would expect from an organization with the word *garden* in its name. In 1987, the Conservation Committee and what had been renamed the National Affairs and Legislation Committee refashioned their annual meeting in Washington to welcome senators and congressmen as speakers and key aides as observers. Thoughtful programs featured lectures by experts in various fields of conservation and roundtable conferences. By 1990, 175 clubs were actively participating, their representatives attending the Washington conference.

So heavy did the work of the Legislative Committee become that Winsome McIntosh, who was chairman of the National Affairs and Legislation Committee, decided it was necessary to employ a consultant familiar with the customs of Congress. "The action of the last fifteen years," she said, "has shifted to the legislative arena." A consultant, however, was not what the two committees really wanted but instead a Washington office with a small staff, a place they could meet, and a clearinghouse for their legislative work. An effort to create this fell short for lack of funding.[43] Winsome McIntosh further created the GCA Conservation Hot Line, which operated for some years, receiving inquiries on legislative matters from members nationwide.

After the successful Washington "seminar"-style meeting in 1987, the two committees agreed that an experienced agent must be obtained to watch over their Washington interests. Mrs. McIntosh's successor, Mrs. Russell S. Wehrle, employed Loretta Neumann as a consultant, emphasizing she was not under any circumstances to be called a "lobbiest," which suggested a commercial instead of a nonprofit interest. "Loretta is our eye and ear in Washington, but let it be clearly understood that she is in no way taking the place of our active and dedicated volunteers," wrote Martha Wehrle. At the same time, the National Affairs and Legislation

Mrs. Clifford Fifield (of the Garden Club of Buzzards Bay, New Bedford, Massachusetts), Horticulture Committee chairman, 1971–73, initiated the plant exchange in 1973 at the Lake Placid annual meeting. Clubs propagated and exchanged plant material nationally for more than thirty years before the activity shifted to the zone level. Mrs. Fifield reached 105 years of age in 2010. *Courtesy of GCA Archive.*

Working with local high school horticulture classes, ladies of the Winchester-Clarke Garden Club rehabilitated a half-mile stand of declining dogwoods along the sixty-seven-year-old Dogwood Carriage Lane at the Virginia State Arboretum. A *Cornus* species is the state tree of Virginia. *Courtesy of GCA Archive.*

Zoe Bevil Talley (of the Magnolia Garden Club, Beaumont, Texas) was instrumental in getting the Winifred Turner Nature Conservancy incorporated into the Big Thicket National Preserve. The twenty-two acres of land have been preserved by Magnolia since 1958 and were given to the U.S. government in January 1994. *Courtesy of the Magnolia Garden Club.*

GCA members "ring around the redwood" in Humboldt Redwoods State Park, California, following a conservation and National Affairs and Legislation Committee meeting in 1993. The park has the greatest expanse of contiguous old-growth redwood forest in the United States and includes the Garden Club of America Grove, now totaling 5,130 acres. *Courtesy of GCA Archive.*

Two recent presidents hailed from Zone III. Jan Pratt (left) (of the Three Harbors Garden Club, East Norwich, New York) and Kay Donahue (of the Little Garden Club of Rye, New York). *Courtesy of GCA Archive.*

Wildings, the beautiful wildflower garden of Mrs. Harry A. Howe, a charter member of the Garden Club of Nashville, was given to the Cheekwood Botanical Gardens and Museum of Art after her death. The entire garden—plants, shrubs, trees, stone walls, paths, and treasures—was lifted and moved to its new home in 1968. *Courtesy of GCA Archive.*

In the 1960s the Garden Club of America commissioned landscape architect Perry Wheeler to design a gazebo at the National Arboretum in Washington, D.C., in honor of its fiftieth anniversary and longstanding affiliation with the arboretum. *Courtesy of GCA Archive.*

A joint millennium project of the Junior Ladies' Garden Club, in Athens, and the Trustees' Garden Club, in Savannah, funded an intern for the GEPSN (Georgia Endangered Plant Stewardship Network) at the Georgia Botanical Garden. The internship program trains teachers and students to protect rare flora and habitats. *Courtesy of GCA Archive.*

In 2007 the Village Garden Club of Sewickley and the Garden Club of Allegheny County, in Pittsburgh, sponsored the planting of an allée of trees leading to the new Walnut Landing boat launch on the Ohio River. *Courtesy of GCA Archive.*

Garden club ladies ford the Eel River in redwood country in 1964. Many were life members of the Save the Redwoods League, committed to saving the last stands of *Sequoia sempervirens* found along the Northern California coast. *Courtesy of Emily Keyes Belt.*

Former GCA presidents attend a quarterly meeting at headquarters in 2005. Left to right: Kitty Ferguson (of the Fox Hill Garden Club, Dover, Massachusetts), Bobbie Hansen (of the Guilford Garden Club, Connecticut), Gina Bissell (of the Garden Club of Wilmington, Delaware), Chris Wilhemsen (of the Garden Club of Morristown, New Jersey), and Ann Frierson (of the Junior Ladies' Garden Club, Athens, Georgia). *Courtesy of GCA Archive.*

Right: The Garden Club of Palm Beach, in Florida, funded the redesign of eight circular flower beds in the median strip of Royal Poinciana Way. The Kaleidoscope Garden, created by Alan Stopek, features low-maintenance, drought-tolerant plants historically linked to Palm Beach County. *Courtesy of Garden Club of Palm Beach. Left:* A circular bed in the Kaleidoscope Garden, as seen from above. *Courtesy of Garden Club of Palm Beach.*

Since 1958 the Little Compton Garden Club, in Rhode Island, has been the steward of Wilbour Woods, fifty-three acres given to the town of Little Compton by Mrs. Henry Lloyd in 1937. Planted as a wildflower sanctuary, Wilbour Woods is popular for passive recreation. Left to right: Jenny Hastings, Ellie Hough, Teenie King, and Peanuts Makepiece. *Courtesy of GCA Archive.*

Former presidents convene for meetings and lunch at headquarters. Left to right: Bobbie Hansen (of the Guilford Garden Club, Connecticut), Gina Bissell (of the Garden Club of Wilmington, Delaware), Millicent Johnson (of the Rumson Garden Club, New Jersey), Alice Mathews (of the Garden Club of Nashville), Jan Pratt (of the Three Harbors Garden Club, East Norwich, New York), and Kitty Ferguson (of the Fox Hill Garden Club, Dover, Massachusetts). *Courtesy of GCA Archive.*

Norma Sutherland (of the Westport Garden Club, Kansas City, Missouri) works on her display, based on the garden of Middleton Place, outside Charleston, for the 1993 Chelsea Flower Show in London. Because of terrorist bombings prior to the show, she could import only the three-hundred-pound framework designed for the exhibit but had to secure flowers locally. *Courtesy of GCA Archive.*

Sara Shallenberger Brown (of the Glenview Garden Club, Louisville, Kentucky) was active and influential in many conservation organizations. In 2010 her family and friends commemorated her hundredth birthday by establishing the Sally Brown GCA National Parks Conservation Scholarship. The annual scholarship funds the field training of a Student Conservation Association apprentice crew leader. *Courtesy of* Visions *magazine from Kentucky Education Television.*

Members of the Carmel-by-the-Sea Garden Club, in California, survey the endangered Yadon's wallflower (*Erysimum menziesii syadonii*) in the Monterey Bay dunes. The Department of Fish and Wildlife uses the information to determine whether Yadon's wallflower still requires endangered status. *Courtesy of GCA Archive.*

Members of the Garden Club of Denver plant the highest alpine rock garden in the world, at 11,152 feet, atop Mt. Goliath with seeds propagated in the Denver Botanic Garden greenhouses. This alpine garden is part of a trail renovation project of the U.S. Forest Service. *Courtesy of GCA Archive.*

The Wildflower Walkers of the Portland Garden Club were organized in 1985 by Phyllis Reynolds to greet the earliest wildflowers in March and to follow the blooming season through August from sea level to Cascade alpine ridges. Shown here in 1999 are enthusiastic hikers on one of their biweekly outings. *Courtesy of GCA Archive.*

In commemoration of the millennium, the Garden Club of America created an outdoor teaching classroom as part of the newly refurbished and enlarged Butterfly Habitat Garden at the Museum of Natural History in Washington, D.C. *Courtesy of GCA Archive.*

Committee opened its Washington hotline, a tool for communication. Having a representative on the scene freed the two GCA committees, which began to hold their joint meetings in other places when it seemed advisable, although still holding the important Washington meeting each year.[44]

In 1999, Mrs. Frank N. Magid, the National Affairs and Legislation chair, convened the yearly Washington meeting in the midcentury modern elegance of the Gold Room of the Rayburn Office Building. One hundred thirty clubs sent representatives to the two-day "legislative conference." Congressmen and senators were there. All who were invited attended, and many who could not attend sent specialist staff members to take notes. Nearly all the relevant federal agencies were represented by their top officials. The group sessions that followed were full-house. Marilyn Magid reflected on the meeting with satisfaction tempered by a savvy bit of hesitation: "Respect for the Garden Club of America and our considerable influence was evident at the small meetings. Amid the excitement, however, there remained an air of caution. . . . Our job of informing legislators was very urgent," for "extreme property rights protections" threatened all that had been accomplished thus far.[45]

The Conservation Committee grew as it moved from one episode to another, strengthening as it proceeded and, in the 1980s, taking on the shape it was still to have in the first decade of the twenty-first century. Its popular publication *Conservation Watch* evolved into the *Real Dirt*, a title to be read two ways. The public purpose of the Conservation Committee, often so different from that of the GCA otherwise, is buoyed by a passion to defend the threatened earth. Ellen Harvey Kelly said in 1979, "Nations finally act rationally when all other possibilities have been exhausted. Until conservation is part of American life, then it will have to be conducted through legislation." Twenty-six years later, Carol Stoddard continued the theme, "What goes on in D.C. today will affect the lives of our children and grandchildren to come."[46]

Chapter Eight
CENTENNIAL

*T*hrough the century of its existence the GCA has faced many crises along the way. The clubs met the challenges of war and economic depression; they battled enemies of the natural world, they struggled to build and create favorable circumstances even when it seemed everyone was against them. It might seem that an organization like the GCA, somewhat toughened to history's twists and turns, would not be easily surprised by misfortune. Yet the drama of 9/11 rocked the GCA, as it did the nation, with a mixture of horror and disbelief and dismay. For the GCA the drama took place very close to home. The Nominating Committee was in session in New York on September 11, 2001. By tradition, headquarters is closed when such committees meet there, to save space, limit distraction, and facilitate confidentiality. On the second day of the session the staff was at work early, staying out of the way, while closed away in the library an accounting firm pored over financial papers.

The session was about to begin. The committee chair, Mercer O'Hara, recalled, "We were all just arriving on Tuesday morning when we heard the news that a plane had crashed into the World Trade Center. Our reaction was that an accident had occurred—terrible, but an accident. Then ten minutes into our meeting Pam Jeanes came in to tell us that a second plane had crashed into the South Tower and with it came the dreadful realization that this was no accident."[1]

There being no television at headquarters, the women crowded around the radio in staff member Cathy Kilroy's office. Telephone service in the city was interrupted, although a few calls did get through to the GCA, bringing scattered details of what was happening. Anne Butler, also a staff member, realized that her son was in the World Trade Center. After the fear of possibility rippled through the crowd, Michael Butler walked through the door, rattled but alive. While tensions did not calm, everyone returned to work—the accounting firm back in the library, GCA staff at their desks. The Nominating Committee dispersed for a few hours, returning to their hotels to call home, watch the events on TV, and try to collect themselves. Pamela Jeanes remembered, "I cannot describe the sorrow and worry we all went through." They returned to the big table in the Executive Room and attended to GCA business until 4:00 P.M.[2]

The committee departed in a group with the staff, several of whom could not make it home and had to stay with relatives in Manhattan. Later that night committee members left their hotels and convened at La Corniche, a restaurant on East Sixty-fourth Street, where they dined among vacant tables, the owner having stayed open for them. Afterward, the committee walked together "through empty streets," to their hotels. No taxis appeared. One member recalled that she could have walked her dog down the middle of Madison Avenue with no distraction. "There was a cop at every subway entrance," wrote Mercer O'Hara, "and everywhere notices about where to go to give blood."

September 11, 2001, brought the grim realization that the safety Americans had enjoyed was probably gone forever. The GCA president at the time, Ann Frierson, spoke to the Zone III meeting in Bedford, New York, soon after the event: "It had been my intent to stand before you today to speak about what being a member of the Garden Club of

America meant to you as a club. I had wanted to foster a sense of pride in your association with this great organization and its many dimensions. Today, in light of current events, my words may have changed, but oh has the significance of the Garden Club of America been heightened." She reviewed the GCA's activities during the world wars: the vegetable gardens, the canning lessons, the landscaping around barracks, assisting in hospitals, the purchase of ambulances to send to the battlegrounds.

"But this," she continued, "is a war far different than any our country has ever known. Canning food, knitting socks, providing seeds and ambulances are not viable aids at the moment. What is there that we can do?" Reminding her audience of the GCA's historical devotion to the natural world, she pointed to the immediate future: "You have been given the opportunity to nourish the battered soul of this country by pursuing the goals of the Garden Club of America. . . . Just as fire rejuvenates the forest, let our work reflect the Phoenix rising from America's ashes—invigorated and determined that the simple beauty of nature will continue to exist for the consolation of those in need."[3]

It was an objective as old as the Garden Club of America itself, phrased anew, for a new time that had come upon Americans with an explosion, actually and figuratively.

The Garden Club of America entered the twenty-first century a larger and more closely organized institution than it had ever been before. Certainly a part of its health was due to efforts at repair and reconstruction in the last decades of the previous century. In the early 1980s Helen Anderson had chaired a long-range planning committee, which was followed in the 1990s by a second long-range planning committee, chaired by Nancy Thomas, with Jane Ward as vice-chair. From these efforts came valuable recommendations for modifying the organization yet keeping its structure; office practices were streamlined in perfect timing with the appearance of technological advances. The launching of an endowment fund campaign in the 1990s, with a goal of three million, was achieved in 2005 with a later increase to five million.

An issue brought before the Long Range Planning Committee in its second phase concerned the headquarters' location in New York. From time to time estates and various other locations were offered in donation to the GCA as headquarters. These were declined. But there was the lingering question of remaining in New York City. Long Range Planning came up with the same decision the board had reached in the 1930s: that the GCA remain in New York if for no other reason than that the far-flung membership was more likely to want to be in New York now and then than elsewhere. For outsiders the shops and other attractions of Manhattan made a fine mix with service to the GCA, not least when the board met in December.[4]

The perspective of the GCA had made its transition from Philadelphia to New York an easy one. Philadelphia's clubs, like those of other zones, addressed themselves first to local projects; the GCA was to be national in scope. In New York, the organization flourished, never seeming "local," in spite of a certain predilection for New York projects in the early days. Headquarters was to move from time to time within the same neighborhood, beginning in 1921 at 598 Madison Avenue in the Bankers Trust Building, in a single room for which the GCA paid a low rent; the organization added a second room in 1924 to separate the library and exhibits from the work areas. The City of New York was persuaded to allow the GCA an "agricultural" tax base, but by 1950 this designation seemed too dubious to defend, and the city permitted a change from nonprofit status to "educational." That designation was right on target.

Headquarters moved on June 1, 1930, to the fifteenth floor of the same building, Bankers Trust, where it remained, in larger rooms, for seventeen years, during which it was treated very well by the building's management. In 1947 the majority of the building was sold to a real estate corporation, and the rent doubled, to two dollars a square foot. Bankers Trust had been a very successful location, and the GCA did not

part from it light heartedly. The building managers had blessed the GCA
with privileges beyond those of other tenants, perhaps at the influence
of J. P. Morgan, who owned a floor in the building. Hetty Harrison, one
of the GCA's most active members, knew Morgan well through her husband, Fairfax Harrison.

When the GCA left Bankers Trust in 1947, all but evicted by the
new owners, the Executive Committee discussed buying a house in midtown, prices being somewhat purchaser-friendly in postwar Manhattan.
The board determined this to be "out of the question." The GCA president at the time, Mrs. Fergus Reid—who was called Edree—strongly
opposed buying property and warned the committee that it was wishing
upon the GCA a dual curse of high expenses and the menacing city regulations that accompanied ownership of property in New York. The GCA,
she said, did not need to become a slave to a building; GCA funds were
needed for its work, not for property. "We need to raise our thinking to
a changed world," said Mrs. Reid, considering the frail economy around
them. "If we are to accomplish anything in the future we must finance
it." It was a "terrible time," she said, to even think of raising dues, and the
board agreed with her.[5]

On November 19, 1947, the Executive Committee signed a rental
agreement for a residential penthouse in the Madison Hotel (now demolished), at 15 East Fifty-eighth Street and Madison Avenue, paying
thirty-five hundred dollars per year. While the rent was in fact lower
than at Bankers Trust, the penthouse was rundown and needed work.
No favors were forthcoming from the Madison Hotel. Very hesitantly the
board raised dues to help pay for the new headquarters, which needed
painting, wallpapering, and much general repair. Even as headquarters
was moving in, it became clear that the space was too small. Nevertheless on June 9, 1948, the new offices were opened with a "house party,"
at which guests admired the familiar vitrines with the display of old gardening books and prints and the elegant, flower-filled terrace open to
the sky.

The penthouse proved more a joy to GCA visitors to New York than convenient to the business operations of the organization. By the fall of 1956 it was deemed unusable. A committee busied itself in the real estate market, soon finding a large co-op suite to buy in a new hotel for twenty-five thousand dollars, with $811.50 to be paid monthly for maintenance. Once again the question of owning real estate made the GCA hesitant, and the committee went out looking for rentals, considering various apartments, both built and not yet built. Welcomed back to the Bankers Trust Building, where the GCA had started out, the board accepted the committee's recommendation, and the office reopened at 598 Madison Avenue, with a tea on October 12, 1959. There the GCA was to remain for almost forty more years, until the building was sold twice over, and it became clear that the privileges enjoyed previously would not be continued.

Attention has always been given to the appearance of the national headquarters, although no effort has ever been made to make the rooms opulent. Board meetings are held there. The business of the club is conducted there. Members visiting New York from local clubs like to drop by their headquarters, if only for a few minutes, and are proud of what they see. A handsome headquarters is good business. No governing board in the GCA has ever denied that or wished a headquarters that is less than appropriate.

Upon the return to the Bankers Trust Building, the GCA faced an interior that was partly finished and partly still being decorated. F. Schumacher & Co., a longtime friend of the GCA, designed special fabrics and papers, a GCA "collection," from which Betty Corning urged all members to buy, because the GCA received a royalty on sales. Laura Dupee Benkard, a former vice president, donated antique French wallpaper for the entrance hall. When Louise Crowninshield died, at about the time of the return to Bankers Trust, one of the rooms was decorated in her memory by friends, including her brother, the noted collector Henry Francis du Pont, who some twenty years earlier had established the Winterthur Museum at their childhood home in Delaware. He supervised every detail of the Louise Crowninshield Room and was in no hurry. The room followed the familiar antiquarian style of the time and included an eighteenth-century paneled fireplace wall from a colonial house. On the completion of the room almost a decade later, in 1968, the House Committee politely reported "a most frustrating project."[6] Nearly twenty years after the room's completion, various members were still making needlepoint seats for the Chippendale-style chairs of the room, the first stitched by the project's originator, Edree Reid. Thirty years after the room's completion, the paneling and the furniture were relocated in the GCA's next move.[7]

At the time when it became clear that another move would be necessary, the Headquarters Committee, established in 1971, supervised the operations of the headquarters, and a subcommittee set to work touring likely relocation sites. New quarters were found in an office building around the corner, at 14 East Sixtieth Street, across from the American office of the American Academy in Rome, and renovation work was undertaken for many months until the GCA relocated there in February 1998.

Members from across the country have made donations of furnishings for headquarters all through the years of the GCA, so a substantial collection of silver and porcelains, prints and paintings, has accumulated at headquarters, together with furniture and, not surprisingly, many containers for flowers. Indeed, headquarters has always been adorned with fresh flower arrangements. It was a courageous Mrs. David B. Borie who stood before the board on June 8, 1994, and announced the House Committee's purchase of a "permanent hall flower arrangement to be used on an on-going basis at all times when fresh plant material is not wanted."[8]

The House Committee attends to the issues involving the physical state of headquarters. Decisions on décor, especially for the meeting rooms and library, are theirs. The Art Committee, a subcommittee of the House Committee, attends to the care and inventory of the valuable art collection of prints and paintings accumulated over the years by donation and, occasionally, by purchase. Archival conservation is the Art Committee's main effort, which involves rematting and framing. Many of the important American botanical artists are represented in the collection, including some who belonged to the GCA. If necessary to make room for new acquisitions, the committee rotates the art displayed on the walls. The Art Committee joins the House Committee in selecting fabrics, wallpaper, and paint. Where interior decorating is concerned the main challenge is a nearly constant process of repair and upgrading, for the rooms receive heavy use.

One of the age-old customs at GCA Headquarters is termed *hospitality*. This consists of a large committee of New York–area members filling the role of caterer for board meetings, teas, openings, and special events. Members from far away look upon this volunteer effort with wonder, amazed to see a buzzing sort of small-town devotion in the glamorous middle of Manhattan. And the tenacity and loyalty of the Hospitality Committee members through the decades have been remarkable. Presented with minimal kitchen facilities in a small space, they turn out lunches, bake cakes, and generally feed their fellow members whenever called upon. Although guests must be charged for the food, it is provided at cost. For the better part of a century the minutes have been laced with reports of the committee's efforts to keep costs down. During one period lunches may be served in several courses; during another the menu might be limited to sandwiches. Sometimes hiring a caterer seems the best solution. In 2010 alone, the volunteer committee served over eight hundred meals at headquarters. The purpose of providing this hospitality at headquarters is to contain groups at meetings, to keep them from scattering at mealtimes, to avoid the tendency of the big city's temptations to interrupt business.[9]

Headquarters employs an executive director, a comptroller, and five or six office staff members, a total that varies from time to time and involves both employed and volunteer staff. The first office had a single secretary. Within a few years, by 1924, she had an assistant part time. The paid staff grew very slowly, always with a female office manager. From the first there has been a constant effort to keep the office modern and efficient. In 1915 Elizabeth Martin "pleaded piteously" to her committee chairs for "typewritten communications." Old Underwood typewriters in the office were donated to the war cause in 1943. The archive records three IBM typewriters stolen from the office in 1977; only one remained. And when the office upgraded to IBM Selectric II machines, they were bolted to the desks.[10]

No office modernization was more complicated than when the computer appeared. Adjustment was apparently difficult as the conversion began its slow progress. In 1986, Mary Barker observed, "The world of floppy disks, print-outs and off-set printing was a voyage of discovery, and gradually the pieces of the giant puzzle [fell] into place, a most rewarding journey." In 1993, as Nancy Thomas's presidency ended, she reported that 480 business letters had been sent from the GCA, although fax and e-mail had begun to be the vehicle for most correspondence within the organization and its member clubs.[11] The annual meeting of 2000 was the first reported upon by computer. Mrs. C. W. Eliot Payne, meeting chair, wrote, "My fond wish is that in the near future, all meeting functions from invitation to registration to transportation will be done electronically, thereby saving a tremendous number of woman-hours, dollars, trees and hand-applied stamps." And so, as Linda Payne had hoped, it very quickly came to be that the GCA's management was completely computerized.[12] A third system was installed in 2011.

Another technological innovation to parallel the computerization of the office was the GCA Web site. After more than a year of arduous planning, Chris Willemsen, GCA president, announced at the last meeting of 1998, "The website is up and running." She told board members and guests, "You are all most welcome to go and view it" down the hall in the president's office, where the site was "pulled up on screen."[13]

Like all innovations of the computer, the Web site took hold quickly. As it grew ever more useful, the existing office computer's effectiveness declined and by 2002 was judged outdated. A staff member, Millie Roman, was made "director of Computer Information Services" and supervised the installation of a new system. Bobbie Hansen, chair of a special committee, inquired of various nonprofit organizations, and her committee selected Imis from Advanced Solutions, explaining, "This system has the fields GCA needs." Mrs. Hansen pronounced the system "fabulous." In conclusion she assured the membership, "The wonderful timesaving world of 21st century technology is within our reach."[14]

But currency with computers is fleeting. In 2010, under the direction of Ann Price Davis, a new computer system and server were installed at headquarters. Meanwhile, Leslie Purple, appointed by the Executive Committee, researched and established computerized printing for the *Bulletin*. This dramatically reduced the cost and raised the physical quality of that vital publication. The Publications Committee has been restyled as the Communications Committee. Two e-mail programs were introduced, one that appeared on the months the *Bulletin* was not published; the other, a red-flag alarm for time-sensitive GCA news.

With modern technology, the issue of privacy has come, along with the questions: Why should state-of-the art horticultural, flower arranging, and conservation materials be available so casually to the public and chance inaccurate transmission and unwelcomed uses? How could the GCA's new technology protect the member clubs? It is the clubs, after all, that fulfill the organization's mission. The questions, new only in their application to computer technology, remain issues very seriously considered but as yet unresolved.

Most days, ordinary days, only officers and committee members with specific duties come in and out of headquarters; the library and the archive nearly always have a member at work. The library that began in Elizabeth Martin's home is today a neat room surrounded by cabinets and centered with a long work table. It is relatively new. Because the GCA has been an organization always on the move, no specific room was allocated as an archive until 2000, the result of the Archive Committee's obtaining a grant for development purposes.[15] The archival holdings at headquarters, such as they were, opened to researchers in 1994. They are managed entirely by volunteers.

Before 1994, the organization, always so much on the move forward, showed only an occasional inclination to save records; even the idea of it probably seemed a packrat interference with the progressive advance. Thus the office manager was left in charge of records, and when there was a need for more room, dead files went to the trash, if sometimes with a basement interlude. Random, gathered-up bundles of letters and writings from such famous people as Gertrude Jekyll further suggest that the files were sometimes purged for curios rather than managed for historical reference. Under the direction of Gail Cooke, the Archive Room took professional form. New filing cases and materials arrived between October 2000 and the spring of 2001 to make a commendable archive. Documents began to appear and were placed under archival care.

Precedent-conscious and history-minded GCA members had for years urged better management of papers and records, to no avail. They had begged the clubs for club histories, which also largely fell on deaf ears. As late as 2005 Gail Cooke made a pioneering appeal for recorded interviews with "older members" of the clubs. Joanne Lenden as historian presented entertaining historical talks to the board, describing early GCA events and personalities she found documented in the records, beckoning board members to take an interest in the preservation of records.[16]

Perhaps most people hesitated to do this because the prospect of an avalanche of papers flooding in from clubs all over the country was daunting, considering the relatively small rented office space. In the past old documents had been usually cleared out to make room. Was everything now to be saved? At this writing the GCA Archive houses papers from two hundred clubs, in varying amounts. Although the logistics of keeping an archive seemed overwhelming, a small group recognized the increasing importance of organizational history for the GCA. The organization had accomplished too many important goals, made too many marks, to allow a silent past.

An event that inspired a general interest in the GCA past was the 1964 discovery of neatly wrapped packages of glass "lantern slides" in the headquarters kitchen pantry. These were the large, archaic, paper-framed glass slides that had once been familiar in academic lecture halls and for many years had been the basis of the GCA's traveling slide shows. These had not gone into the trash. Somehow they had made the transition from headquarters to headquarters.[17]

A heavy and cumbersome lot, perhaps the lantern slides seemed more important than ordinary paper files. However they may have survived, their fortunes greatly improved with a new generation. They found a champion in Harriet J. Phelps, who had them removed from their pantry storage, cleaned, and properly packed. She found that the most immediately interesting and distinctive of the pictures were views of GCA members' gardens in the early twentieth century, captured in high-quality glass plate negatives, many in color.[18]

Taken to the Smithsonian Institution's Horticultural Services Division for evaluation, the pictures were acclaimed for their rarity, and the GCA donated the entire collection to the institution in 1987, more than three thousand images. They are the principal feature of the Smithsonian's Archives of American Gardens, an ongoing program for documenting gardens and the basis for a groundbreaking book, *The Golden Age of American Gardens,* by GCA members Mac Griswold and Eleanor Weller, published in 1991. The Archives of American Gardens Research Station was opened to researchers by the Smithsonian in January 1994.

Through the lantern slides the GCA rather backed into the history business. The revival of a long and successful association with America's premier museum institution was rightly a source of pride to the GCA.

The recording of gardens continues with the GCA's Garden History and Design Committee, which still meets with officials of the Smithsonian's Archives of American Gardens. GCA members continue to collect and encourage other GCA members to seek out early garden pictures and plans, furthering the Smithsonian's programs of garden study, as well as a broad range of garden scholarship. Over time, the cooperative venture caught members' attention, and the archive was created at headquarters. Revealing details of a century of gardening and garden subjects, as well as the projects and organization of the GCA, it grows constantly in quantity and value, not only to gardening and landscape design, but also to women's history.

The only lingering question with the GCA Archive is: How long can limited space in a Manhattan office suite hold the rising mountain of material? GCA Headquarters space, never large, will one day have to find other provisions for storing files. An archive with no access for research is dead indeed. Here again, the computer has come to call at the GCA. The Archive Committee in 2005 enlarged the storage capacity of the Archive Room and completed the first CD scan of early issues of the *Bulletin,* to be used at headquarters. At this writing the committee has advanced a step further, and back issues of the *Bulletin* are now available online. With a touch of the "find" key, a resource amazingly rich opens up. Yet for all the blessings of technology, GCA archivists are wary of leaning upon it entirely for preservation purposes. Edie Loening finds that "hard copies are the only things that seem to survive the years."[19]

Publicly oriented projects of the Garden Club of America are usually carried out by the local clubs as individual efforts. An exception, for example, was the International Flower Show, the early showcase for GCA talent. For this event headquarters aided the participation of the GCA clubs. Another very visible project of national scope has been Partners for Plants, a joint venture of the Horticulture and Conservation committees, launched in 1991. Describing itself as "a grass roots, hands-on volunteer initiative,"[20] over two decades the Partners for Plants Committee has narrowed its address to "endangered plant needs" on federally managed public lands, including those of the National Park Service, the U.S. Forest Service, the U.S. Fish and Wildlife Service, and the Bureau of Land Management. The federal government has not been generous in funding botanical studies, so GCA member clubs, in cooperation with the government scientists, have not only undertaken the research and identification of plants threatened with oblivion but also developed programs by which these plants might be replenished, such as the attempt of the Mill Mountain Garden Club, of Roanoke, Virginia, to revive and replace the dying native chestnut population. The GCA's role in mapping, monitoring, and transplanting has been highly significant. At the end of two years, in 1992, fifty projects proved the program's great success, and twenty years later it continues as one of the GCA's most successful public endeavors.

Apart from flower shows and meetings, most GCA public projects have nearly always been of a horticultural sort: parks, botanical gardens, historical gardens. Projects given the annual Founders Fund Award present a good cross section of the GCA's public work in clubs across the country. The Founders Fund Committee meets once a year at headquarters in New York. Many entries are reviewed, and three are selected as finalists. As a result of balloting through the clubs, one finalist receives the twenty-five-thousand-dollar Founders Fund Award, and the runners up receive seventy-five hundred dollars each. Announcement of the awards is a major event at the annual meeting.

The sorts of projects vary. For example, horticultural projects are sometimes canted toward a humanitarian approach in helping some group in need, such as the sunken garden built during 1941–43 by the Chestnut Hill Garden Club at Cushing General Hospital, Framingham, Massachusetts, a wartime and postwar rehabilitation facility for veterans. Projects of this character began in World War I and became a familiar part of the GCA's program during World War II. A Chicago garden center for the disabled was built by the Kenilworth Garden Club in 1974, a model for others. In the early 1980s the Garden Clubs of Evanston, Illinois, and Lookout Mountain, Chattanooga, Tennessee, equipped nature parks for the handicapped with raised beds, special tools, and knotted-rope railings guiding the visitor along a level floor to stops augmented with tape-recorded interpretations.

In 1985 the Little Garden Club of Memphis planted a "sensory garden," with plants selected to serve the blind by arousing the senses of smell, taste, and touch. Again in Tennessee the Knoxville Garden Club in 1990 created a rooftop garden at a local rehabilitation center so that patients using wheelchairs could actually dig in the dirt themselves using special tools the club provided. The Garden Club of Honolulu in 2004 helped inmates at a women's prison develop abandoned grounds into productive vegetable gardens. The produce was sold in local markets.

Before the 1980s, when conservation's strong influence began to be felt significantly, GCA club projects centered largely in horticulture as it applied either to garden design or educational facilities. An early example of the latter was the French Broad River Garden Club's wildflower plantings at the Asheville-Biltmore Botanical Gardens, in North Carolina, designed to increase public appreciation for Smoky Mountain wildflowers. Another was the walled garden at the Newark Museum, redesigned and planted by the Garden Club of Somerset Hills, New Jersey, for "increased public use" and educational purposes, with plants labeled for study. The Garden Club of Honolulu helped create Prehistoric Glen, at the Foster Botanic Garden.

Projects have sometimes been tied to historic restoration sites, particularly in the era of the United States Bicentennial. During that period seven of the Founders Fund Awards went to projects related to historic houses, but historical projects had already attracted applications to the fund in the 1930s, usually with the goal of embellishing the grounds of historic house museums with trees and plantings. During 1948–50 the Garden Study Club of New Orleans restored the flower garden at Oakley Plantation, near St. Francisville, Louisiana, where John James Audubon, as family tutor, painted more than fifty of his birds. Some applications have reflected even more ambitious projects. In 1967, the Amateur Gardeners Club of Maryland became a major player in the resurrection of boxwood parterres at the Paca House garden, in Annapolis, an eighteenth-century ornamental landscape whose restoration required removal of a hotel structure that had subsequently covered the entire site. During 1982–85 the West Chester Garden Club helped with the early stages of the restoration of the eighteenth-century botanist John Bartram's ancient nursery and garden near Philadelphia. Bartram's garden was a longtime interest of Philadelphia clubs and of international interest to scholars of the history of transatlantic horticulture.

For all the horticultural focus, conservation has been a theme, if a lesser one, in GCA projects since the 1920s and none on a grander scale than the fight to save the giant redwoods of California. Ethel Lansdale's 1929 donation of a redwood grove in memory of her husband has inspired over the years the donation of more than 950 additional memorial groves among the California redwood forests. We have seen how GCA members across the nation joined with the Pacific Coast clubs to assure preservation of as much of the forests as possible. This trend has lasted for nearly a century and still continues when a forest is threatened. The earliest conservation quests were to preserve areas for parks, such as Barthomolew's Cobble, in Massachusetts, a site saved in part by the Worcester Garden Club in the late 1930s and following World War II. The Rochester Garden Club in New York extended the protection of Bergen Swamp in the late 1940s, and at about the same time the Portland Garden Club in Oregon purchased and thus saved 160 acres of rare old myrtle trees, famed for their beauty and sharp camphor fragrance, adjacent to Loeb State Park, of which the tract is now part. Virgin forests, old ponds, swamps, marshes all felt the GCA conservationists' presence through the 1970s.

It was in the 1980s that conservation, as a theme for club projects, really came into its own. Preservation of Fresh Pond Reservation, a bird habitat near Cambridge, Massachusetts, was researched and planned by the Cambridge Plant and Garden Club in 1980. In 1983 the Magnolia Garden Club in Beaumont, Texas, already having been active in the creation of the Big Thicket National Park, took leadership in creating wildlife preserves along the Gulf of Mexico, where migrating birds come up from the South and rest in the trees, under the protection of alligators who inhabit ditches and swamps below. At Virginia Beach in 1993 the Virginia Beach Garden Club helped preserve a nearby great salt marsh. Many projects have reflected the longtime interest in preserving native plants and wildflowers, such as the 2005 Woodland Project of the Hancock Park Garden Club, in Los Angeles. In 2003, the Lake and Valley Garden Club of Cooperstown, New York, undertook the conservation of part of the shore of Otsego Lake through an innovative water conservation system.

By far the greatest interest the projects have shown, however, has been in education. Some of this has naturally involved publications. From early books on horticulture and history to articles in the *Bulletin* and lectures sponsored, club projects with educational purposes are the overwhelming majority. Indeed, it could be argued that all the projects— from restored gardens to preserved swamps—have been educational at the root.

An educational publication received the first Founders Fund Award. The Amateur Gardeners Club, of Maryland, was given the award for publishing a facsimile of the sixteenth-century Badianus Manuscript. No one thought the facsimile would be a best seller or make money. It was published purely to communicate a valuable South American botanical document that has been priceless to pre-Columbian studies. Publications have not been typical of most club projects, because their printing is costly, their profits are tenuous, and much labor is involved, but club publications have nonetheless been issued all along, ranging from garden guides to regional planting guides, from monographs on one species to fund-raising cookbooks. In recent years club histories have been popular, including *The Garden Club of Philadelphia: One Hundred Years* (2004) by Maria Willing, et al, and Elizabeth Craig Weaver Proctor's *A History of the Garden Club of Nashville* (2010).

The Wissahickon Garden Club in 1971 sponsored a children's botanical film, *Room to Grow*, at the Pennsylvania Horticultural Society. The Portland Garden Club, in Oregon, built a greenhouse at the Rae Selling Berry Botanic Garden to house and interpret a rare collection of "alpines, primulas, rhododendrons and native plants."[21] The Des Moines Founders Garden Club created a six-acre "urban demonstration of Iowa's botanical heritage" during 1990–94.[22] The Perennial Planters Garden Club, of Providence, Rhode Island, created an "educational garden," a "microcosm of the state," a "green oasis in an industrial area," at the city's Childrens Museum during 1995–99.[23] The eleven GCA clubs of New Jersey sponsored a conference, Hotter Times Ahead, at Princeton University in the fall of 2007 in cooperation with the Princeton Environmental Institute and Environmental Defense; the objective was to supply current information in the science of global warming.

The above is a sampling of some outstanding projects among hundreds of others conducted by GCA clubs toward the end of the twentieth century and at the beginning of the new century. In the past decade nearly all the projects reported by the individual clubs were educational in character, the vast majority concerning horticulture and its relation to conservation. The interpretation of outdoor spaces from a horticultural point of view has been a strong inclination of the clubs in their projects. About 40 percent of the clubs have scholarship programs, and these can be added to the twenty-five scholarships and fellowships offered by the national organization. This further carries out the dedication of the GCA to its original principle of 1913 and its credo, "to stimulate the knowledge and love of gardening." In 1980, to the original was added: "to share the advantages of association by means of educational meetings, conferences and publications, and to restore, improve, and protect the quality of the environment through educational programs and action in the fields of conservation and civic improvement."[24]

Early in the twenty-first century the Garden Club of America, anticipating the year 2013, began making plans to celebrate its centennial. Alice Matthews, president, asked former presidents Chris Willemsen and Ann Frierson in the fall of 2005 to address the subject and urged all members to contact them with ideas. Members voted to make the restoration and landscaping of the Sixty-ninth Street entrance to Central Park the centennial Founders Fund gift. With a project well in hand and money to raise, a Centennial Committee was duly appointed, with Mrs. W. Michael Thompson Jr. as chair.

Under Ray Thompson's leadership, the Centennial Committee has undertaken to restore the Sixty-ninth Street entrance to the park and immediate areas inside it, located at Sixty-ninth Street and Fifth Avenue. Plans were being finalized in 2011. The project will include new plantings of trees and native plants as a resurrection of the ideas of Olmsted and Vaux to suggest romantic rural landscapes of earlier times, although Olmsted himself had an interest in interpreting the idea more through exotics than through native trees and shrubbery. To bring sunlight to the shady area, the GCA plan called for a thinning of the overgrown population of volunteer trees and a cultivation of specimens, given plenty of room and planted with such native flowering shrubs as witch hazel for undergrowth. A widening of the Sixty-ninth Street entrance was considered but abandoned in the face of required approvals by many city commissions. Natasha Hopkinson expressed the original idea of Central Park and the GCA's commitment to it: "Most important was the idea of a democratic garden used by all social classes, and the elevation of man's nature through the exposure to nature—a real or created version."[25]

Soon the question of the annual meeting for 2013 and its location required an answer. By a sequence long-established the annual meeting of that year was to fall to Zone VII, states of the upper South, but when Philadelphia understandably wished to hold the annual meeting in the centennial year, Zone VII traded 2013 for Philadelphia's earlier date. Committees in the ten clubs of Greater Philadelphia set to work, as any zone would with any annual meeting. However, this one had a new, reflective twist.

First the obvious question: What was left of the Philadelphia known to the founders that might add interest to the centennial meeting? Elizabeth Martin's house on Rittenhouse Square has become a shop. Stenton remains a Colonial Dames museum and, like the GCA, has weathered with distinction a full century in its original role. Andalusia retains its Greek-temple grandeur; no longer a private residence, it is preserved by a family foundation as a museum. Germantown still has some of its old gardens. The house Wyck, where the founders had eaten their lunch amid artistic flower arrangements on the day of the preliminary meeting, just prior to the GCA's founding, still stands and also has become a museum. Although the Garden Club of America has never been one to pay much attention to its past, so busy has it been moving forward, a certain reverence has settled over the GCA across the country as the hundredth year draws near.

Planning for the centennial meeting in Philadelphia is underway, under the direction of Leslie Purple and Laura Gregg, cochairs of the 2013 annual meeting. To all appearances this is to be simply an annual meeting, which is a business meeting with embellishments; what will make this one inevitably exceptional is the attachment to the hundredth year of the Garden Club of America. The committee in Philadelphia has no formal connection with the Centennial Committee of the national organization in New York, although the two have exchanged ideas. Some of the annual meeting plans, like those for any annual meeting, have been subject to approval by the Executive Committee. In 2010 the

Philadelphia committee selected Loew's Philadelphia Hotel for the occasion, a converted art deco–style bank building downtown, a block and a half from City Hall. Dramatically modern, Loew's has the "right tone" for the centennial meeting. The theme agreed upon is GCA history and the achievement of "many goals over the years."[26]

In conjunction with the 2013 annual meeting, a premeeting tour for the board of associates has been scheduled as well as a postmeeting tour for which GCA members can sign up. A major flower show has been envisioned as the central feature of the event, a larger show than the ones that usually accompany the annual meetings. The idea of a handwritten invitation has met with a favorable response from the committee. A commemorative bowl, decorated symbolically, has been commissioned from Tiffany & Company. An acorn charm has also been commissioned. A major feature of the celebration will be an exhibition of rare books from the Garden Club of America library, under the direction of the Grolier Club Library, in New York. Many ideas have been on the table, including the design and manufacture of a silk scarf in addition to the charm and the bowl. These will be sold at the shop that is customarily set up at annual meetings.[27]

It would have interested the founders to know that the centennial of their Garden Club of America will be held in the city of centennials, Philadelphia. If they ever thought of an organization largely of and by women extending through a century, they never said so, at least in writing. But they believed from the start that what they were doing was important. They had no crystal ball through which to see the evolution of their creation, now with thousands of members scattered through clubs that are clustered in twelve zones. The long shadow of the Garden Club of America extends west over the Pacific to Hawaii, south to Mexico, and east over the Atlantic to Bermuda. Headquarters in midtown Manhattan provides national services for clubs, which are in themselves autonomous.

What is the real significance of being one hundred years old, beyond reaching a milestone? A hundred years can be a badge. Old buildings, taken quite for granted, suddenly gain stature and sometimes even museum status when their years finally add up to a century. Once, when there were fewer of these, the admiration was greater; now, as our civilization ages, there are more hundred-year-old buildings, and they are less distinctive. For the GCA the centennial calls for a pause to consider an organization that, heretofore, has never been much interested in historical reflection. Hence this book has been an attempt to chronicle the organization and its shape through its century history.

How has the GCA lived so long and kept on such an even keel? The explanation for the organization's early firm foundation probably lies in its development in the East and the far West at the same time. While the GCA was being kindled in Philadelphia and New York, a not insignificant group of its members, spending winters in California, carried their interests west. Concurrently, on the West Coast the conservation movement was taken up by garden clubs, creating a powerful and effective western GCA to balance the organization in the East, laying the ground for the rapid development of clubs in between. As seen with the participation of GCA clubs all over the nation in the rescue of the California redwoods, the two coasts of the nation joined hands very effectively. The national outlook the GCA has maintained would not have been likely without this early union east and west.

Yet, for all the excellence of that historical basis, the GCA's major crises might have involved survival in the context of the changing place of women in the American culture. For the first half century, the GCA was made up largely of housewives. By the twenty-first century this traditional majority has been joined by members who are doctors, scientists, businesswomen, interior decorators, architects, landscape architects and designers, artists, writers, lawyers, bankers, mayors, city council members, legislators, inventors, teachers, shop owners, manufacturers, real estate agents, and more—indeed by members in a whole spectrum of careers that before the last quarter of the twentieth century were fields occupied primarily by men. There being only so much time in a day, a planner in, say, 1965 might have predicted that the Garden Club of America would dwindle in membership, not for lack of interested people, but because there were to be so many other options for women. To the contrary, the GCA has grown.

That women's lives are busy cannot be considered news, but the scope of what they do outside the home has definitely enlarged. They have not emerged anew, only cut new facets in the same stone. Protection under civil rights law in the 1960s certainly stimulated a female presence, but for many women the "women's movement" was well underway when Elizabeth Martin and Ernestine Goodman had their idea for the GCA, and it never turned back. In the stronger context of modern women in the workplace, the GCA does not generally lose members because of career obligations; membership continues to grow in the clubs, which are themselves the members of the GCA. The binding principles and advantages of garden education among friends have the same appeal they always had.

The GCA's contributions to the betterment of American life have been substantial. Upon this laurel the GCA may rest happily in its one hundredth year. The achievement has many parts, the credit belonging to the clubs, and the clubs *are* the GCA. Every club is a local club but a fitted piece of the national puzzle as well. The main work of the clubs is in their areas: local projects, local meetings, information shared locally. They spread their efforts in zones to achieve a broader level of the same thing, and the zones band together under the national officers at the top, who change with specified regularity. The GCA knows no dynasties. In the interest of preventing a headquarters domination through convenience of place, the creation of a New York City club has been historically avoided. The New York Area Committee was established in 1977 by members of area clubs to engage specifically in city projects.

The Garden Club of America is like a great beehive with glass walls. Just as any GCA member seeking information, precedent, or opportunity may easily look upward through the levels of the club and zone for ready answers, the national organization can look down along the same route for whatever reason there might be, not least to seek out prospective national officers and committee members. GCA members are expected to work and to work together. Through work in projects, legislation, flower shows, and other organizational endeavors, the individual member follows the route of service first in the club, then in the zone, and at last on the national level. At every step the GCA provides a learning experience. Education in the GCA is based upon standards in many different domains, the most obvious being the formal judging in horticulture and flower arranging; in conservation, lessons may lie in the joy or heartbreak of a final verdict on a quest to preserve.

By the time an officer is elected or appointed to a national office or position, the candidate has risen through the ranks, so to speak, and is no stranger to what the GCA stands for. The simple, strict organizational structure this represents has suffered no assaults, no efforts to change, which attests its effectiveness. Within the edifice the GCA enjoys admirable fluidity. From top to bottom and back, no voice that wishes to be heard is muffled. The strength of the GCA, the sovereignty, lies in the forums of the member clubs.

The Garden Club of America was founded near the halfway point of the second decade of the twentieth century. Half a century of post–Civil War nation building marked the era. During that transitional fifty years, America had incubated apart from the rest of the world. Beatrix Farrand's aunt Edith Wharton called this American period "the Age of Innocence" in one of her books. And in truth, one recalls the founding of the GCA in a certain frame of innocence, of blooming flower gardens set in a romantic place, a group of ladies espousing simple ideals that naturally would have appealed to women favored by protected lives.

The founders loved their gardens and their beautiful flowers as emblems of the America they had known all their lives. They would not have been so eager to protect the beauty of that America had they not sensed it slipping away. Mrs. Wharton's "innocence" might well apply to them, although it should not be taken to imply either weakness or a narrow focus. The principles the founders set down in their garden were solid.

Even after the founding generation was gone and the world opened up, with its good and bad, the original principles they set down have prevailed. The GCA has lived on and thrived. Reshaped and expanded in scope, the original objectives remain today the elements of purpose that have sustained the GCA for a century, through times that were by no means ages of innocence. Through two world wars, the Great Depression, and many subsequent recessions and wars, the GCA's structural timbers have remained sound. The house Elizabeth Martin and Ernestine Goodman imagined for their friends a century ago in Germantown still holds together. But the house itself is bigger and greater than either of them probably ever could have imagined.

Afterword

In the centennial year, the Garden Club of America has 17,500 members in two hundred clubs nationwide. The clubs represent forty-one states of the Union as well as Washington, D.C., and eight additional courtesy member clubs are in Canada, Bermuda, Germany, Jamaica, New Zealand, and Uruguay.

Acknowledgments

I wish to acknowledge those who gave time and energy to this project, and I begin with Edie Loening. Without her devoted attention to details in research, her familiarity with the GCA Archive, and her originality in finding sources, researching this book would often have been a stumbling process. She was a vigilant reader of manuscripts. For all her assistance and advice I am grateful.

Nancy Murray, chair, Book Committee of the Garden Club of America, guided this book from an idea to realization. Her committee included Nancy D'Oench, Ann Frierson, Corbin Harwood, Janet Robertson, and Chris Willemsen.

The picture research was conducted by Anne Myers, Sally Cummins, Ellen Morris, and Jane Vanderzee. With Edie Loening they composed the captions. For completing this daunting task I thank them. And for factual assistance, I thank also Gail Cooke and Joanne Lenden. Additional thanks to Sally Cummins for her invaluable research on the history of all of the GCA committees from their inception.

It was our good fortune to have a hundred years of illustrations copied and conserved by the distinguished photographer David Godichaud of Paris. In the archive they vary from Kodak to studio. Their evenness here is a tribute to his skill.

Office staff at headquarters of the Garden Club of America, in New York, was always cheerfully at hand. Millie Roman, executive administrator, and Monro M. Bonnell, database and Web site coordinator, were especially helpful, as was Anne Butler.

Nancy Murray and I wish to thank the GCA presidents who presided over the organization and gave us every kind of encouragement while the book came to be: Alice Mathews, Maryjo Garre, Joan George, and Marian Hill. We remember fondly Kitty Ferguson's urging that a history be written for the centennial.

For a wide variety of favors, my thanks to Norene Alexander, Marcia Anderson, Elaine Burke, Torrey Cooke, Susan Everitt, Amy Freitag, Laura Gregg, Penny Horne, Jane Keuskamp, Marnie Laird, Bonny Martin, Polly Moore, Jeanne Payson, Lula Potter, Leslie Purple, Lucinda Seale, Libby Smith, Sally Squire, Katie Stewart, Nancy Thomas, Kingslea Thomas, Susan Wilmerding, and Fran Wolfe.

Publication of this book reaffirms a nearly ninety-year occasional publishing association between the Garden Club of America and the Smithsonian Institution. On behalf of myself and Nancy Murray I want to thank Carolyn Gleason, director of Smithsonian Books, for welcoming the manuscript. Assisted by her Smithsonian colleague Christina Wiginton, she oversaw the many details of producing the book, not least in engaging the wise, eagle-eyed editor, Robin Whitaker.

Appendix 1

INDIVIDUAL CLUBS AND YEAR OF JOINING
THE GARDEN CLUB OF AMERICA, BY STATE

Alabama
Little Garden Club of Birmingham, 1950, Birmingham
Red Mountain Garden Club, 1933, Birmingham

Arizona
Columbine Garden Club, 1989, Scottsdale

Arkansas
Little Rock Garden Club, 1960, Little Rock

California
Carmel-by-the-Sea Garden Club, 1986, Carmel
Diggers Garden Club, 1927, Pasadena
Garden Club of Santa Barbara, 1918, Santa Barbara
Hancock Park Garden Club, 1996, Los Angeles
Hillsborough Garden Club, 1929, Hillsborough
Marin Garden Club, 2011, Marin County
Orinda Garden Club, 1980, Orinda
Pasadena Garden Club, 1920, Pasadena
Piedmont Garden Club, 1926, Piedmont
Woodside-Atherton Garden Club, 1934, San Francisco

Colorado
Broadmoor Garden Club, 1941, Colorado Springs
Garden Club of Denver, 1920, Denver

Connecticut
Connecticut Valley Garden Club, 1933, West Hartford
Fairfield Garden Club, 1923, Fairfield

Garden Club of Darien, 1942, Darien
Garden Club of Hartford, 1919, Hartford
Garden Club of New Haven, 1954, New Haven
Green Fingers Garden Club, 1913, Greenwich
Greenwich Garden Club, 1920, Greenwich
Guilford Garden Club, 1948, Guilford
Hortulus, 1936, Greenwich
Litchfield Garden Club, 1952, Litchfield
Middletown Garden Club, 1920, Middletown
New Canaan Garden Club, 1920, New Canaan
New London Garden Club, 1962, New London
Ridgefield Garden Club, 1916, Ridgefield
Sasqua Garden Club, 1939, Fairfield
The Stamford Garden Club, 1946, Stamford
Stonington Garden Club, 1999, Stonington
Washington Garden Club, 1917, Washington

Delaware
Garden Club of Wilmington, 1920, Wilmington

Florida
Founders Garden Club of Sarasota, Inc., 1984, Sarasota
Garden Club of Halifax County, 1952, Ormond Beach
Garden Club of Palm Beach, 1931, Palm Beach
The Grass River Garden Club, 1998, Delray Beach
Jupiter Island Garden Club, 1957, Jupiter Island
Late Bloomers Garden Club, 2003, Jacksonville

Georgia
Cherokee Garden Club, 1956, Atlanta
Junior Ladies' Garden Club, 1958, Athens
Peachtree Garden Club, 1920, Atlanta
Sand Hills Garden Club, 1929, Augusta
Trustees' Garden Club, 1941, Savannah

Hawaii
Garden Club of Honolulu, 1932, Honolulu

Illinois
Garden Club of Barrington, 1940, Barrington
Garden Club of Evanston, 1921, Evanston
Garden Guild of Winnetka, 1949, Winnetka
Kenilworth Garden Club, 1923, Kenilworth
Lake Forest Garden Club, 1913, Lake Forest
Winnetka Garden Club, 1935, Winnetka

Indiana
Indianapolis Garden Club, 1939, Indianapolis

Iowa
Cedar Rapids Garden Club, 1956, Cedar Rapids
Des Moines Founders Garden Club, 1942, Des Moines

Kentucky
Garden Club of Lexington, 1924, Lexington
Glenview Garden Club, 1932, Louisville
Paducah Garden Club, 1929, Paducah

Louisiana
Garden Study Club of New Orleans, 1939, New Orleans
The Monroe Garden Study League, 1991, Monroe
New Orleans Town Gardeners, Inc., 1952, New Orleans
Shreveport Garden Study Club, 2008, Shreveport

Maine
Garden Club of Mount Desert, 1926, Mount Desert
Piscataqua Garden Club, 1930, York Harbor

Maryland
Amateur Gardeners Club, 1913, Baltimore
Catonsville Garden Club, 1952, Catonsville
Garden Club of Chevy Chase, 1955, Chevy Chase
Garden Club of Twenty, 1915, Baltimore
Green Spring Valley Garden Club, 1913, Garrison / Green Spring Valley
Halten Garden Club, 1927, Baltimore
Hardy Garden Club, 1920, Ruxton
St. George's Garden Club, 1938, Baltimore
Talbot County Garden Club, 2004, Baltimore

Massachusetts
Beacon Hill Garden Club, 1972, Boston
Berkshire Garden Club, 1921, Berkshire
Cambridge Plant and Garden Club, 1968, Cambridge
Chestnut Hill Garden Club, 1920, Chestnut Hill
Cohassett Garden Club, 1927, Cohasset
Fox Hill Garden Club, 1971, Dover
Garden Club of Buzzards Bay, 1935, New Bedford
The Lenox Garden Club, 1913, Lenox
Milton Garden Club, 1927, Milton
Nantucket Garden Club, 1966, Nantucket Island
Noanett Garden Club, 1923, Noanett
North Shore Garden Club of Massachusetts, 1931, Manchester by the Sea
Worcester Garden Club, 1928, Worcester

Michigan
Bay City Garden Club, 1954, Bay City
Garden Club of Michigan, 1913, Grosse Pointe

Minnesota
Lake Minnetonka Garden Club, 1929, Wayzata
St. Paul Garden Club, 1933, St. Paul

Mississippi
The Garden Club of Jackson, 2007, Jackson
Greenville Garden Club, 1951, Greenville
Laurel Garden Club, 1942, Laurel
Pilgrimage Garden Club, 1950, Natchez

Missouri
Garden Club of St. Louis, 1921, St. Louis
Ladue Garden Club, 1953, St. Louis
Westport Garden Club, 1956, Kansas City

Nebraska
Loveland Garden Club, 1997, Omaha

New Hampshire
Garden Club of Dublin, 1935, Dublin
Monadnock Garden Club, 1928, Swanzey

New Jersey
Garden Club of Englewood, 1923, Englewood
Garden Club of Madison, 1949, Chatham
Garden Club of Morristown, 1917, Morristown
The Garden Club of Princeton, 1913, Princeton
Garden Club of Somerset Hills, 1915, Somerset Hills
Garden Club of the Oranges, 1923, South Orange
Garden Club of Trenton, 1913, Trenton
Plainfield Garden Club, 1944, Plainfield
Rumson Garden Club, 1952, Rumson
Short Hills Garden Club, 1913, Short Hills
Summit Garden Club, 1920, Summit

New Mexico
Santa Fe Garden Club, 1982, Santa Fe

New York
Allyn's Creek Garden Club, 1937, Rochester
Bedford Garden Club, 1913, Bedford Hills
Essex County Adirondack Garden Club, 1933, Keene Valley
Fort Orange Garden Club, 1925, Albany
Garden Club of East Hampton, 1915, East Hampton

Garden Club of Irvington-on-Hudson, 1936, Irvington-on-Hudson
Garden Club of Lawrence, 1937, Lawrence
Garden Club of Orange and Duchess Counties, 1913, Warwick
Lake and Valley Garden Club, 1938, Cooperstown
The Little Garden Club of Rye, 1948, Rye
Millbrook Garden Club, 1915, Millbrook
North Country Garden Club of Long Island, 1914, Oyster Bay
North Suffolk Garden Club, 1931, Stony Brook
Philipstown Garden Club, 1918, Philipstown
Rochester Garden Club, 1925, Rochester
Rusticus Garden Club, 1952, Bedford
Rye Garden Club, 1915, Rye
Southampton Garden Club, 1937, Southampton
South Side Garden Club of Long Island, 1921, Islip
Stony Brook Garden Club, 1945, Stony Brook
Syracuse Garden Club, 1975, Syracuse
Three Harbors Garden Club, 1959, East Norwich
Ulster Garden Club, 1915, Kingston

North Carolina
French Broad River Garden Club, 1930, Asheville
Twin City Garden Club, 1951, Winston-Salem

Ohio
Akron Garden Club, 1945, Akron
Cincinnati Town & Country Garden Club, 1951, Cincinnati
Country Garden Club, 1942, Perrysburg
Garden Club of Cincinnati, 1914, Cincinnati
Garden Club of Cleveland, 1913, Cleveland
Garden Club of Dayton, 1926, Dayton
Little Garden Club of Columbus, 1994, Columbus
Shaker Lakes Garden Club, 1920, Cleveland

Oregon
Portland Garden Club, 1928, Portland

Pennsylvania
Carrie T. Watson Garden Club, 2008, Fairview
Four Counties Garden Club, 1924, Philadelphia
Garden Club of Allegheny County, 1916, Pittsburgh
Garden Club of Philadelphia, 1913, Philadelphia
The Gardeners, 1913, Philadelphia
The Garden Workers, 1969, Philadelphia
The Planters, 1938, Philadelphia
Providence Garden Club of Pennsylvania, 1946, Wallingford

Village Garden Club of Sewickley, 1961, Sewickley
The Weeders, 1913, Philadelphia
West Chester Garden Club, 1935, West Chester
Wissahickon Garden Club, 1942, Philadelphia

Rhode Island
Little Compton Garden Club, 1952, Little Compton
Newport Garden Club, 1914, Newport
Perennial Planters Garden Club, 1967, Providence
South County Garden Club of Rhode Island, 1924, Warwick

South Carolina
Carolina Foothills Garden Club, 1952, Greenville
Palmetto Garden Club, 1941, Columbia

Tennessee
Garden Club of Lookout Mountain, 1923, Chattanooga
Garden Club of Nashville, 1932, Nashville
Knoxville Garden Club, 1932, Knoxville
The Little Garden Club of Memphis, 1949, Memphis
Memphis Garden Club, 1925, Memphis

Texas
Alamo Heights–Terrell Hills Garden Club, 1978, San Antonio
Founders Garden Club of Dallas, 1940, Dallas
The Garden Club of Houston, 1932, Houston
The Gertrude Windsor Garden Club, 1974, Tyler
Magnolia Garden Club, 1949, Beaumont
River Oaks Garden Club, 1933, Houston

Vermont
Bennington Garden Club, 1928, Bennington

Virginia
Albemarle Garden Club, 1915, Charlottesville
The Augusta Garden Club, 1927, Staunton
Dolley Madison Garden Club, 1922, Orange
Fauquier & Loudoun Garden Club, 1918, Warrenton
Garden Club of Alexandria, 1955, Alexandria
Garden Club of Norfolk, 1922, Norfolk
James River Garden Club, 1920, Richmond
Mill Mountain Garden Club, 1957, Roanoke
Tuckahoe Garden Club of Westhampton, 1952, Westhampton
The Virginia Beach Garden Club, 1976, Virginia Beach
Warrenton Garden Club, 1913, Warrenton
Winchester-Clarke Garden Club, 1928, Winchester

Washington
Seattle Garden Club, 1923, Seattle
Tacoma Garden Club, 1928, Tacoma

Washington, D.C.
Georgetown Garden Club, 1955
Perennial Garden Club, 1960
The Trowel Club, 1955

West Virginia
Huntington Valley Garden Club, 1959, Huntington
Kanawha Garden Club, 1923, Charleston

Wisconsin
Green Tree Garden Club of Milwaukee, 1936, Milwaukee
Kettle Moraine Garden Club, 1964, Nashota
Lake Geneva Garden Club, 1920, Lake Geneva
Town and Country Garden Club, 1969, Sheboygan

Appendix 2

NATIONAL PRESIDENTS OF THE

GARDEN CLUB OF AMERICA

Mrs. J. Willis Martin (Elizabeth "Lizzie" Price), 1913–20

Mrs. S. R. V. Crosby (Henrietta Marion Grew), 1920–21

Mrs. Samuel Sloan (Katharine "Kitty" Colt), 1921–25

Mrs. John A. Stewart Jr. (Anne Thomas), 1925–29

Mrs. William A. Lockwood (Elizabeth Edwards), 1929–32

Mrs. Jonathan Bulkley (Sarah Tod), 1932–35

Mrs. Robert H. Fife (Sarah Gildersleeve), 1935–38

Mrs. Samuel Seabury (Maud Richey), 1938–41

Miss Aline Kate Fox, "Kate," 1941–44

Mrs. Harry T. Peters (Natalie Wells), 1944–47

Mrs. Hermann G. Place (Angela Moore), 1947–50

Mrs. Melvin E. Sawin (Edith Moulton), 1950–53

Mrs. Fergus Reid (Etheldreda "Edree" Seabury), 1953–56

Mrs. Randolph C. Harrison (Mary Hawes), 1956–59

Mrs. Charles D. Webster (Natalie Peters), 1959–62

Mrs. Erastus Corning II (Elizabeth "Betty" Platt), 1962–65

Mrs. Thomas M. Waller (Wilhelmina "Willie" Kirby), 1965–68

Mrs. Jerome K. Doolan (Elvira Broome), 1968– 71

Mrs. Frederick C. Tanner (Dorelle Moulton), 1971–73

Mrs. Nicholas R. du Pont (Genevieve "Bunny" L. Estes), 1973–75

Mrs. George P. Bissell Jr. (Georgina "Gina" Miller), 1975–77

Mrs. Benjamin M. Belcher (Nancy Knapp), 1977–79

Mrs. R. Henry Norweb Jr. (Elizabeth Gardner), 1979–81

Mrs. Samuel M. Beattie (Catherine "Kay" Hamrick), 1981–83

Mrs. Niels W. Johnsen (Millicent Mercer), 1983–85

Mrs. Frank M. Donahue (Katherine "Kay" Haley), 1985–87

Mrs. Charles G. Ward Jr. (Jane Downing), 1987–89

Mrs. Edward A. Blackburn Jr. (Sadie Gwin Allen, "Sadie Gwin"), 1989–91

Mrs. Sellers J. Thomas (Nancy Stallworth), 1991–93

Mrs. Robert W. Freitag (Christine "Chris" Dietrich), 1993–95

Mrs. Richardson Pratt Jr. (Mary "Jan" Offett), 1995–97

Mrs. Alan M. Willemsen (Christine "Chris" Schroeder), 1997–99

Mrs. Frederik C. Hansen Jr. (Barbara "Bobbie" Pettit), 1999–2001

Mrs. Joseph C. Frierson Jr. (Ann Smith), 2001–3

Mrs. David L. Ferguson (Katharine "Kitty" Crowninshield), 2003–5

Mrs. Robert C. H. Mathews Jr. (Alice Casey), 2005–7

Mrs. Samuel Garre III (Maryjo Simjian), 2007–9

Mrs. George J. Harris (Joan Marie Hogg), 2009–11

Mrs. Benjamin A. Hill (Marian Weldon), 2011–13

Chapter 1: The Founding Generation

1. Elizabeth Martin, "History of the Garden Club of America since Its Founding in May 1913," *Bulletin of the Garden Club of America* (hereafter cited as *Bulletin*), July 1920, 2–7; Ernestine Goodman, "The Garden Club of America: History 1913–1938," *Bulletin*, November 1938, 22–96.

2. Quoted phrase from Alice Morse Earle, *Old Time Gardens* (New York: Macmillan Company, 1901), 4–41.

3. As with nearly all biographical details in this book, the information on Miss Goodman is found in many local sources and not least the *Bulletin*'s obituaries and others on her death on January 19, 1952. Her social and civic involvements are occasionally unearthed in Philadelphia newspapers or reports on the projects themselves. Again, as with all the players in this history, some are easier to trace than others. Mrs. Martin, for example, was Philadelphia's main woman civic leader, so articles about or referring to her and her husband, Judge Martin, are numerous. Relatively few directly involve the GCA, but they are useful in a general way.

4. Martin, "History," 6–7.

5. Ibid., 3–5; minutes of meetings, April 30 and May 1, 1913, Garden Club of America Archive (located in the headquarters in New York City; hereafter cited as GCA Archive).

6. Original statement by Ernestine Goodman, GCA Archives; see also Goodman, "The Garden Club of America," 23–24.

7. Martin, "History," 3–4; Ellen P. Williams "Notes Taken at the Meeting of Garden Clubs April 30, 1913," ms., GCA Archive; "List of Those Present at the Foundation Meeting of the Garden Club of America, April 10, 1913, Philadelphia," typescript, GCA Archive.

8. *Bulletin*, first issue, n.d. [1913].

9. *Bulletin*, September 1917, 22–24.

10. Martin, "History," 9.

11. Minutes, May 22, 1914.

12. Wilson's neutrality speech to the 63rd U.S. Congress, August 20, 1914.

13. Martin, "History," 6.

14. Ibid., 6–7.

15. Ibid., 7.

16. Goodman, "The Garden Club of America," 24–25.

17. Elizabeth Martin to the membership, Philadelphia, July 27, 1917, GCA Archive.

18. Goodman, "The Garden Club of America," 27.

19. See Stephanie A. Carpenter, *On the Farm Front: The Women's Land Army in World War I* (DeKalb,: Northern Illinois University Press, 2003).

20. Kate Brewster quoted in Goodman, "The Garden Club of America," 22.

21. Marjorie Gibbon Battles and Catherine Colt Dickey, *Fifty Blooming Years: The Garden Club of America, 1913–1963* (New York: Garden Club of America, 1963).

22. Goodman, "The Garden Club of America," 28.

23. Minutes, June 13, 1917.

24. Kate Brewster, editorial in *Bulletin*, November 1919.

Chapter 2: The GCA Defines Itself

1. Goodman, "The Fifth Annual Meeting," in "The Garden Club of America: History 1913–1938," *Bulletin,* November 1938, 23–24; minutes, June 13, 1917, GCA Archive; *Bulletin,* November 1919, 42.

2. Martha Hutcheson, "A Wider Program for Garden Clubs," 1919, GCA Archive.

3. Minutes, June 17, 1919.

4. See Robin Karson, *Fletcher Steele, Landscape Architect: An Account of the Garden-maker's Life, 1885–1971* (New York: Harry N. Abrams, 1989).

5. Minutes, [November?] 1916.

6. See minutes, November 14, 1923.

7. The billboard issue was introduced to the GCA in its founding year, 1913. In that year the American Association of Highway Improvement (founded in 1911) reported 1,258,060 automobiles on the as-yet-sparse paved roads and highways in America. The GCA established the Billboard Committee on November 12, 1923.

8. This is not to imply that the Garden Club of America burned billboards. There was a very strong local protest against billboards in the New York City environs, both in Westchester County and in the Bronx, leading to burnings. See the *New York Times,* November 21, 1920, for a billboard burning in the latter site; also see Catherine Gudis, *Billboards, Automobiles, and the American Landscape* (New York: Routledge, 2004), for a description of the war and its "dynamics of gender," women opposing the advertisers they called the "billboard boys." As for the chauffeur chopping down the billboards, many have claimed the honor, but for present purposes, this history will accept the claim of the Garden Club of Allegheny County, Pennsylvania, as posted on its Web site.

9. "Eighth Annual Meeting Report," May 10, 1921; and minutes, January, March, May 1921, mention reports from the Wildflower Committee, but the original reports appear to be lost.

10. *Bulletin,* May 1922, 267; minutes, January 9, 1922.

11. "Suggestion for Letters That Might Be Sent to Individuals or Officers of Local Clubs and Organizations," typescript, n.d., GCA Archive.

12. This is well covered in the minutes of 1922–24 and indeed to 1933; it is compiled in Betty Pinkerton, *The Conservation Committee History, 75 Years, 1924–1999: The Garden Club of America* (New York: Garden Club of America, 1999), 7–18 and passim.

13. Harriet Barnes Pratt's papers are not abundant, but a substantial collection is housed in the Office of the Curator, the White House, Washington, D.C., and like the other leaders in the GCA, various reports, letters, and references are found in the *Bulletin*, minutes, and files in the GCA Archive. The absence of personal papers for most of these women is lamentable. Today past presidents are solicited by GCA Archive for their papers, but to date the harvest is slim.

14. This account comes from Harriet Pratt herself in a 1950 letter to Mrs. Nightingale, GCA Archive; also see *Bulletin*, July 1947, 19.

15. Minutes, October 1924.

16. *New York Times*, April 26, 1916.

17. Minutes, December 1926.

18. When the two Fifth Avenue hotels the Waldorf and the Astoria were joined in 1897, they were connected by a bridge corridor. This bridge was commemorated in the name by using an equal sign between "Waldorf" and "Astoria." The symbol was retained when the hotel moved from Fifth to a new building on Park Avenue in 1931 but was gradually replaced by a hyphen after World War II.

19. The models presented to the Smithsonian were on display there until 1946, when they were deaccessioned because of their deteriorated condition. They were then transferred to the architecture school at Catholic University in Washington. For their transfer to the Smithsonian, see Horace W. Peaslee to Mrs. William A. Lockwood, Washington, D.C., November 2, 1925, GCA Archive. For their removal to Catholic University, see Rev. James A. Magner, treasurer, Catholic University, to the Smithsonian, November 12, 1946, Smithsonian Archive.

20. Scrapbooks of the International Flower Show, GCA Archive.

21. Minutes, October 10, 1928.

22. *Bulletin*, March 21, 1928.

23. The whole run of the *Bulletin* is available online.

24. Charles Scribner to Alice Lockwood, New York, March 21, 1932, GCA Archive.

25. Both volumes of *The Gardens of Colony and State* were republished by the GCA and the University of Pennsylvania Press in 2000.

26. The last issue of the *Almanac* appeared on February 11, 1931.

27. Louisa King greatly aided the British landscape designer Gertrude Jekyll (1843–1932) in Jekyll's later years. The two, having worked in designing King's garden and probably others, were close friends. When Jekyll's fortunes shrank after World War I, Mrs. King stood by her. Gertrude Jekyll wrote a series of articles for the *Bulletin* through the 1920s for a hundred dollars each, for which Mrs. King privately reimbursed the GCA. They remain articles of great interest for the philosophy expressed in them. Some of Gertrude Jekyll's papers can be found in the GCA Archive.

28. Margaret McPherson, *How to Stage a Flower Show*, brochure, 1926 and subsequent editions published by the GCA, GCA Archive.

29. *Bulletin,* November 1919.

30. Louise du Pont Crowninshield's papers are extensive and housed at the Hagley Museum and Library, in Wilmington, Delaware.

31. This pamphlet was sent out with the March 1924 issue of the *Bulletin,* copy in the Louise du Pont Crowninshield Papers, Hagley Museum and Library.

32. Minutes, May 12, 1925.

33. Ibid.; Dr. Lee J. Strong, address to the Quarantine Committee of the GCA, January 11, 1939, GCA Archive.

34. Minutes, November 10, 1925.

35. Carol Stoddard, "A Fond Look at Margorie Sale Arundel, a GCA Legend," *Bulletin,* December 2010–January 2011; *Trillium undulatum* has been on the Endangered Species List of the U.S. Fish and Game Service in three different states since 1988.

Chapter 3: Policies

1. In that the zone partitioning required a change in the by-laws, those who favored it worked toward the change in advance, one supposes privately, leaving no record as yet to be found. See minutes, January 14, March 18, and April 8, 1931; and the presentation on January 13, 1932.

2. Minutes, January 13, 1932.

3. Executive Committee minutes, October ?, 1922.

4. The issue that might be called the "GCA and the eyes of the world" was a strong and lingering one. It appeared several times at early stages but never more emphatically than at the annual meeting in Detroit in 1924, where all public involvement was questioned, even sending letters of support to good causes. The board became sensitive to the issue and turned down many invitations to join outside projects. For example, in 1924 Mrs. Herbert Hoover's request that the GCA sponsor gardening with the Girl Scouts of America was gently rejected; also, the board declined to share in the restoration of George Washington's ancestral home, Sulgrave Manor, in England, and Thomas Jefferson's Monticello, in Virginia. Other projects and events met with the same refusal. In every instance, becoming partners with other organizations on such a high-profile level made the board hesitate. The hesitation was purely practical, in the interest of preserving what the GCA had as an organization. In 1924 the Executive Committee established rules to govern this sort of participation. More will be seen of this later.

5. Minutes, February 11, 1931.

6. Members-at-large were established as "associate members" in 1916 and were soon renamed. While records do not say so, this type of membership may have been a means by which men could join the GCA. At the annual meeting in Richmond in 1924 the admissions report noted two hundred of members-at-large status and feared that they were "fast encroaching upon the club membership and should be curbed." There were then forty-two hundred members in the GCA, and members-at-large were nominated by the individual clubs and the Executive Committee. Report, April 23, 1924, GCA Archive.

At the board meeting January 12, 1927, a men's advisory was approved for the GCA; at the next meeting, February 8, after some debate, it was decided to list the three men's names on the letterhead.

7. Mrs. Lansdale, a member-at-large in the GCA, presented the idea of a GCA redwood grove at the July 1930 annual meeting in Seattle, but the die was cast already with the organization. Mrs. John A. Stewart had taken the chairmanship of a Redwood Committee more than a year before and by the previous February had already raised $83,728.92. Working with Mrs. Lansdale, whom she called her "inspiration," she benefited from Mrs. Lansdale's broad previous experience with Save the Redwoods League.

8. *Bulletin,* December 10, 1931, and Summer 1982. After 1931 the redwoods were to become a staple in GCA committee and board business for decades to follow, as the GCA commitment enlarged.

9. *Bulletin,* Summer 1982; also see Joanne Lenden, "Redwoods: Timeline and Bibliography," 2001, GCA Archive.

10. Minutes, October 8 and November 12, 1923. The substance of the discussion is all that survives, but it was extensive, footed in the old idea of the GCA's presenting a gentler, more aloof face to the public and avoiding controversy. Neither Mrs. Noyes nor Mrs. Harrison seemed to care, although they must have found the new title a little apart from the subject.

11. See Richard Longstreth, ed., *The Mall in Washington, 1791–1991* (Washington DC: National Gallery of Art, 1991), 79–141.

12. Minutes, December 8, 1925.

13. Minutes, September 9, 1925.

14. Minutes, January 14, 1931.

15. Minutes, November 9, 1932; committee report, December 10, 1931, GCA Archive.

16. James M. Goode, *Capital Lossses: A Cultural History of Washington's Destroyed Buildings* (Washington DC: Smithsonian Institution Press, 1979), 298–99, details the fortunes of the War Department columns, set up at Arlington Cemetery in the 1870s as commemorative gates. They stood until 1971, when, disassembled in pieces, they were discarded in a woods area adjacent to the cemetery. The only columns Grant and Mrs. Noyes could have been dealing with were those from the old State Department, torn down in 1866 to make way for expansion of the U.S. Treasury Building. The GCA's other Washington project at this time was to participate in the erection of granite landmarks that defined the original boundaries of the federal district as established in 1792.

17. Minutes, December 15, 1933.

18. Minutes, January 11, 1928.

19. I shall not attempt to document my opinion in any detailed way but only say that after a thorough reading of the minutes and the *Bulletin* for the first quarter century of the GCA, I found the ideas expressed in the texts to be quite evident.

20. John Russell Pope, quoted in Charles Moore, *The Life and Times of Charles Follen McKim* (Boston: Houghton Mifflin Company, 1929), 150.

21. Minutes, May 12 and June 11, 1925. See also Gorham P. Stevens, director, to Mrs.

Harrison, American Academy in Rome, April 3, 1925, and other letters relevant to the early days of the fellowship, GCA Archive.

22. Minutes, May 12 and June 11, 1925.

23. Gorham P. Stevens to Mrs. Harrison, American Academy in Rome, April 3, 1925, GCA Archive.

24. Minutes, January 12, 1927.

25. Minutes, May 14, 1930.

26. Henrietta Maria Stout (Mrs. Charles H. Stout) was active in horticultural pursuits from the early 1900s until World War II. An expert on the dahlia, she published on her favorite flower and promoted its use in gardens. Marilyn Worseldine is a graphic artist with a Georgetown, D.C., studio, Market Sights, which opened in 1976.

27. The history of the medals at this time is well chronicled in the minutes for the relevant years and in articles in the *Bulletin*.

28. Minutes, April 10, 1935.

29. Minutes, October 8, 1986, January 8, 1936.

30. Minutes, April 13, 1938.

31. Alice Lockwood wrote a day-by-day report and kept scrapbooks on the first GCA Visiting Gardens trip in 1929; Marion M. Davison published a lively account of the 1935 tour to Japan, also supported by scrapbook pictures; a transcript was made of the 1939 trip to England; all in the GCA Archive. The GCA Archive also houses an excellent and detailed diary of a GCA tour of Mexico kept by Anne Burrage, a GCA director from Massachusetts. Most Visiting Gardens trips were covered briefly in the *Bulletin,* and some useful articles also came from information gleaned on trips. In general, however, there has been little comprehensive coverage of GCA tours, except that which is scattered through personal scrapbooks and collections through the generations of participants.

32. Sarah Bulkley's scrapbook records the trip to Japan in numerous photographs, notes, and mementos. The collection also contains the text of her radio address to the Japanese people. GCA Archive.

Chapter 4: Coming of Age

1. Minutes, July 8, 1930.

2. Minutes, March 19, 1940.

3. Minutes, February 13, 1941; *New York Times,* January 19, 1941.

4. Ibid.

5. Minutes, January 8, 1941.

6. Minutes, April 9, 1941.

7. Edith Kohlsaat, "Zones Ask What Can We Do to Help?" *Bulletin,* January 8, 1941.

8. Ibid.

9. *Bulletin,* December 1942, 8.

10. *New York Herald Tribune,* December 31, 1939; Margaret Anne Tockarshewsky, "Lost Flowers of the Fair," Queens Botanical Garden Archives, Queens, New York,

available at Queens Botanical Garden Web site; "World's Fair Edition" of the *New York Times*, April 30, 1939.

11. Eleanor Roosevelt, "My Day," *New York Herald Tribune*, June 13, 1940.

12. A partial record of the activities of the individual clubs can be gleaned from the wartime minutes and the relatively few histories we have of member clubs. I am left with an impression that the GCA participation was far more significant than the scant records suggest.

13. *Bulletin*, December 1942, 14.

14. Kate Fox, "The Garden Club of America in relation to War Emergency," *Bulletin*, January 1942, 2–4.

15. Minutes, December 10, 1941.

16. M. L. Wilson, assistant director, Department of Defense, to Miss Fox, Washington, D.C. [December 1941?], GCA Archive; also see minutes, January 14, 1942.

17. *Bulletin*, January 1942, 35–37.

18. Minutes, January 14, 1942.

19. The exhibit was reduced in size for travel elsewhere. Minutes, February 10, 1943; see also *Bulletin*, December 1942, 8.

20. Minutes, June 10, 1942.

21. Minutes, October 9, 1940.

22. Minutes, February 19, 1941, and December 12, 1942.

23. Minutes, December 12, 1942.

24. Ibid.

25. Dorothy Falcon Platt, "Annual Report to the Garden Club of Philadelphia," October 1944, GCA Archive.

26. *Bulletin*, January 14, 1942.

27. *Bulletin*, December 1942, 14.

28. Minutes, June 10, 1942.

29. Minutes, June 10, 1942, and January 10, 1945, as reported by Sarah Fife.

30. Minutes, July 8, 1942.

31. David Swain to his mother, [Des Moines?] Iowa, January 10, 1945, GCA Archive.

32. Mrs. Tileston, memorandum, copy, n.d., GCA Archive.

33. Minutes, December 13, 1944.

Chapter 5: The Horticulturists

1. *Bulletin*, May 1943, 32–33.

2. Lantern slides taken of the Crystal Palace Exhibition are in the GCA Archive.

3. Robert C. Post, ed., *1876: A Centennial Exhibition* (Washington DC: National Museum of History and Technology, Smithsonian Institution, 1976), 66–73; see also, J. S. Ingram, *The Centennial Exposition: Described and Illustrated* (Philadelphia: Hubbard Bros., 1976); and John Maass, *The Glorious Enterprise: The Centennial Exposition of 1876* (Watkins Glen, NY: American Life Foundation, 1973).

4. Minutes, May 16, 1946, GCA Archive.

5. The two prongs of interest within this committee become evident in the minutes beginning in 1922; in January 1925 the Subcommittee on Quarantines presented its essay "Plant Quarantine Policies and World Progress," which was printed in the March issue of the *Bulletin*. Meanwhile, both the minutes and the *Bulletin* chronicle a still-dominant interest in plants and their propagation on the part of the Conservation Committee.

6. Minutes, January 9, December 11, 1935; see Dr. Lee A. Strong, report [January 11, 1939], GCA Archive.

7. Minutes, January 11 and February 8, 1939.

8. Minutes, October 9, 1940; Emma Thatcher, report, October 1940.

9. Minutes, October 11, 1944.

10. Minutes, December 11, 1946, and November 19, 1947.

11. Mrs. Allinson, "Report on United Horticulture," 1946, GCA Archive; minutes, December 11, 1946.

12. Minutes, October 8, 1947, January 14, 1948, November 16, 1949.

13. Minutes, December 10, 1947.

14. Minutes, February 10, 1925.

15. Minutes, April 11, 1928.

16. Mrs. Donald H. McGraw, "The Interchange Fellowship," October 5, 1994, GCA Archive; "History of the Garden Club of America Fellowships," n.d., GCA Archive, and noted in minutes, January 10, 1967.

17. Minutes, February 10 and March 10, 1982; October 12 and December 7, 1983; February 8, 1984. See also "A History of Fellowships in the Garden Club of America," typescript, January 10, 1968, GCA Archive.

18. Minutes, February 10, 1960, and June 13, 1973.

19. Mrs. Edward King Poor III, "Plants That Merit Attention," Report to the Board, March 22, 1982, GCA Archive.

20. Mrs. Edward King Poor III, "Plants That Merit Attention," report to the board, March 22, 1982, GCA Archive.

21. Minutes, March 10, 1971; see also papers related to the nursery issue, GCA Archive.

22. Minutes, April 3, 1952; horticultural scholarship files, GCA Archive.

23. "Alice Ires, 89, Dies," *New York Times,* December 17, 2000.

24. The Committee for the National Capital became the National Affairs Committee and at this writing is the National Affairs and Legislation Committee.

25. Minutes, March 8, 2000; "The Butterfly Habitat Garden," report, 1999, GCA Archive.

26. Bobbie Hansen to Nancy Murray, memorandum, November 1, 2010, GCA Archive.

27. Author interviews with Nan King, October 17 and November 10, 2010, GCA Archive.

28. Louise Wrinkle, "Report to the Board," February 11, 1987, GCA Archive; Nancy

Thomas, "Report to the Board from the Horticulture Committee," June 10, 1987, GCA Archive.

29. Mrs. Alan Willemsen, report, October 9, 1991, GCA Archive.

30. Minutes, March 6, 1998. Reports of some of the regional committees are found in the GCA Archive.

31. Philadelphia Committee, report, March 6, 1998, GCA Archive.

32. Minutes, December 4, 1991.

33. Mrs. Henry S. Streeter, report, "National Projects," March 1988, GCA Archive.

34. Minutes, December 4, 1991.

Chapter 6: The Flower Arrangers

1. Jessie Benton Fremont, *Souvenirs of My Time* (Boston: D. Lothrop and Company, 1887), 95.

2. The actual establishment of the Art Committee was in the summer of 1922. It first appears in the October 9, 1922 minutes. Mrs. Lockwood's Flower Show Committee was already at work a year before. See *Bulletin* July 1922.

3. Minutes, December 8, 1926, and October 10, 1928.

4. The term *applied art* was often used in the 1920s and 1930s to mean art in practical use, such as decorative arts. Thus, applied art was different from "fine art," which was "art for art's sake." For enough flexibility to allow for many entries, the flower show classes were under the umbrella of applied art and not as specific as the fine art would be.

5. Minutes, December 14, 1932.

6. Minutes, October 10, 1945.

7. Minutes, January 9 and November 13, 1946.

8. *Bulletin*, February 1985, 32–33; Greenwich Garden Club, news release, "Mrs. Yoneo Arai," September 1967; Polly Moore and Lynda Chase, eds., *A History of the Des Moines Founders Garden Club, the Garden Club of America, Des Moines, Iowa* (Des Moines: Des Moines Founders Garden Club, 2008), 15, 23.

9. *New York Times*, March 19, 1952.

10. Minutes, February 9, 1955.

11. Minutes, December 12, 1956; Mrs. Reynolds's committee report, fall 1956, GCA Archive.

12. The flower-arranging rules were first published in the *Bulletin*, March 1957, then published separately in 1961 as *The Flower Show Judging Guide* and were available from headquarters and the Flower Show Committee.

13. Minutes, October 14, 1959; author interview with Mrs. David B. Martin, October 19, 2010, GCA Archive.

14. "Commercial Appeal," clipping, October ?, 1959, GCA Archive.

15. Minutes, February 10, 1960.

16. This process was designed at the Memphis meeting in 1959.

17. Elvira Doolan, "Report of the Flower Show Committee," minutes, May 10, 1967.

18. Participation in the International Flower Show is documented rather thoroughly with photographs and some text in scrapbooks, GCA Archive.

19. Minutes, October 11, 1978.

20. Bonny Martin, report, March 5, 1997, GCA Archive.

21. Minutes, February 9, 1972

22. Author interviews with Arabella Dane, by telephone, May 10, 2009, and in person, July 17, 2010.

23. Author interview with Arabella Dane, May 10, 2010.

24. Author interview with Penny Horne, June 12, 2010.

25. Minutes, March 5 and December 10, 1997; quotations from the latter minutes.

26. Mrs. Samuel Garre III, report on photography, October 8, 1997, GCA Archive.

27. Minutes, March 5, 2003. The chair of the Photography Committee was to be a member of the Flower Show Judging Committee.

28. Author interview with Bonny Martin, October 21, 2010, GCA Archive.

Chapter 7: The Conservationists

1. Minutes, December 12, 1924.

2. Fanny Farwell to the board, December 12, 1924, GCA Archive.

3. Photo of advertisement napkin, GCA Archive. Mrs. Farwell sold twenty-nine thousand of these napkins.

4. Mary Vaux Walcott, *North American Wildflowers* (Washington DC: Smithsonian Institution, 1925).

5. Minutes, November 19, 1924; copy of Rev. Reiland letter, GCA Archive.

6. See copy of original in GCA Archive.

7. Minutes, October 10, 1928.

8. Minutes, October 10 and November 14, 1928.

9. Minutes, October 10, 1928.

10. Minutes, January 8, 1930.

11. Stephen Trimble, *Desert Reflections: Joshua Tree National Park* (Joshua Tree National Park Association, 1979), 37–40; *Bulletin,* March 1928.

12. Minutes, December 14, 1932.

13. Minutes, January 9 and March 20, 1935.

14. Minutes, February 10, 1937.

15. Minutes, December 14, 1938.

16. *Bulletin,* December 1942, 40.

17. Minutes, June 12, 1946.

18. Minutes, March 23, 1947.

19. *Bulletin,* December 1942, 3.

20. Minutes, April 9, 1958.

21. Minutes, October 14, 1959.

22. Minutes, April 9, 1958.

23. Minutes, April 9, 1959.

24. There are other claimants to inventing the term *litterbug*, but Louise McKeon is usually the accepted creator. Other adaptations of "litter" were current in the 1960s, including a GCA brochure entitled "Annie Doesn't Litter Anymore."

25. Betty Pinkerton, *The Conservation Committee History, 75 Years, 1924–1999: The Garden Club of America* (New York: Garden Club of America, 1999), 22–24.

26. Minutes, March 12, 1958, and January 13, 1960; "Student Conservation Program," report, n.d., GCA Archive.

27. See Garden Club of Palm Beach, *The Plan of Palm Beach: Prepared under the Direction of the Garden Club of Palm Beach Approved by the Town Council* (Chicago: Bennett, Parsons & Frost, Consulting Architects, 1929).

28. Executive Committee minutes, December 3, 1954, cited in Pinkerton, *The Conservation Committee History*, 23–24.

29. Minutes, December 9, 1953. Denunciation of the Army Corps of Engineers was fairly continual from the 1930s onward but occurred especially frequently in the 1950s and 1960s with the building of the great dams that blocked rivers in many states. The GCA always opposed those dams as destructive to a region's ecology and natural beauty; moreover, they claimed, not without validity, that private economic gain was the real source of most of the projects.

30. Minutes, December 14, 1955; Mrs. Taylor's report, GCA Archive.

31. Minutes, June 10, 1959, January 13, 1960, and November 15, 1961.

32. Minutes, February 13, 1963. The war against the atomic energy plant at Bodega Bay produced some flamboyant "heroines" on the conservation scene: Rose Gaffney, a passionate landowner who lived near the proposed plant site; Hazel Mitchell, who was a café waitress; and Professor Doris Sloan, from the University of California, Berkeley, all of whom worked closely with the GCA.

33. George Avery, "Remarks," Waldorf=Astoria Hotel, New York, November 13, 1963, copy in GCA Archive.

34. Minutes, June 10, 1964.

35. Minutes, February 10, 1965.

36. Minutes, May 10, 1967.

37. The McMillan Plan was a vast master plan for the modernization and redesign of monumental Washington, produced in 1902 by architects working under Senator James McMillan's Senate Parks Committee. The official document on this plan is Charles Moore, ed., *The Improvement of the Park System of the District of Columbia*, 57th Congress, 1st session, 1902. See also Thomas Hines, "The Imperial Mall: The City Beautiful Movement and the Washington Plan of 1901–1902," in *The Mall in Washington, 1791–1991*, ed. Richard Longstreth (Washington DC: National Gallery of Art, 1991), 79–99.

38. Dr. Norman Borlaug, a Nobel scientist, denounced environmentalists before the United Nations, comparing them to "boll weevils and locusts as new farm pests." He predicted, "The world would starve to death if there were a return to organic farming."

When the Conservation Committee reported this to the GCA it noted that Borlaug even endorsed the use of DDT. His support for these products was in the context of the need for their quick work in third world countries, not in the United States.

39. Minutes, March 20, November 21, and December 10, 1969. President Nixon signed the Endangered Species Act in 1969 and by that time had committed to banning DDT and to an "airport act" that would end a Florida airport project that was threatening the Everglades.

40. Elizabeth Glore, "Report to the Board of Directors," February 20, 1982, GCA Archives.

41. Minutes, November 10, 1982, statement of Elizabeth Glore, minutes, November 11, 1982.

42. Minutes, March 9, 1983; copies of instructions, GCA Archive.

43. Minutes, March 13, 1986.

44. Pinkerton, *The Conservation Committee History,* 63–66; minutes, December 9, 1992, March 6, 1996.

45. Minutes, March 8, 1995.

46. Minutes, March 9, 1979, and March 9, 2005.

Chapter 8: Centennial

1. Mercer O'Hara, reminiscence of the event, n.d., GCA Archive.

2. Pamela Jeanes, reminiscence of the event, n.c., GCA Archive.

3. Ann Frierson, address, [misdated March 5, 2003], typescript, GCA Archive.

4. See long-range planning reports, GCA Archive.

5. Minutes, October 8, 1947.

6. Minutes, November 13, 1968.

7. Mrs. Benkard's historical wallpaper, mounted directly onto the plaster wall, proved too costly for the GCA to even attempt to rescue. Concerned about preserving the paper, Barbara Hinrichs, who was in charge, determined to donate it to someone willing to go to the labor and expense of removing it, and it was accordingly rescued in December 1997. See Barbara B. Hinrichs, "The Palais Royal Paper," report, December ?, 1997, GCA Archive.

8. Minutes, June 8, 1994.

9. When a new kitchen was completed in 1998, Mrs. Peter Moffitt said to the Hospitality Committee, "If you're happy, we're happy!" Minutes, June 2, 1998.

10. Several thefts of office machinery recommended the bolting of the typewriters to the desks. Mrs. Martin made her plea at an Executive Committee meeting, Philadelphia, n.d., June 1915.

11. Nancy Thomas, report, June 9, 1993, GCA Archive.

12. Minutes, June 7, 2000. Linda Payne, report on office technology, May 2000, GCA Archive.

13. Minutes, December 8, 1998.

14. Minutes, March 6, 2002.

15. Minutes, March 7, 2001; Archive Room papers file, GCA Archive.

16. Lenden, reports to the board, GCA Archive. At a board meeting on March 9, 1994, Mrs. Henry U. Harris Jr. said, "As of March 7 at 11:00 A.M. we are happy to announce that an Archive Restoration Fund has been launched!" This was set up to bring out, process, microfilm, and preserve the boxes of papers randomly kept in the basement of the office building. Mary Jeanne Harris's husband Henry funded the Archive room in her honor.

17. Eleanor Weller, a member of the Library Committee, called the lantern slides "a gold mine of landscape design and garden history." See minutes, March 9, 1994.

18. Minutes, March 9, 1994.

19. Edie Leoning in conversation with the author, September 5, 2011.

20. *Partners for Plants* brochure, n.d., GCA Archive.

21. Rae Selling Berry Botanical Garden, tourist brochure, n.d., GCA Archive.

22. Text of Founders Fund Award, 1994, GCA Archive.

23. Providence Children's Museum, text of Founders Fund Award, 1999, GCA Archive.

24. The mission statement was edited and enlarged in 1981 to accommodate the GCA's more proactive approach to public issues. Minor change in the interest of brevity had been made in 1973. Little record of discussions involving either revision survives in the board or Executive Committee minutes. The later alterations were made in the Policy Committee on October 13, 1981, and the result is the mission statement today. See relevant notes and papers from the October meeting 1981, Emma Henry Tomkins Matheson Papers, GCA Archive; and Laura Gregg to author, e-mail, September 19, 2010, GCA Archive..

25. Natasha Hopkinson to the author, e-mail, October 28, 2011, GCA Archive.

26. Emma Henry Tomkins Matheson Papers, GCA Archive.

27. Author telephone interview with Leslie Purple and e-mail correspondence with Leslie Purple and Laura Gregg, variously in October and November 2010.

A Note on the Sources

Only in recent years has the Garden Club of America moved to assemble a formally managed archive. The development of this aspect of the national organization is described in the text. Notwithstanding the former absence of archival management, documents that must be kept, as with any business, have survived largely intact since the start. The spine of this history is the minutes of the board of directors meetings and the minutes of the Executive Committee. The board's minutes can be said to be complete from 1913, several thousand pages in typescript, whereas the executive minutes, often kept as summations and in less detail, have gaps. To both, this work is deeply indebted.

In addition to these voluminous papers are committee reports, some correspondence, and reports from various projects. The *Bulletin of the Garden Club of America*, established by Elizabeth Martin soon after the founding, has continued through the century to today. The *Bulletin* as commenced and continued for its first half century was more a journal than the name suggests. In it one found monographs, firsthand accounts, obituaries, and other materials of use to the historian. The *Bulletin* today is also useful but in a different way, as a printed medium of communication to all the clubs that compose the GCA.

Individual characters sometimes have been difficult to trace. A few I could not find in sufficient detail to give complete names in the text. In one or two cases I had to resort to gravestones for information. In the main I have gone to state and local historical societies to trace those I could not find in GCA records, where, at least in the early years, no first names were used, only "Mrs. ____" or "Miss ____." Relevant local newspapers had to be searched; pay dirt might be found in a wedding announcement or a husband's obituary. Personal papers of the various players have been rare, but there are bright spots, and I think this will increase with the greater visibility of the GCA Archive. All the usual ancillary sources have been consulted, such as newspapers and congressional reports. I have gone to the clubs where particular information was needed about an event or personality. Their historical papers are usually spotty, sometimes scrapbooks only, yet at certain points a scrapbook can be useful as well. A few clubs have regular archives, such as the Garden Club of Philadelphia with its excellent collection at the Pennsylvania Historical Society. These are the exceptions, but now that the GCA's national headquarters has an archive, clubs have begun sending papers to New York. Others seek local colleges and city libraries as their repositories. All two hundred clubs are already represented in the GCA Archive, in one way or another.

Several histories of the national organization have gone before this one, and while they are named in the notes, I also want to acknowledge them here. Elizabeth Martin's "History of the Garden Club of America since Its Founding in May 1913," appeared in the *Bulletin* in 1920, followed in that same journal eighteen years later by Ernestine Goodman's *The Garden Club of America: History 1913–1938*. For the half-century anniversary Marjorie Gibbon Battles and Catherine Colt Dickey published *Fifty Blooming Years: The Garden Club of America, 1963*. Diana Morgan Olcott published *Winds of Change: 75th Anniversary Chronicle 1963–1988*. Betty Pinkerton's *The Conservation Committee History, 75 Years, 1924–1999*, belongs with those above as a basic source. These books and articles have been at my side for the duration of this project. The very few club histories that exist have been assembled as well for specific inquiry. Their number is increasing, and it is hoped more will appear.

The usual source-by-source bibliographical listing has been omitted. Where a reference seems to me necessary an endnote is supplied. When material comes from reports or minutes, the date in which it occurs in the narrative will indicate its location in the GCA Archive.

Index

Garden Club of Nashville (TN), 205
Garden Club of New Bedford (MA), 101
Garden Club of Palm Beach (FL), 173
Garden Club of Philadelphia (PA), 1, 3, 4,
  62, 79, 90–91, 101–102
Garden Club of St. Louis (MO), 50
Garden Club of Somerset Hills (NJ), 202
Garden Club of Virginia, 36–37, 77
Garden Club of Wilmington (DE), 76,
  89–90
garden clubs, 3, 13, 18, 22, 40. *see also*
  member clubs
garden design, 5, 8, 42, 61, 106–107,
  117–118, 123. *see also* landscape
  architecture/design
gardener, public perception of, 42
The Garden Guild, 4, 5. *see also* Garden
  Club of America
gardening, public perception of, 63
gardens: butterfly, 121; "colonial," 2,
  4, 110–111; emotional role during
  wartime, 14, 79–80, 91, 190; fragrance
  and sensory, 120, 202; "gardens of
  distinction," 49–50, 98; historic,
  17, 36–37, 110–111, 202–203, 206;
  humanitarian projects, 201–202; ivy,
  120–121; Japanese, 167, 168; *Locator,*
  67; models created for flower shows,
  32–33, 40, 120–121; naturalistic, 40;
  peace, 75; prison, 202; public, 19, 202,
  205 (*see also* landscape architecture/
  design, civic); rooftop, 202; rose, 2,
  120; tours (*see* tours); transition from
  flowers to vegetables, 8, 9, 13, 76–77,
  84, 89; transition from vegetables to
  flowers, 1–2; Victorian era, 2; victory,
  89–91, 110; "Virginia," 111, 112
Garden Study Club of New Orleans (LA),
  203
Garre, Mary Jo, 148, 149
Garrett, Ethel, 166, 168, 169
GCA. *see* Garden Club of America
Georgia, 147
Germany, 82, 83, 100, 213
Gibbons, Mrs. John H., 70
global warming, 205

Glore, Mrs. Robert H., 184–185
Goodman, Ernestine: background,
  3; creation of mission statement,
  6, 26, 48; as first secretary and first
  treasurer, 5; founding of the Garden
  Club of Philadelphia, 1; garden, 1–2;
  Pennsylvania School of Horticulture,
  62; views on the Woman's Land Army,
  12; vision for the GCA, 1, 212; during
  World War I, 11, 12, 14
Grand Canyon, 177, 180
Grand Central Station, 32
grants. *see* Founders Fund
grazing on public lands, 163, 177
Great Britain, 66, 76–78, 108, 113–115,
  135
Greece, 110
greenery, Christmas, 24, 85, 93, 103,
  153–154, 161
Greenleaf, James Leal, 64
Greenwich Garden Club (CT), 134
Gregg, Laura, 207
Griswold, Mac, 199
Grolier Club Library (NY), 208

habitat conservation, 53, 158, 163, 203,
  204
habitat degradation, 160, 176. *see also*
  Army Corps of Engineers
Hancock, Walter, 70
Hancock Park Garden Club (Los Angeles,
  CA), 204
Hansen, Bobbie, 121–122, 197
Hare, Mrs. Montgomery, 85
Harrison, Hetty (Mrs. Fairfax), 54, 58, 59,
  60, 64–65, 192
Harwood, Ellie, 137
Hawaii, 74, 143
headquarters in New York City:
  advantages of, 28, 191; decoration
  and furnishings, 193–194, 195; East
  Fifty-eighth St. and Madison Ave.,
  192–193; East Sixtieth St., 194; East
  Sixty-seventh St., 27; Fifth Ave., 27–28;
  Madison Ave., 29, 34, 191–192, 193–
  194; move from Philadelphia to, 27–28,